Spreadsheet Applicatio
in Managerial Accountin

Spreadsheet Applications in Managerial Accounting

Angelo E. DiAntonio

Professor of Accountancy
Clarion University
Clarion, Pennsylvania

Reston Publishing Company, Inc.
A Prentice-Hall Company
Reston, Virginia

Library of Congress Cataloging in Publication Data

DiAntonio, Angelo.
Spreadsheet applications in managerial accounting.

1. Managerial accounting—Data processing.
2. Electronic spreadsheets. I. Title.
HF5679.D53 1985 658.1'511'0285425 84-27607
ISBN 0-8359-6962-2

A Prentice-Hall Company
Reston, Virginia 22090

10 9 8 7 6 5 4 3 2 1

PRINTED IN THE UNITED STATES OF AMERICA

Contents

Acknowledgments

The manual is the result of the activity of many individuals. My appreciation is offered to those students who participated in the development of this work. Their enthusiasm served as motivation for me and their honest criticism helped make this a better product. The accounting practitioners that used this technique in my mini-courses rendered valuable comments and suggestions. Gratitude is extended to my university colleagues who were exposed to this technique during presentations and workshops as well as one-to-one. They were especially supportive of the effort to develop a technique to integrate computers into the accounting classroom.

A special thanks to John N. Sigler, Ulrich C. Toensmeyer and Dolores B. Truitt who offered ideas, suggestions and support during the development and preparation of this manual.

I am especially grateful to Theodore Buchholz, Reston Publishing Company, Inc. for understanding the concept as well as recognizing the need for this work.

This manual is dedicated to Marianne, Edmond and Mark.

Angelo E. Di Antonio

Preface

This manual is designed to assist you to use the computer in a very practical and useful manner. The book will prove useful to the computer novice as well as the experienced computer programmer. Students, instructors and accounting practitioners will benefit from the techniques and procedures discussed in this book.

There are many books in the marketplace that offer instruction in accounting and computer science. The thrust of this manual is to harness the speed, accuracy and power of the computer to perform managerial accounting tasks.

USING THE MANUAL

It is assumed that the user of the manual has access to a computer, a spreadsheet program and a managerial accounting book. There are over 160 items included in this manual that give detailed instruction for immediate input into a computer. Over 1750 problems with solutions assist you to confirm the accuracy of the programs that you key into the computer. The manual will aid you in acquiring the valuable skills of using the computer with minimal time and effort.

ABOUT THE BOOK

This book was written to help you to become familiar with practical applications of electronic worksheets. The models in this book were developed for the field of managerial accounting. After the techniques and procedures in this book are mastered, they may be extrapolated to other fields.

The electronic spreadsheet is a grid or a matrix with which computations may be made using the power and speed of the computer. The use of electronic worksheets does not require an extended background in computer science. One of the main features of our book is that it is completely devoid of computer technical terms. Electronic spreadsheets are truly "user friendly." This means that the user may utilize the computer without the intercession of an analyst, programmer and computer operator. The use of electronic spreadsheets may be learned rapidly. The programs may be designed in a short period of time and may be changed with minimal time and effort expended. The power of the computer is truly placed in control of the ultimate user. We have included over 160 models in this book that are designed to assist you. Our detailed instructions will help you to input these items into your computer. There are over 1750 solved problems in this book that will aid you to verify the accuracy of the items after you input them into your computer.

THE GENERIC NATURE OF THIS BOOK

The format of the book has been designed such that it is generic in nature. There are many computers, spreadsheets and textbooks in the marketplace and many more of these are arriving on the scene. Our book may be used with any computer, spreadsheet or textbook. We recognize that the grid and arithmetical operators have been used for at least 500 years. We do not discern anything in the immediate future that will cause us to abandon these basic tools. The electronic spreadsheet is simply a grid with the capability of performing arithmetical computations.

ABOUT YOUR COMPUTER

We do not refer to a specific computer in this book. You are obliged to spend a little time with your computer manual. You are not obliged to know very much about your computer to use a spreadsheet. You should know how to turn the computer on and off. It is also necessary to become familiar with the technique to bring up your spreadsheet on your computer. The use of electronic spreadsheets is more than a typing exercise. You will be using the electronic spreadsheet for some very sophisticated exercises. The computer keyboard is similar to the typewriter keyboard. It is not necessary for you to know how to type to use a computer. As you practice with our models, you will become sufficiently familiar with the keyboard.

ABOUT YOUR SPREADSHEET

Our instructions are compatible with the spreadsheets that are on the market. Because of the thrust of this book, we do not utilize all of the power of your spreadsheet. The models included in this manual solve each individual problem using few and limited commands. We want to help you to become familiar with electronic spreadsheets. In this manual we are using the spiral learning approach. Initially, you will become familiar with a few commands. In a short time, you will become comfortable with our technique and procedures. As you progress and sense the need for additional commands, consult the manual for the spreadsheet that you are using. In this manner, as you find the need for commands you will become familiar with them.

ABOUT YOUR MANAGERIAL ACCOUNTING TEXTBOOK

The subjects in our manual are fully discussed in your managerial textbook. Our manual makes little or no effort to discuss the individual topics. In this book, we are primarily and solely concerned with providing instructions on the electronic spreadsheets. The task of detailed instruction in managerial accounting has been relegated to the managerial accounting textbooks. Our book will be most helpful if it is used in concert with one of the many fine managerial textbooks that are in the marketplace. Consult your managerial accounting textbook for detailed discussion of the items in our book. The items included in our book are common to managerial accounting textbooks. After you gain facility with our technique, you will be able to develop your own templates for any problem in any managerial accounting textbook.

PRACTICE . . . PRACTICE . . . PRACTICE

The only way to acquire a skill is by practice. There are many items in this book with which you may practice. It is necessary to use a computer as you proceed through this book. Chapter one includes a model with detailed instructions for you. Use this model to help you to begin study of electronic spreadsheets.

Summary
Condensed List of Items

No. of Items	*Chapter Number*		*No. of Problems*
	1	Introduction	
25	2	Concepts and terms	200
21	3	Process Costing	105
10	4	Cost behavior	200
16	5	Break-even sales	115
15	6	Segments	150
		Absorption and Direct Costing	
16	7	Contribution Margin	75
9	8	Budgets	225
17	9	Variance Analysis	120
12	10	Capital Budgeting	300
10	11	Service Department Allocation	146
		Percent Basics	
17	12	Statement Analysis	155
168		Totals	1791

To the Teacher

Computers are the wave of the future. This is an expression that is frequently heard. I would like to alter this statement to:

Computers are the wave of the present.

Even though projections for the use of computers may reach fantasyland, the use of computers at the present time astounds most people in the business world. Electronic spreadsheets are responsible for making computers really "user friendly." They may be learned rapidly and easily. They are versatile and lend themselves to accounting computations.

As instructors, we have an obligation to reach out and help our students to become aware of the happenings in the world of the commerce. It could be that many of our students are more aware than we are. Many of our students have used computers prior to their post-secondary educational experience. They are familiar and comfortable with computers. We are remiss if we do not build on the computer foundation that they possess.

Our book will help you to integrate computers into your classroom. Encourage your students to use the computers that you have available. The instructions in our book are sufficient to get you and your students working on electronic spreadsheets with very little difficulty. Do not be overly concerned about the mistakes that you or your students make. Determine the nature of the problem and with a little effort you will correct the situation. The resolution of these errors may be classified as learning.

The instructions described in this book have been used successfully by many students. It is an especially worthwhile experience to observe students learn the use of electronic spreadsheets. After they become familiar with electronic spreadsheets, students are anxious to work problems using them. Students really enjoy the experience. Incidentally, they will also spend more time in your subject area and consequently they will learn more.

To the Student

Our book will aid you to become familiar with electronic worksheets. We have helped many students to learn the procedures and techniques that are discussed in this book. After a little experience with our instructions, you will be able to input the problems that are in your textbook. You will also be able to use the computer for most of the business problems that you encounter. The time and effort that you expend to acquire this technique will assist immensely with your schoolwork and with your career no matter what your profession. Our students have found the experience worthwhile and pleasurable.

1 Introduction

The advent of spreadsheets represented a breakthrough in the use of computers. Spreadsheets may be mastered with little effort and in minimal time and a variety of chores may be relegated to the computer without intensive programming and sophisticated expertise. Spreadsheets prove especially useful in the field of managerial accounting. Spreadsheets will satisfy most managerial accounting needs. Break-even, budgeting, capital budgeting, direct costing, process costing, statement analysis and other facets of managerial accounting may be benefitted with the use of spreadsheets. Reports can be easily designed, changed, saved, loaded and printed. The user of information may input a program into a computer and then engage in "what if" activity with relative ease.

In this manual we describe a technique that offers you the opportunity to acquire the skill of the use of spreadsheets. This book was written for the computer novice as well as the experienced programmer. Students, public and private accountants, instructors and everyone that makes computations may be benefitted by the use of spreadsheets on the computer.

The instructions that are included in this book have been used by students, instructors and practitioners. The individuals who participated in classes, workshops and one-to-one instruction awarded a positive reception to the procedures and techniques described in this manual. Individuals were able to utilize spreadsheets in meaningful activity after a relatively short period of time. Accounting students were encouraged to assign themselves exercises and problems directly from their textbook and complete them on the computer using the spreadsheet. The assignments were completed by the students with little or no difficulty. Instructors were able to use these techniques for instruction as well as classroom management. Accounting practitioners were able to use spreadsheets in their daily activity. The overall reaction by participants indicated that learning to use the spreadsheet on the computer was a worthwhile and pleasurable experience.

An algorithm according to Webster is, "any particular procedure for solving a certain type of problem." There are over 160 algorithms included in this manual. After you have completed several of our algorithms, you are encouraged to develop your own programs using our techniques and procedures. The formats that you develop may be considered patterns or templates. These templates may be used to complete similar problems by merely changing the variable data. After you have learned to use a spreadsheet, you will be able to engage in sensitivity analysis with little effort.

Spreadsheets are an excellent aid in the classroom. Students may use prepared templates or they may develop their own. After students gain some experience with prepared templates, they are able and anxious to design their own templates. We encourage instructors to turn their students loose on the computer. The development of the template by a student is a learning experience. Not only do students become comfortable with spreadsheets and computers, they learn subject material in an environment different from the traditional lecture classroom mode. In order to complete the template, it is necessary to understand the solution to the problem. The student may focus on the concepts of the problem since the computer performs the tedious arithmetical computations.

The thrust of this manual is to assist the user to become familiar with the use of spreadsheets in the area of managerial accounting. It is assumed that the manual will be used in concert with a managerial accounting textbook. The content material of this manual has been designed to be compatible with any one of the fine managerial accounting textbooks that exist in the marketplace. The order of content material varies with the several textbooks. The items that are in our book may be found in your managerial book by an examination of the index or the table of contents. After you learn the technique, you will be able to design a template for any problem in your textbook.

There are a number of spreadsheets in existence at the present time and many more arriving on the scene. We have designed this manual such that the algorithms in this book may be used with any spreadsheet. The generic nature of our instructions are applicable to any of the spreadsheets in the marketplace. We have developed algorithms using a matrix and a few commands. This has proved to be very satisfactory for instructional purposes. After you have mastered the commands offered in this book, we encourage you to expand your repertoire with commands from the specific spreadsheet that you are using. As the need for a command arises, examine the spreadsheet manual for the answer or consult someone familiar with your spreadsheet.

In this manual, we have concentrated on the use of spreadsheets for managerial accounting. It is assumed that you are familiar with some of the fundamental operations of your computer. You should know how to turn it on and off and be able to bring up the spreadsheet on the monitor. A short period of time spent with your computer operating manual will prove to be sufficient. Better yet, spend a few minutes with someone who is familiar with your computer and your spreadsheet. It is not necessary to become a "computer jock" in order to use a spreadsheet.

MATRIX DESCRIPTION

The spreadsheet takes the form of a grid or matrix. The matrix consists of columns (vertical) and rows (horizontal). The number of columns and rows depends upon the specific spreadsheet that you are using. There will be over 60 columns and over 250 rows included in your spreadsheet. The size does not concern us since we will be using an extremely small part of the spreadsheet.

THE MATRIX

MATRIX SEGMENTS

Massive spreadsheets are difficult to handle. Our approach is to apportion the matrix into screens or pages called segments. We define segments in this manual as 6 columns and 12 rows. You may change the dimensions of our segment to be compatible with your monitor. First, input our program exactly as it appears in the book. Then you may insert rows and columns. The computer will automatically make the appropriate changes in the formulas. This is an indication of the flexibility that you will enjoy with electronic spreadsheets.

FACTS AREA

The contents of a cell will be destroyed as new data or formulas are typed into a cell. In order to preserve the contents of a cell, segregate the facts of the problem from the solution. The facts of the problem are typed on the matrix in one area. Facts include each of the variables in the problem. There are no formulas or computations in the facts segment of your matrix.

SOLUTION AREA

We also create an area on the spreadsheet reserved for the solution. The solution area includes headings, labels, formulas computations. As the facts are changed, the solution will be recalculated. In this manner, a template is prepared that will solve an infinite number of problems merely by altering the variable data without the danger of erasing the formulas. Each of the over 160 algorithms in this book have been designed in this manner and will serve as models for this technique.

CELL IDENTIFICATION

The columns and rows are given names. In most spreadsheets, the names of the columns (vertical) are usually alphabetic characters and the rows (horizontal) are usually named with numbers. A cell is the coordinate or the intersect of the column and row. Each cell is identified by its position on the matrix. The cell in the upper left corner of the matrix is called A1 (column A - row 1). In similar manner, each cell is referred to by the name of the column and the name of the row of the intersect.

Examples

B14 . . . 2nd column . . . 14th row
K34 . . . 11th column . . . 34th row
M78 . . . 13th column . . . 78th row

The procedures and techniques discussed in this text are designed to assist you to develop programs or templates of your own. You will be able to examine a problem and solve it on an electronic worksheet. You may or may not save time preparing the solution on the computer. The real advantage to the prepared template is that you may solve an infinite number of similar problems with little effort. Repeating the task with the prepared template is at computer speed. The accuracy of the solution is devoid of human frailty. We encourage you to make every attempt to prepare templates of your own after you work with several of the items in this book.

There are several steps that will assist you to design a program.

1. Define the problem.
   You should understand the problem that you are going to put on the computer. It is well to spend a few minutes to understand the program.
2. Isolate the facts.
   As you get an understanding of the problem, isolate the facts. With our technique, one area of the matrix will be devoted to the facts. You may write your facts on paper or place them directly on the spreadsheet. After you gain experience with the spreadsheet, you will find it easier to type your facts on the spreadsheet rather than writing them on paper. Either method is satisfactory.
3. Format the solution.
   Another portion of the matrix will display your solution to the problem. In the solution, you will be using the data included in the facts area. The solution includes heading, labels, formulas and computations. Our manual includes many examples for you to follow. Do not hesitate to create your solution directly on the spreadsheet, but be prepared to make changes as you see a better way. You must be persistent and tenacious to complete the project.
4. Test the program.
   Prepare several sets of facts with solutions that you know are correct. Type the facts into your template and check the solution with your prepared solution. Then try other facts and determine if the solution is correct.
5. Evaluate the program.
   Print the program and determine if it meets your expectations. Examine the headings, labels and the format. Work on your printout

and make the changes until you are satisfied that the reader will be able to understand it.

6. Document the program.
Documentation may be included in a special area of your matrix or may be prepared in a hard copy and kept in a binder. The documentation should assist the user as well as the designer and include the program rationale and objectives. Author name and the date prepared should also be part of the documentation. Keep a printed copy (hard copy) of the program. Your spreadsheet program will print the monitor display as well as the cell content for your program.
It is well to prepare a log for changes that are made to the program. The log should include author, date, the nature of the change and the reason for the change.
The extra time that you spend to document your program will result in a big payoff as you use, evaluate and change the template.

DESIGN A PROGRAM

1. DEFINE PROBLEM
2. ISOLATE FACTS
3. FORMAT SOLUTION
4. TEST PROGRAM
5. EVALUATE PROGRAM
6. DOCUMENT PROGRAM

HOW TO USE THIS BOOK

The way to learn about spreadsheets is to work with them on a computer. The instructions in this book will help you if you input them in a computer and observe the results. One of the advantages of the use of spreadsheets is that it is not necessary to have a background in computer science to use them. After you have selected the item that you desire to work, follow these procedures.

Input the CELL CONTENT of the item into your computer exactly as we have indicated.

In order to make certain that you have copied the CELL CONTENT, we have provided you with a number of items that you may use to check your work. Change the FACTS of the item that you pressed in your computer with the data that we have supplied.

Compare your SOLUTION with the SOLUTION that we have provided. If they are the same, save the project.

Input your own FACTS and observe the changes in the SOLUTION. You may focus on the concepts in the problem without the tedium of arithmetical computations. You have the opportunity to work an infinite number of problems and the computer will make the computations. You may observe trends and the impact of the changes of the FACTS on the SOLUTION.

DIRECTION KEYS

The cursor moves in four directions:

up, down, left, right

Some computers have four direction keys and others have two. Determine how to control the cursor on your computer.

The direction keys will cause you to move the cursor one cell at a time and are sufficient to move the cursor short distances on the matrix. Your spreadsheet has the capability of moving the cursor large distances in a more efficient manner than pressing the direction keys. Examine your spreadsheet manual and practice with the command that will automatically move the cursor to a specific cell anywhere on the matrix with a few keystrokes. If you cannot locate it in your manual, ask someone who is familiar with your spreadsheet.

OPERATORS USED IN THIS BOOK

The operators used in this book are listed below:

+	ADD
–	SUBTRACT
*	MULTIPLY
/	DIVIDE
	EXPONENTIATION
@ADD	ADD a column of numbers
@SQRT	SQUARE ROOT

OTHER OPERATORS

Your spreadsheet includes many other operators. We have concentrated on algorithms in this book rather than using all of the possible operators in every spreadsheet. Our book uses only a few of the operators that are available in your spreadsheet. After you gain some experience with the items in this book, please explore some of the other operators that are described in the instruction manual that came with your spreadsheet.

Some of the other operators that will be of interest to you are included in the following list.

1. Blank a cell
2. Clear the screen
3. Delete a column or row
4. Edit a cell
5. Format a cell
   integer, dollar, justify left or right
6. Global . . . format the entire matrix
7. Insert . . . a column or row
8. Move . . . column or row
9. Print the matrix or a portion of the matrix
10. Replicate (copy) rows or columns
11. Storage commands . . . save, load
12. Window . . . create a window or windows

NAMING CONVENTION

You must assign a name to your file at the time you save it on a disk. It is well to use a designation that is meaningful so that it is easy to remember. However, do not be concerned if you can't remember the name. The spreadsheet and your operating system have a directory that you may examine to get the name. In most systems, eight characters is the limit for a filename and the filename must begin with an alphabetic character. Examine your spreadsheet manual to determine the constraints on filenames.

In this book we have used a naming convention that includes the number of the chapter and the number of the problem in that chapter.

Examples

Chapter 2 Problem 3 . . . CH02PR03
Chapter 3 Problem 5 . . . CH03PR05
Chapter 4 Problem 1 . . . CH04PR01

Note that each filename begins with an alphabetic character and there is a limit of eight characters in each name. Beware of the numeric 0 (zero) and the alphabetic O. Data processing people normally place a diagonal through the numeric 0 (zero) to distinquish it from the alphabetic O.

THE MODEL

We have developed a model to assist you to become familiar with spreadsheets. The model is a four year forecast. Please complete the tasks in this assignment on a computer and refer to the printout of the model. The printout includes two screen displays and the cell content of these displays.

The matrix (grid) includes columns (vertical) and rows (horizontal). The columns bear the names of alphabetic characters and the rows are numbered. The intersect of the column and row serves as the name of the cell. Therefore the cell at column A and Row 5 is referred to as A5.

Examine the printout of the model on the next page. The upper half of the model includes two figures that are each entitled SCREEN DISPLAY. After you have completed this exercise, the monitor of your computer will appear exactly as the figures entitled SCREEN DISPLAY. The bottom half of the printout is entitled CELL CONTENT. This area includes the specific instructions that cause the screen displays.

The upper screen display is labeled FACTS. Included in this screen are the basic premises of the problem. The initial year of the forecast is 1987 and the sales of the initial year amount to $10,000. Also assume that there will be a 10% increase in sales each year. The other facts are cost of sales, 60% of sales, and the expenses, 15% of sales. The tax rate is 40% of income. There are no computations or formulas in the FACTS area.

The SOLUTION area displays the completed forecast for the four years. The headings, labels, computations and formulas will be included in the SOLUTION area of the matrix. Some of this information is invisible on the monitor. If you place the cursor on top of a cell, you may examine the cell content on the edit line. If any of the facts are changed, the solution will automatically recalculate the appropriate cells in the forecast. Spreadsheets are ideal for "what if" exercises. They are rapid, accurate and easy to modify.

Now let us examine the portion of the page that is called CELL CONTENT. The contents of each cell is printed in the form of the matrix that you see on the monitor. The cell contents include headings, labels, formulas and computations. The printout of the cell content of the model will serve as detailed instructions to type in our model.

Examine the cell contents of the model in detail. Type the contents of the cells into your spreadsheet exactly as they appear in CELL CONTENT area. When you are finished typing in the contents of each cell, the SCREEN DISPLAY will be exactly as it appears at the top of the model.

Type in the model as follows:

In Cell A1 . . . type . . . MODEL
In Cell A2 . . . type . . . Initial Y
In Cell A3 . . . type . . . Sales

Complete all of the cells of the model up to and including Row 9. Type exactly what you see and place it in the appropriate cell.

Row 10 is the line that has the name of the years.

In Cell C10 . . . type . . . +C2
The content of cell C2 will appear in cell C10.

The other years will be dependent on the value in cell C10.

In Cell D10 . . . type . . . +C10+1

This will cause 1 to be added to the 1987 in C10. D10 will display 1988.

Type in the cell content for the remainder of the cells on row 10. Note that the names of the years are displayed in each of the cells that you complete.

After you have completed the above, type 1990 in cell C2 and observe the changes in each of the other years. Now type 1987 in cell C2.

Row 11 includes the sales data.

In Cell A11 . . . type Sales
In Cell C11 . . . type +C3
Contents of Cell C3 will be transferred to C11
In Cell D11 . . . type +C11*(1+(D3*.01)
This notation will cause the value in C11 to be multiplied by 1.10. (The value in D3 is 10 . . . this is multiplied by .01 and the product is added to 1.) Sales are projected to increase by 10% each year.

The printout of the cell content is limited to 10 characters per cell in a column. The cell may contain more than 10 characters. The characters in excess of 10 will scroll to the next line of the column. Examine the printout of cell D11 in the model. Note the manner in which the characters over 10 scroll to the next line of column D.

The content of cell D11 is as follows:

+C11*(1+(D3*.01)

After you have completed typing in the contents of the cells, try some "what-ifs." Place your cursor on cell C2. This is the cell that has the amount of sales for the initial year. If you change this cell, each of the other cells will change. Assume that the sales for the initial year is 50000. Type 50000 in C2. Notice the effect of this change on the remainder of the model. Now type other numbers in C2 and observe the results.

The matrix is designed so that any number in the FACTS area (Rows 1-6) may be changed and the SOLUTION will be affected.

Change the values in these cells:

C2, C3, C4, C5, C6 and D3

Observe the changes in the SOLUTION portion of the matrix. We have prepared several additional models. Practice with these until you begin to get comfortable with the technique. Our book includes over 160 models that you may use for practice. With sufficient practice with our models, you will be able to develop your own models.

SCREEN DISPLAY

MODEL NO. 1

SCREEN DISPLAY

```
MODEL        FACTS      FACTS      FACTS      FACTS   MODEL
Initial Year              1987     Each Year
Sales                    10000           10 % Increase
Cost of Sales               60 % of sales
Expenses                    15 % of sales
Income tax rate             40 % of income
```

SCREEN DISPLAY

```
SOLUTION              SOLUTION              SOLUTION
             RESTON COMPANY......FORECAST
          Four years Ended December 31, 1990
                          1987      1988      1989      1990
Sales                    10000     11000     12100     13310
Cost of Sales             6000      6600      7260      7986
Gross Profit              4000      4400      4840      5324
Expenses                  1500      1650      1815      1997
Net Income                2500      2750      3025      3328
Income Tax                1000      1100      1210      1331
Income after Tax          1500      1650      1815      1997
```

CELL CONTENT

	A	B	C	D	E	F
1	MODEL	FACTS	FACTS	FACTS	FACTS	MODEL
2	Initial Y	ear	1987	Each Ye	ar	
3	Sales		10000	10	% Increa	se
4	Cost of S	ales	60	% of sal	es	
5	Expenses		15	% of sal	es	
6	Income ta	x rate	40	% of inc	ome	
7	SOLUTION		SOLUTION		SOLUTION	
8		RESTO	N COMPANY	......FOR	ECAST	
9		Four yea	rs Ended	December	31, 1990	
10			+C2	+C10+1	+D10+1	+E10+1
11	Sales		+C3	+C11*(1+(D 3*.01)	+D11*(1+(D 3*.01)	+E11*(1+(D 3*.01)
12	Cost of S	ales	+C11*C4*.0 1	+D11*C4*.0 1	+E11*C4*.0 1	+F11*C4*.0 1
13	Gross Pro	fit	+C11-C12	+D11-D12	+E11-E12	+F11-F12
14	Expenses		+C11*C5*.0 1	+D11*C5*.0 1	+E11*C5*.0 1	+F11*C5*.0 1
15	Net Incom	e	+C13-C14	+D13-D14	+E13-E14	+F13-F14
16	Income Ta	x	+C15*C6*.0 1	+D15*C6*.0 1	+E15*C6*.0 1	+F15*C6*.0 1
17	Income af	ter Tax	+C15-C16	+D15-D16	+E15-E16	+F15-F16

MODEL NO. 2

The heading, labels, formulas and computations are identical to the previous model. We have made one change. We changed the sales in cell C3 from 10000 to 50000. Examine the SOLUTION and observe how the four year forecast changed. The user may input a series of projected sales in cell C3 and the solution will be recalculated. Each of the solutions may be stored and a printout may be obtained. This is an example of the power of electronic worksheets.

SCREEN DISPLAY

MODEL	FACTS	FACTS	FACTS	FACTS	MODEL
Initial Year		1987	Each Year		
Sales		50000	10 % Increase		
Cost of Sales		60 % of sales			
Expenses		15 % of sales			
Income tax rate		40 % of income			

SCREEN DISPLAY

SOLUTION	SOLUTION		SOLUTION	
RESTON COMPANY......FORECAST				
Four years Ended December 31, 1990				
	1987	1988	1989	1990
Sales	50000	55000	60500	66550
Cost of Sales	30000	33000	36300	39930
Gross Profit	20000	22000	24200	26620
Expenses	7500	8250	9075	9983
Net Income	12500	13750	15125	16638
Income Tax	5000	5500	6050	6655
Income after Tax	7500	8250	9075	9983

Type in your own numbers in Cell C3. Observe the effect of a change in sales on cost of goods sold, gross profit, expenses, income tax and income after tax. Type in a series of numbers and observe the results.

MODEL NO. 3

The heading, labels, formulas and computations are identical to the initial model. We have made one change. We changed the percent increase in D3 from 10% to 5%. Examine the SOLUTION and observe how the four year forecast changed. The user may input a series of projected percent change in sales in cell D3 and the solution will be recalculated. Each of the solutions may be stored and a printout may be obtained. This is another example of the power of èlectronic worksheets.

SCREEN DISPLAY

MODEL	FACTS	FACTS	FACTS	FACTS	MODEL
Initial Year		1987	Each Year		
Sales		10000	5 %	Increase	
Cost of Sales		60 %	of sales		
Expenses		15 %	of sales		
Income tax rate		40 %	of income		

SCREEN DISPLAY

SOLUTION SOLUTION SOLUTION

RESTON COMPANY......FORECAST

Four years Ended December 31, 1990

	1987	1988	1989	1990
Sales	10000	10500	11025	11576
Cost of Sales	6000	6300	6615	6946
Gross Profit	4000	4200	4410	4631
Expenses	1500	1575	1654	1736
Net Income	2500	2625	2756	2894
Income Tax	1000	1050	1103	1158
Income after Tax	1500	1575	1654	1736

Type your own numbers in cell D3 and observe the manner in which the model changes. Put in a series of numbers in cell D3 and observe the results in each of the cells in the solution. Look at the change income from 1987 to 1990.

MODEL NO. 4

The heading, labels, formulas and computations are identical to the initial model. We have made three changes. We changed the amount of sales in cell C3 from 10000 to 50000 and the percent increase in D3 from 10% to 5%. In addition we changed the cost of sales % in cell C4 from 60% to 70%. Examine the SOLUTION and observe how the four year forecast changed. The user may input a series of changes of any of the numbers in the FACTS area and the solution will be recalculated. Each of the solutions may be stored and a printout may be obtained. This is another example of the power of electronic worksheets.

SCREEN DISPLAY

```
MODEL      FACTS      FACTS      FACTS      FACTS  MODEL
Initial Year              1987   Each Year
Sales                    50000         5 % Increase
Cost of Sales               70 % of sales
Expenses                    15 % of sales
Income tax rate             40 % of income
```

SCREEN DISPLAY

```
SOLUTION            SOLUTION            SOLUTION
               RESTON COMPANY......FORECAST
            Four years Ended December 31, 1990
                          1987      1988      1989      1990
Sales                    50000     52500     55125     57881
Cost of Sales            35000     36750     38588     40517
Gross Profit             15000     15750     16538     17364
Expenses                  7500      7875      8269      8682
Net Income                7500      7875      8269      8682
Income Tax                3000      3150      3308      3473
Income after Tax          4500      4725      4961      5209
```

Practice changing the matrix by making changes in the FACTS area of the matrix. Change the number in C3 which is sales for the initial year. Change the percent of cost of sales in cell D3 and percent change in sales in cell C4. Note how the SOLUTION changes. Especially observe the change in inocme each and compare the inocme in the first year with the income in the fourth year. Continue to change these numbers and make observations. You will observe the relationships among the several items on the matrix. This is another example of the power of electronic worksheets. You may save or print out each of these solutions.

MODEL NO. 5

The heading, labels, formulas and computations are identical to the initial model. We have changed each of the variables. The year in C2 has been changed from 1987 to 1990. Sales in C3 has been changed to 50000 and the percent increase in D3 has been changed from 10% to 5%. Cost of sales has been changed from 60% in Cell C4 to 70%. The expenses have been changed from 15% of sales to 12% of sales in Cell C5. The income tax rate has been changed in Cell C6 from 40% to 35% of income.

SCREEN DISPLAY

```
MODEL        FACTS     FACTS     FACTS     FACTS   MODEL
Initial Year             1990    Each Year
Sales                   50000            5 % Increase
Cost of Sales              70 % of sales
Expenses                   12 % of sales
Income tax rate            35 % of income
```

SCREEN DISPLAY

```
SOLUTION             SOLUTION              SOLUTION
              RESTON COMPANY......FORECAST
           Four years Ended December 31, 1990
                          1990      1991      1992      1993
Sales                    50000     52500     55125     57881
Cost of Sales            35000     36750     38588     40517
Gross Profit             15000     15750     16538     17364
Expenses                  6000      6300      6615      6946
Net Income                9000      9450      9923     10419
Income Tax                3150      3308      3473      3647
Income after Tax          5850      6143      6450      6772
```

Examine the SOLUTION and observe how the four year forecast changed. The user may input a series of changes of any of the numbers in the FACTS area and the solution will be recalculated. Each of the solutions may be stored and a printout may be obtained. This is another example of the power of electronic worksheets.

2 Concepts and Terms

Condensed List of Items

Item No.		*Problems*
CH02PR01	Cost of goods manufactured—format	5
CH02PR02	Cost of goods manufactured—extended	5
CH02PR03	Cost of goods sold—format	5
CH02PR04	Cost of goods sold—extended	5
CH02PR05	Prime cost	5
CH02PR06	Conversion cost	5
CH02PR07	Prime cost, conversion cost and total cost	5
CH02PR08	Cost of direct material	5
CH02PR09	Cost of direct labor	5
CH02PR10	Cost of overhead	5
CH02PR11	Cost of direct material—per unit	5
CH02PR12	Cost of direct labor—per unit	5
CH02PR13	Cost of overhead—per unit	5
CH02PR14	Cost per unit—total	5
CH02PR15	Cost per unit—total	5
CH02PR16	Cost per unit—total by period	5
CH02PR17	Overhead—predetermined rate—machine hour	5
CH02PR18	Overhead—predetermined rate—labor hour	5

CH02PR19	Overhead—predetermined rate—labor dollars	5
CH02PR20	Overhead—predetermined rate—combined	5
CH02PR21	Overhead—predetermined rate—by dept.	—
CH02PR22	Total Cost—machine hours	25
CH02PR23	Total Cost—labor hours	25
CH02PR24	Total Cost—labor dollars	25
CH02PR25	Total Cost—labor dollars (per unit)	25
		200

HOW TO USE THE MATERIAL IN THIS CHAPTER

Input the CELL CONTENT of the item into your computer. Change the FACTS of the item that you pressed in your computer with the data that we have supplied. Compare your SOLUTION with the SOLUTION that we have provided. If they are the same, save the project. Input your own FACTS and observe the changes in the SOLUTION. You may focus on the concepts in the problem without the tedium of arithmetical computations. You have the opportunity to work an infinite number of problems and the computer will make the computations. You may observe trends and the impact of the changes of the FACTS on the SOLUTION.

OVERVIEW

The Statement of Cost of Goods Manufactured is one of the basic statements that is studied in managerial accounting. CH02PR01 and CH02PR02 will assist you to study this statement. After you have typed these problems into the computer, you may change the numbers in the FACTS area and observe the change in the SOLUTION.

Another basic statement is the Statement of Cost of Goods Sold. CH02PR03 and CH02PR04 offer you the opportunity to practice with this statement. Input different numbers for the beginning and ending inventory so that you may understand the impact of these numbers on cost of goods sold.

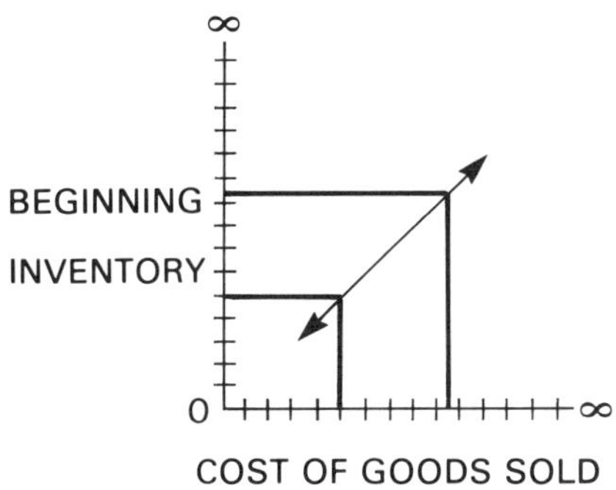

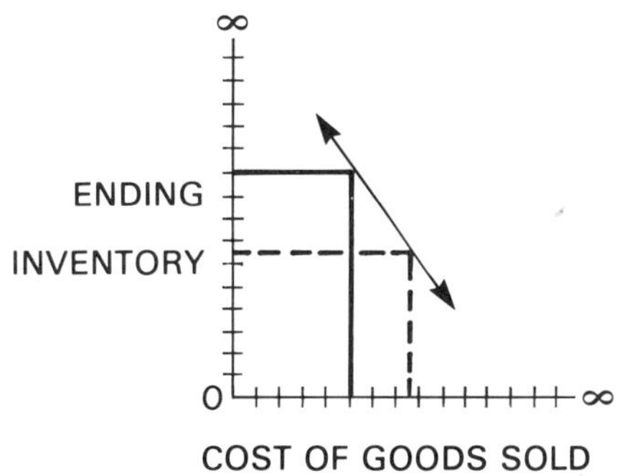

CH02PR05, CH02PR06 and CH02PR07 involve the concepts of prime cost and conversion cost. Prime cost (direct material + direct labor) and Conversion cost (direct labor + overhead) are basic concepts discussed in managerial accounting.

Direct material, direct labor and overhead are the three elements of cost. CH02PR08 to CH02PR16 are concerned with the three elements of cost.

It is necessary to predetermine an overhead rate and there are several techniques to accomplish this. CH02PR17 to CH02PR25 show several ways to compute the estimated overhead cost.

```
CH02PR01          Chapter 2 Problem 1
Prepare a Condensed Statement of Cost of Goods Manufactured
Format
         Work in Process - Beginning
       + Direct Materials
       + Labor and Overhead
       - Work in Process - Ending
         Cost of Goods Manufactured
```

SCREEN DISPLAY

```
        FACTS  Cost of Goods Manufactured-Condensed
           5000  Work in Process Inventory - Beg.
          20000  Direct Materials
          30000  Labor and Overhead
           3000  Work in Process Inventory - End
      SOLUTION
           5000  Work in Process Inventory - Beg.
          20000  Direct Materials
          30000  Labor and Overhead
          55000  Total
           3000  Work in Process Inventory - End
          52000  Cost of Goods Manufactured
```

CELL CONTENT

	A	B	C	D	E
1	FACTS	Cost of G	oods Manu	factured-	Condensed
2	5000	Work in	Process	Inventory	- Beg.
3	20000	Direct	Materials		
4	30000	Labor a	nd Overhe	ad	
5	3000	Work in	Process	Inventory	- End
6	SOLUTION				
7	+A2	Work in	Process	Inventory	- Beg.
8	+A3	Direct	Materials		
9	+A4	Labor a	nd Overhe	ad	
10	+A7+A8+A9	Total			
11	+A5	Work in	Process	Inventory	- End
12	+A10-A11	Cost of	Goods Ma	nufacture	d

CH02PR02

SCREEN DISPLAY

```
FACTS  Cost of Goods Manufactured-Extended

  5000  Work in Process Inventory - Beg.
  3000  Work in Process Inventory - End
 20000  Direct Materials
 30000  Direct Labor
  3000  Cleaning Expense-Factory
  4000  Depreciation-Machinery
 10000  Insurance-Factory
 10000  Rent-Factory
  3000  Utilities-Factory
```

SCREEN DISPLAY

```
SOLUTION
      5000  Work in Process Inventory - Beg.
     20000  Direct Materials
     30000  Direct Labor
      3000  Cleaning Expense-Factory
      4000  Depreciation-Machinery
     10000  Insurance-Factory
     10000  Rent-Factory
      3000  Utilities-Factory
     85000  Total
      3000  Work in Process Inventory - End
     82000  Cost of Goods Manufactured
```

CELL CONTENT

	A	B	C	D	E
1	FACTS	Cost of G	oods Manu	factured-	Extended
2	5000	Work in	Process	Inventory	- Beg.
3	3000	Work in	Process	Inventory	- End
4	20000	Direct	Materials		
5	30000	Direct	Labor		
6	3000	Cleanin	g Expense	-Factory	
7	4000	Depreci	ation-Mac	hinery	
8	10000	Insuran	ce-Factor	y	
9	10000	Rent-Fa	ctory		
10	3000	Utiliti	es-Factor	y	
11					
12	SOLUTION				
13	+A2	Work in	Process	Inventory	- Beg.
14	+A4	Direct	Materials		
15	+A5	Direct	Labor		
16	+A6	Cleanin	g Expense	-Factory	
17	+A7	Depreci	ation-Mac	hinery	
18	+A8	Insuran	ce-Factor	y	
19	+A9	Rent-Fa	ctory		
20	+A10	Utiliti	es-Factor	y	
21	+A13+A14+A 15+A16+A17 +A18+A19+A 20	Total			
22	+A3	Work in	Process	Inventory	- End
23	+A21-A22	Cost of	Goods Ma	nufacture	d

CH02PR03

Chapter 2 Problem 3

Determine Cost of Goods Sold from the data supplied.

Format

```
    Finished Goods Inventory - Beginning
  + Cost of Goods Manufactured
  + Goods Available for sale
  - Finished Goods Inventory - End
    Cost of Goods Sold
```

SCREEN DISPLAY

```
  FACTS  Cost of Goods Sold-Condensed
     5000  Finished Goods Inventory  - Beg.
     3000  Finished Goods Inventory  - End
    20000  Cost of Goods Manufactured

SOLUTION
     5000  Finished Goods Inventory  - Beg.
    20000  Cost of Goods Manufactured
    25000  Goods Available for sale
     3000  Finished Goods Inventory  - End
    22000  Cost of Goods Sold
```

CELL CONTENT

	A	B	C	D	E
1	FACTS	Cost of G	oods Sold	-Condense	d
2	5000	Finishe	d Goods I	nventory	- Beg.
3	3000	Finishe	d Goods I	nventory	- End
4	20000	Cost of	Goods Ma	nufacture	d
5					
6	SOLUTION				
7	+A2	Finishe	d Goods I	nventory	- Beg.
8	+A4	Cost of	Goods Ma	nufacture	d
9	+A7+A8	Goods A	vailable	for sale	
10	+A3	Finishe	d Goods I	nventory	- End
11	+A9-A10	Cost of	Goods So	ld	

SCREEN DISPLAY

CH02PR04

```
FACTS  Cost of Goods Sold-Extended
   5000  Finished Goods Inventory  - Beg.
   3000  Finished Goods Inventory  - End
   4000  WIP - Beg
   6000  WIP - End
  20000  Direct Materials
  30000  Direct Labor
  40000  Overhead
```

SCREEN DISPLAY

```
SOLUTION
     4000  WIP - Beg
    20000  Direct Materials
    30000  Direct Labor
    40000  Overhead
    94000  Total
     6000  WIP - End
    88000  Cost of Goods Manufactured
     5000  Finished Goods Inventory  - Beg.
    93000  Goods Available for sale
     3000  Finished Goods Inventory  - End
    90000  Cost of Goods Sold
```

CELL CONTENT

	A	B	C	D	E
1	FACTS	Cost of G	oods Sold	-Extended	
2	5000	Finishe	d Goods I	nventory	- Beg.
3	3000	Finishe	d Goods I	nventory	- End
4	4000	WIP - B	eg		
5	6000	WIP - E	nd		
6	20000	Direct	Materials		
7	30000	Direct	Labor		
8	40000	Overhea	d		
9					
10					
11					
12					
13	SOLUTION				
14	4000	WIP - B	eg		
15	20000	Direct	Materials		
16	30000	Direct	Labor		
17	40000	Overhea	d		
18	+A14+A15+A 16+A17	Total			
19	6000	WIP - E	nd		
20	+A18-A19	Cost of	Goods Ma	nufacture	d
21	+A2	Finishe	d Goods I	nventory	- Beg.
22	+A20+A21	Goods A	vailable	for sale	
23	+A3	Finishe	d Goods I	nventory	- End
24	+A22-A23	Cost of	Goods So	ld	

CH02PR05

Chapter 2 Problem 5
Determine Prime Cost from the data supplied

Formula

```
     Direct Materials      10000
   + Direct Labor          14000
                       ---------
     Prime Cost            24000
                       =========
```

SCREEN DISPLAY

```
Prime Cost
FACTS              FACTS

    10000 Direct Material
    14000 Direct Labor

SOLUTION           SOLUTION

         Prime Cost              24000
```

CELL CONTENT

	A	B	C	D
1	Prime Cos	t		
2	FACTS		FACTS	
3				
4	10000	Direct M	aterial	
5	14000	Direct L	abor	
6				
7	SOLUTION		SOLUTION	
8				
9		Prime Cos	t	+A4+A5

CH02PR06

```
                  Chapter 2 Problem 6
Determine Conversion Cost from the data supplied

Formula
       + Direct Labor           14000
         Overhead               10000
                            ---------
         Conversion Cost        24000
                            =========
```

SCREEN DISPLAY

```
Conversion Cost
FACTS                FACTS


    14000 Direct Labor
    10000 Overhead
SOLUTION             SOLUTION

         Conversion Cost        24000
```

CELL CONTENT

	A	B	C	D
1	Conversio	n Cost		
2	FACTS		FACTS	
3				
4				
5	14000	Direct L	abor	
6	10000	Overhead		
7	SOLUTION		SOLUTION	
8				
9		Conversio	n Cost	+A5+A6

CH02PR07

Chapter 2 Problem 7

Determine Prime Cost, Conversion Cost and Total Cost from the data supplied.

Formula	Prime Cost	Conversion Cost	Total Cost
Direct Material	12000		12000
+ Direct Labor	14000	14000	14000
Overhead		10000	10000
Total	26000	24000	36000

SCREEN DISPLAY

```
Prime Cost and Conversion Cost
FACTS              FACTS
    12000 Direct Material
    14000 Direct Labor
    10000 Overhead
SOLUTION                      Prime       Conv.     Total
                              Cost        Cost       Cost
         Material                 12000               12000
         Labor                    14000     14000     14000
         Overhead                           10000     10000
         Total                    26000     24000     36000
```

CELL CONTENT

	A	B	C	D	E	F
1	Prime Cos	t and Con	version C	ost		
2	FACTS		FACTS			
3	12000	Direct M	aterial			
4	14000	Direct L	abor			
5	10000	Overhead				
6	SOLUTION			Prime	Conv.	Total
7				Cost	Cost	Cost
8		Material		+A3		+A3
9		Labor		+A4	+A4	+A4
10		Overhead			+A5	+A5
11		Total		+D8+D9	+E9+E10	+F8+F9+F10

CH02PR08

SCREEN DISPLAY

```
Determine cost of material
FACTS              FACTS
     4000 Raw Material Inventory - Beg
    50000 Material Purchased
     3000 Returned Purchases
     5000 Freight in
     6000 Raw Material Inventory - End
```

SCREEN DISPLAY

```
SOLUTION           SOLUTION
          Raw Mat. Inv. -  Beg.                        4000
          Purchases Materials               50000
          Returned Purchases                 3000
           Net Purchases                              47000
          Freight in                                   5000
          Available for use                           56000
          Raw Material Inventory - End                 6000
          Cost of Direct Materials                    50000
```

CELL CONTENT

	A	B	C	D	E	F
1						
2						
3						
4	Determine	cost of	material			
5	FACTS		FACTS			
6	4000	Raw Mate	rial Inve	ntory - B	eg	
7	50000	Material	Purchase	d		
8	3000	Returned	Purchase	s		
9	5000	Freight	in			
10	6000	Raw Mate	rial Inve	ntory - E	nd	
11						
12						
13						
14	SOLUTION		SOLUTION			
15		Raw Mat.	Inv. -	Beg.		+A6
16		Purchase	s Materia	ls	+A7	
17		Returned	Purchase	s	+A8	
18		Net Pur	chases			+E16-E17
19		Freight	in			+A9
20		Availabl	e for use			+F15+F18+F 19
21		Raw Mate	rial Inve	ntory - E	nd	+A10
22		Cost of	Direct Ma	terials		+F20-F21

CH02PR09

Chapter 2 Problem 9

Determine Cost of Direct Labor from the data supplied.

Formula

```
       Total Cost                          30000
       Direct Material          10000
       Overhead               +  7500
                              ---------
         Total                         -   17500
                                        ---------
       Direct Labor                        12500
                                        =========
```

SCREEN DISPLAY

```
Determine Cost of Labor
FACTS              FACTS

    10000 Direct Material
     7500 Overhead
    30000 Total Cost
SOLUTION           SOLUTION

         Cost of Direct Labor           12500
```

CELL CONTENT

	A	B	C	D	E
1	Determine	Cost of	Labor		
2	FACTS		FACTS		
3					
4	10000	Direct M	aterial		
5	7500	Overhead			
6	30000	Total Co	st		
7	SOLUTION		SOLUTION		
8					
9		Cost of D	irect Lab	or	+A6-A4-A5

CH02PR10

```
                  Chapter 2 Problem 10
Determine Cost of Overhead from the data supplied.
Formula
         Total Cost                           30000
         Direct Material         10000
         Direct Labor     +       7500
                              ---------
           Total                       -      17500
                                          ---------
         Cost of Overhead                     12500
                                          =========
```

SCREEN DISPLAY

```
Determine Cost of Overhead
FACTS              FACTS

    10000 Direct Material
     7500 Direct Labor
    30000 Total Cost
SOLUTION           SOLUTION

         Cost of  Overhead              12500
```

CELL CONTENT

	A	B	C	D	E
1	Determine	Cost of	Overhead		
2	FACTS		FACTS		
3					
4	10000	Direct M	aterial		
5	7500	Direct L	abor		
6	30000	Total Co	st		
7	SOLUTION		SOLUTION		
8					
9		Cost of	Overhead		+A6-A4-A5

CH02PR11

Chapter 2 Problem 11

Determine Cost of Materials used per unit.

Formula

	Direct Material	25000
Divide by	Number of Units	6250
	Cost per unit	4

SCREEN DISPLAY

```
Cost of Materials used per Unit
FACTS                FACTS

    25000 Direct Material

     6250 Number of Units

SOLUTION
         Cost Per Unit            4
```

CELL CONTENT

	A	B	C	D
1	Cost of M	aterials	used per	Unit
2	FACTS		FACTS	
3				
4	25000	Direct M	aterial	
5				
6	6250	Number o	f Units	
7				
8	SOLUTION			
9		Cost Per	Unit	+A4/A6

CH02PR12

Chapter 2 Problem 12

Determine Cost of Direct Labor per unit.

Formula		
	Direct Labor	31625
Divide by	Number of Units	6250
	Cost per unit	5.06

SCREEN DISPLAY

```
Cost of Labor - Cost per Unit
FACTS                FACTS

    31625 Direct Labor

     6250 Number of Units

SOLUTION
         Cost Per Unit          5.06
```

CELL CONTENT

	A	B	C	D
1	Cost of L	abor - Co	st per Un	it
2	FACTS		FACTS	
3				
4	31625	Direct L	abor	
5				
6	6250	Number o	f Units	
7				
8	SOLUTION			
9		Cost Per	Unit	+A4/A6

CH02PR13

Chapter 2 Problem 13
Determine Cost of Overhead per unit.
FORMULA

Overhead	42000
Divide by Number of units	5495
Cost per unit	7.643312

SCREEN DISPLAY

```
Cost of Overhead  Cost per Unit
FACTS             FACTS

    42000 Overhead

     5495 Number of Units

SOLUTION
         Cost Per Unit       7.643312
```

CELL CONTENT

	A	B	C	D
1	Cost of O	verhead	Cost per	Unit
2	FACTS		FACTS	
3				
4	42000	Overhead		
5				
6	5495	Number o	f Units	
7				
8	SOLUTION			
9		Cost Per	Unit	+A4/A6

CH02PR14

Chapter 2 Problem 14

Determine total cost per unit from data supplied.

Formula

	Total	Per Unit
Number of Units	10000	
Direct Materials	28000	2.80
Direct Labor	37500	3.75
Overhead	50000	5.00
Total Cost	115500	11.55

SCREEN DISPLAY

FACTS FACTS	
Direct Materials	28000
Direct Labor	37500
Overhead	50000
Number of Units	10000
SOLUTION Unit Cost	
Direct Materials	2.80
Direct Labor	3.75
Overhead	5.00
Total	11.55

CELL CONTENT

	A	B	C	D
1	FACTS	FACTS		
2	Direct Ma	terials		28000
3	Direct La	bor		37500
4	Overhead			50000
5	Number of	Units		10000
6				
7	SOLUTION	Unit Cost		
8	Direct Ma	terials		+D2/D5
9	Direct La	bor		+D3/D5
10	Overhead			+D4/D5
11	Total			+D8+D9+D10

CH02PR15

Chapter 2 Problem 15

Determine total cost per unit from data supplied.

Formula

Number of Units	15000	
	Total	Per Unit
Direct Materials	19000	1.27
Direct Labor	25000	1.67
Overhead	50000	3.33
Total Cost	94000	6.27

SCREEN DISPLAY

FACTS FACTS	
Direct Materials	19000
Direct Labor	25000
Overhead	50000
Number of Units	15000
SOLUTION	Unit Cost
Direct Materials	1.27
Direct Labor	1.67
Overhead	3.33
Total	6.27

CELL CONTENT

	A	B	C	D	E	F
1	FACTS	FACTS				
2						
3	Direct Ma	terials				19000
4	Direct La	bor				25000
5	Overhead					50000
6	Number of	Units				15000
7	SOLUTION					Unit Cost
8	Direct Ma	terials				+F3/F6
9	Direct La	bor				+F4/F6
10	Overhead					+F5/F6
11	Total					+F8+F9+ F10

CH02PR16

SCREEN DISPLAY

FACTS	Compute unit cost		Period	
	1st	2nd	3rd	4th
Direct Materials	75000	38000	19000	10500
Direct Labor	100000	60000	25000	37500
Overhead	50000	50000	50000	46875
Number of units	25000	12500	6250	9375
SOLUTION	1st	2nd	3rd	4th
Direct Materials	3	3.04	3.04	1.12
Direct Labor	4	4.8	4	4
Overhead	2	4	8	5
Total Cost	9	11.84	15.04	10.12

CELL CONTENT

	A	B	C	D	E	F
1	FACTS	Compute u	nit cost		Period	
2			1st	2nd	3rd	4th
3	Direct Ma	terials	75000	38000	19000	10500
4	Direct La	bor	100000	60000	25000	37500
5	Overhead		50000	50000	50000	46875
6	Number of	units	25000	12500	6250	9375
7	SOLUTION		1st	2nd	3rd	4th
8	Direct Ma	terials	+C3/C6	+D3/D6	+E3/E6	+F3/F6
9	Direct La	bor	+C4/C6	+D4/D6	+E4/E6	+F4/F6
10	Overhead		+C5/C6	+D5/D6	+E5/E6	+F5/F6
11	Total Cos	t	+C8+C9+C10	+D8+D9+D10	+E8+E9+E10	+F8+F9+F10

CH02PR17

Chapter 2 Problem 17
Determine predetermined overhead rate.

Formula

Overhead	182500
Machine Hours	50000
Predetermined Rate per hour	3.65

SCREEN DISPLAY

FACTS FACTS FACTS

Manufacturing overhead	182500
Machine Hours	50000

SOLUTION

Predetermined Rate	3.65

CELL CONTENT

	A	B	C	D	E
1	FACTS	FACTS	FACTS		
2					
3	Manufactu	ring over	head		182500
4	Machine H	ours			50000
5					
6					
7	SOLUTION				
8	Predeterm	ined Rate			+E3/E4

CH02PR18

Chapter 2 Problem 18

Determine predetermined overhead rate.

Formula

	Overhead	91250
Divide by	Labor Hours	50000
	Predetermined Rate per hour	1.825

SCREEN DISPLAY

```
FACTS     FACTS     FACTS

Manufacturing overhead                    91250
Labor   Hours                             50000


SOLUTION
Predetermined Rate                        1.825
```

CELL CONTENT

	A	B	C	D	E
1	FACTS	FACTS	FACTS		
2					
3	Manufactu	ring over	head		91250
4	Labor	ours			50000
5					
6					
7	SOLUTION				
8	Predeterm	ined Rate			+E3/E4

CH02PR19

Chapter 2 Problem 19
Determine predetermined overhead rate.

FORMULA

Overhead	45625
Divide by Labor dollars	50000
Predetermined Rate	.9125

SCREEN DISPLAY

```
FACTS     FACTS     FACTS

Manufacturing overhead                     45625
Labor dollars                              50000


SOLUTION
Predetermined Rate                         .9125
```

CELL CONTENT

	A	B	C	D	E
1	FACTS	FACTS	FACTS		
2					
3	Manufactu	ring over	head		45625
4	Labor dol	lars			50000
5					
6					
7	SOLUTION				
8	Predeterm	ined Rate			+E3/E4

CH02PR20

Chapter 2 Problem 20
Determine predetermined overhead rate.

FORMULA

Overhead 200000

	Total	Rate
Machine Hours	15000	13.33
Labor Hours	24000	8.33
Labor Dollars	80000	2.50

SCREEN DISPLAY

FACTS FACTS	
Units to be produced	16000
Machine Hours	15000
Direct Labor Hours	24000
Direct Labor Cost	80000
Manufacturing overhead	200000
SOLUTION	OH Rate
Machine Hours	13.33
Direct Labor Hours	8.33
Direct Labor Cost	2.50

CELL CONTENT

	A	B	C	D	E
1					
2	FACTS	FACTS			
3	Units to	be produc	ed		16000
4	Machine H	ours			15000
5	Direct La	bor Hours			24000
6	Direct La	bor Cost			80000
7	Manufactu	ring over	head		200000
8					
9	SOLUTION				OH Rate
10	Machine H	ours			+E7/E4
11	Direct La	bor Hours			+E7/E5
12	Direct La	bor Cost			+E7/E6

CH02PR21

Chapter 2 Problem 21
Determine predetermined overhead rate.

FORMULA

Overhead	200000		
		Total	Rate
Machine hours		15000	13.33
Labor Hours		24000	8.33
Labor Dollars		80000	2.50

SCREEN DISPLAY

FACTS FACTS	Dept. 1	2	3
Units to be produced	20000	16000	24000
Machine Hours	60000	15000	45000
Direct Labor Hours	12000	24000	48000
Direct Labor Cost	120000	80000	40000
Manufacturing overhead	200000	200000	200000
SOLUTION			
Machine Hours	3.33	13.33	4.44
Direct Labor Hours	16.67	8.33	4.17
Direct Labor Cost	1.67	2.50	5.00

CELL CONTENT

	A	B	C	D	E	F
1	FACTS	FACTS			Dept.	
2				1	2	3
3	Units to	be produc	ed	20000	16000	24000
4	Machine H	ours		60000	15000	45000
5	Direct La	bor Hours		12000	24000	48000
6	Direct La	bor Cost		120000	80000	40000
7	Manufactu	ring over	head	200000	200000	200000
8						
9	SOLUTION					
10	Machine H	ours		+D7/D4	+D7/E4	+D7/F4
11	Direct La	bor Hours		+D7/D5	+D7/E5	+D7/F5
12	Direct La	bor Cost		+D7/D6	+D7/E6	+D7/F6

CH02PR22

CH02PR22 Chapter 2 Problem 22

Determine Cost per Unit from the data supplied.

Formula

	Direct Materials		150
	Direct Labor		200
Estimated Overhead		10000	
Estimated Machine Hours		5000	
	Rate per hour	2	
	Machine Hours	20	
	Overhead		40
	Total Cost		390

SCREEN DISPLAY

```
FACTS     FACTS     Based on machine hours
Direct Materials                150
Direct Labor                    200
Machine Hours         --->       20
Estimated Overhead            10000
Estimated Machine Hours        5000
SOLUTION
Direct Materials             150.00
Direct Labor                 200.00
Overhead - machine hours      40.00
Overhead - rate per hour                 2.00
Total                        390.00
```

CELL CONTENT

	A	B	C	D	E
1	FACTS	FACTS	Based on	machine h	ours
2	Direct Ma	terials		150	
3	Direct La	bor		200	
4	Machine H	ours	--->	20	
5	Estimated	Overhead		10000	
6	Estimated	Machine	Hours	5000	
7	SOLUTION				
8	Direct Ma	terials		+D2	
9	Direct La	bor		+D3	
10	Overhead	- machine	hours	+D4*(D5 /D6)	
11	Overhead	- rate pe	r hour		+D5/D6
12	Total			+D8+D9+ D10	

CH02PR23

Chapter 2 Problem 23

Determine Cost per unit from the data supplied.

```
FORMULA
          Direct Materials                    300
          Direct Labor                        200
Estimated Overhead                 20000
Estimated Labor Hours               5000
           Rate per hour               4
           Labor hours               100
           Overhead                           400
                                        ---------
          Total Cost                          900
                                        =========
```

SCREEN DISPLAY

```
FACTS     FACTS     Based on Labor Hours
Direct Materials                        300
Direct Labor                            200
Labor Hours                    --->     100
Estimated Overhead                    20000
Estimated Labor Hours                  5000

SOLUTION
Direct Materials                     300.00
Direct Labor                         200.00
Overhead  - rate per hour     4.00   400.00
Total                                900.00
```

CELL CONTENT

	A	B	C	D	E
1	FACTS	FACTS	Based on	Labor Hou	rs
2	Direct Ma	terials			300
3	Direct La	bor			200
4	Labor Hou	rs		--->	100
5	Estimated	Overhead			20000
6	Estimated	Labor Ho	urs		5000
7					
8	SOLUTION				
9	Direct Ma	terials			+E2
10	Direct La	bor			+E3
11	Overhead	- rate p	er hour	+E5/E6	+E4*(E5 /E6)
12	Total				+E9+E10 +E11

CH02PR24

Chapter 2 Problem 24

Determine Cost per unit from the data supplied.

```
FORMULA
         Direct Materials                  150
         Direct Labor                      200
Estimated Overhead             10000
Estimated Labor Dollars         5000

SOLUTION
Direct Materials              150.00
Direct Labor                  200.00
Overhead rate %         200   400.00
                           ---------
         Total                750.00
                           =========
```

SCREEN DISPLAY

```
FACTS    FACTS    Based on Labor dollars
Direct Materials                150
Direct Labor            --->    200
Estimated Overhead            10000
Estimated Labor Dollars        5000

SOLUTION
Direct Materials             150.00
Direct Labor                 200.00
Overhead rate %        200   400.00
Total                        750.00
```

CELL CONTENT

	A	B	C	D	E
1	FACTS	FACTS	Based on	Labor dol	lars
2	Direct Ma	terials		150	
3	Direct La	bor	--->	200	
4	Estimated	Overhead		10000	
5	Estimated	Labor Do	llars	5000	
6					
7	SOLUTION				
8	Direct Ma	terials		+D2	
9	Direct La	bor		+D3	
10	Overhead	rate %	(+D4/D5)*1 00	+D3*(D4 /D5)	
11	Total			+D8+D9+ D10	

```
CH02PR25
                    Chapter 2 Problem 25
          Determine total costs
          FORMULA
                                           Per Unit
          Direct Materials                     6.25
          Direct Labor                         9.23
          Overhead
           (% of labor)                  50    4.615
                                           ---------
          Total Cost per unit                  20.10
                                           =========
          Number of units                      10000
          Total Cost                                     200950
```

SCREEN DISPLAY

```
FACTS             FACTS                              CH02PR25
     6.25 Direct Materials
     9.23 Direct Labor
       50 Overhead (% of Labor)
    10000 Number of Units
        5 % rate of change
SOLUTION Unit Costs       1st       2nd       3rd       4th
 # of units             10000     10500     11025     11576
 Direct Materials       62500     65625     68906     72352
 Direct Labor           92300     96915    101761    106849
 Overhead               46150     48458     50880     53424
Total Costs            200950    210998    221547    232625
```

CELL CONTENT

	A	B	C	D	E	F
1	FACTS		FACTS			"CH02PR25
2	6.25	Direct M	aterials			
3	9.23	Direct L	abor			
4	50	Overhead	(% of La	bor)		
5	10000	Number o	f Units			
6	5	% rate o	f change			
7	SOLUTION	Unit Cost	s 1st	2nd	3rd	4th
8	# of uni	ts	+A5	+C8*(1+(A6 *.01)	+D8*(1+(A6 *.01)	+E8*(1+(A6 *.01)
9	Direct M	aterials	+C8*A2	+D8*A2	+E8*A2	+F8*A2
10	Direct L	abor	+C8*A3	+D8*A3	+E8*A3	+F8*A3
11	Overhead		+C10*(A4*. 01)	+D10*(A4*. 01)	+E10*(A4*. 01)	+F10*(A4*. 01)
12	Total Cos	ts	@SUM(C9... C11	@SUM(D9... D11	@SUM(E9... E11	@SUM(F9... F11

Chapter 2

Problem 1 PRACTICE PRACTICE PRACTICE PRACTICE PRACTICE PRACTICE

Determine Cost of Goods Manufactured from the data supplied.

Format

  Work in Process - Beginning
+ Direct Materials
+ Labor and Overhead
- Work in Process - Ending
  Cost of Goods Manufactured

Item No.	WIP-Beg	Mat.	Lab & OH.	WIP-End	Cost of Goods Mfg
1	5000	20000	30000	3000	52000
2	6000	20000	30000	3000	53000
3	7000	20000	30000	3000	54000
4	8000	20000	30000	3000	55000
5	9000	20000	30000	3000	56000

Problem 2 PRACTICE PROBLEMS

Determine Cost of Goods Manufactured from the data supplied.

Format

  Work in Process - Beg
+ Direct Materials
+ Labor and Overhead
- Work in Process - End
  Cost of Goods Manufactured

Item No.	WIP-Beg	Material	Labor	OH	WIP-End	Goods Mfg
1	5000	20000	30000	30000	3000	82000
2	6000	20000	30000	30000	3000	83000
3	7000	20000	30000	30000	3000	84000
4	8000	20000	30000	30000	3000	85000
5	9000	20000	30000	30000	3000	86000

Problem 3 PRACTICE PRACTICE PRACTICE PRACTICE PRACTICE PRACTICE

Determine Cost of Goods Sold from the data supplied.

Format

  Finished Goods Inventory - Beg
+ Cost of Goods Manufactured
+ Goods Available for sale
  Finished Goods Inventory - End
- Cost of Goods Sold

Item No.	F.G.-Beg	Cost of Gds Mfd	F.G.-End	COGS
1	5000	20000	3000	22000
2	6000	20000	3000	23000
3	7000	20000	3000	24000
4	8000	20000	3000	25000
5	9000	20000	3000	26000

PRACTICE PROBLEMS

Problem 4

Determine Cost of Goods Sold from the data supplied.

Format

```
  Finished Goods Inventory - Beginning
+ Cost of Goods Manufactured
+ Goods Available for sale
- Finished Goods Inventory - End
  Cost of Goods Sold
```

Item No.	F.G.-Beg	Cost of Gds Mfd	F.G.-End	COGS
1	0	20000	0	20000
2	0	20000	3000	17000
3	0	25000	3000	22000
4	3000	20000	0	23000
5	3000	25000	0	28000

Problem 5 PRACTICE PRACTICE PRACTICE PRACTICE PRACTICE PRACTICE

Determine Prime Cost from the data supplied

Formula

```
  Direct Materials        10000
+ Direct Labor            14000
                      ---------
  Prime Cost              24000
                      =========
```

Item No.	Direct Material	Direct Labor	Prime Cost
1	10000	14000	24000
2	11000	14000	25000
3	12000	14000	26000
4	13000	14000	27000
5	14000	14000	28000

Problem 6

Determine Conversion Cost from the data supplied

Formula

```
+ Direct Labor            14000
  Overhead                10000
                      ---------
  Conversion Cost         24000
                      =========
```

Item No.	Direct Labor	Overhead	Conversion Cost
1	15000	14000	29000
2	16000	14000	30000
3	17000	14000	31000
4	18000	14000	32000
5	19000	14000	33000

Problem 7 PRACTICE PRACTICE PRACTICE PRACTICE PRACTICE PRACTICE

Determine Prime Cost and Conversion Cost from the data supplied.

FORMULA

	Prime Cost	Conv. Cost
Direct Material	12000	
+ Direct Labor	14000	14000
		10000
Total	26000	24000

Item No.	Direct Material	Direct Labor	Overhead	Prime Cost	Conv. Cost
1	15000	15000	14000	30000	29000
2	16000	16000	14000	32000	30000
3	17000	17000	14000	34000	31000
4	18000	18000	14000	36000	32000
5	19000	19000	14000	38000	33000

Problem 8 PROBLEMS WITH SOLUTIONS

Determine Cost of Direct Material from the data supplied.

Format

Raw Material Inventory - Beginning	4000
+ Material Purchased	50000
- Returned Purchases	3000
+ Freight In	5000
= Material Available for Production	56000
- Raw Material Inventory - End	6000
= Cost of Direct Materials	50000

Item No.	Beg. Inv.	Net Purch.	Freight In	End Inv.	Cost of D. M.
1	4000	47000	5000	6000	50000
2	5000	47000	5000	6000	51000
3	6000	47000	5000	6000	52000
4	7000	47000	5000	6000	53000
5	8000	47000	5000	6000	54000

Problem 9 PRACTICE PRACTICE PRACTICE PRACTICE PRACTICE PRACTICE

Determine Cost of Direct Labor from the data supplied.

Formula

Total Cost		30000
Direct Material	10000	
+ Overhead	7500	
Total	-	17500
Direct Labor		12500

Item No.	Direct Material	Direct Overhead	Total Cost	Direct Labor
1	10000	7500	30000	12500
2	10500	7500	30000	12000
3	11500	7500	30000	11000
4	12500	7500	30000	10000
5	13500	7500	30000	9000

Please work these problems
Check your answers with the solution

Problem 10

Determine Cost of Overhead from the data supplied.
Formula

Total Cost		30000
Direct Material	10000	
Direct Labor +	7500	

Total		- 17500

Cost of Overhead		12500
		=========

Item No.	Direct Material	Direct Labor	Total Cost	Overhead
1	15000	7500	30000	7500
2	15500	7500	30000	7000
3	16500	7500	30000	6000
4	17500	7500	30000	5000
5	18500	7500	30000	4000

Problem 11

Determine Cost of Materials used per unit.
Formula

	Direct Material	25000
Divide by	Number of Units	6250
	Cost per unit	4

Item No.	Direct Material	Number of Units	Cost Per Unit
1	15000	300	50.00
2	15500	300	51.67
3	16500	300	55.00
4	17500	300	58.33
5	18500	300	61.67

Problem 12

Determine Cost of Direct Labor per unit.
Formula

	Direct Labor	31625
Divide by	Number of Units	6250
	Cost per unit	5.06

Item No.	Direct Labor	Number of Units	Cost Per Unit
1	8000	250	32.00
2	8500	250	34.00
3	9500	250	38.00
4	10500	250	42.00
5	11500	250	46.00

Problem 13

Determine Cost of Overhead per unit.
Formula

	Overhead	42000
Divide by	Number of Units	5495
	Cost per unit	7.643312

Item No.	Overhead	Number of Units	Cost Per Unit
1	600	200	3.00
2	1100	200	5.50
3	2100	200	10.50
4	3100	200	15.50
5	4100	200	20.50

Problem 14

Determine total cost per unit from data supplied.
Formula

Number of Units 10000

	Total	Per Unit
Direct Materials	28000	2.80
Direct Labor	37500	3.75
Overhead	50000	5.00
Total Cost	115500	11.55

Item No.	Direct Materials	Direct Labor	Overhead	Number of Units	Cost Per Unit
1	28000	37500	50000	10000	11.55
2	29000	37500	50000	10000	11.65
3	30000	37500	50000	10000	11.75
4	31000	37500	50000	10000	11.85
5	32000	37500	50000	10000	11.95

Problem 15

Determine total cost per unit from data supplied.
Formula

Number of Units 15000

	Total	Per Unit
Direct Materials	19000	1.27
Direct Labor	25000	1.67
Overhead	50000	3.33
Total Cost	94000	6.27

Item No.	Direct Materials	Direct Labor	Overhead	Number of Units	Unit Cost
1	19000	25000	50000	10000	9.40
2	20000	26000	52000	10000	9.80
3	21000	27000	54000	10000	10.20
4	22000	28000	56000	10000	10.60
5	23000	29000	58000	10000	11.00

Problem 16 Please work these problems
Check your answers with the solution

Given
Direct Material
Direct Labor
Overhead
Units
Compute
Cost per unit

Item No.	Direct Material	Labor	Overhead	Units	Cost per Unit
1	75000	100000	50000	25000	9.00
2	85000	100000	50000	25000	9.40
3	95000	100000	50000	25000	9.80
4	105000	100000	50000	25000	10.20
5	115000	100000	50000	25000	10.60

Problem 17 PRACTICE PRACTICE PRACTICE PRACTICE PRACTICE PRACTICE

Determine predetermined overhead rate.

Formula

Overhead	182500
Machine Hours	50000
Predetermined Rate per hour	3.65

Item No.	Overhead	Machine Hours	Overhead Per Unit
1	182500	50000	3.65
2	180000	50000	3.60
3	177500	50000	3.55
4	175000	50000	3.50
5	172500	50000	3.45

Problem 18 PRACTICE PROBLEMS

Determine predetermined overhead rate.

Formula

Overhead	91250
Divide by Labor Hours	50000
Predetermined Rate per hour	1.825

Item No.	Overhead	Labor Hours	Overhead Per Unit
1	91250	50000	1.83
2	91350	50000	1.83
3	91450	50000	1.83
4	91550	50000	1.83
5	91650	50000	1.83

Chapter 2

Please work these problems.
Compare your results with the prepared solution.

Problem 19

Determine predetermined overhead rate.

FORMULA

Overhead	45625
Divide by Labor dollars	50000
Predetermined Rate	.9125

Item No.	Overhead	Labor Dollars	Overhead Per Unit
1	45625	50000	0.91
2	46625	50000	0.93
3	47625	50000	0.95
4	48625	50000	0.97
5	49625	50000	0.99

PRACTICE PRACTICE PRACTICE PRACTICE PRACTICE PRACTICE

PRACTICE PROBLEMS

Problem 20

Determine predetermined overhead rate.

FORMULA

Overhead 200000

	Total	Rate
Machine Hours	15000	13.33
Labor Hours	24000	8.33
Labor Dollars	80000	2.50

Overhead 200000

	Machine Hours		Labor Hours		Labor Dollars	
Item No.	Hours	Rate	Hours	Rate	Dollars	Rate
1	15000	13.33	24000	8.33	80000	2.50
2	14000	14.29	23000	8.70	79000	2.53
3	13000	15.38	22000	9.09	78000	2.56
4	12000	16.67	21000	9.52	77000	2.60
5	11000	18.18	20000	10.00	76000	2.63

Chapter 2 Problem 22

CH02PR22

Determine Cost per Unit from the data supplied.

Formula

	Direct Materials		150
	Direct Labor		200
Estimated Overhead		10000	
Estimated Machine Hours		5000	
	Rate per hour	2	
	Machine Hours	20	
	Overhead		40
	Total Cost		390

Please work these problems.
Compare your results with the prepared solution.

Item No.	Material+ Labor	Overhead	Estimated Hours	Number of Hours	Cost Per Unit
1	350	10000	50000	20	354.00
2	360	10000	50000	20	364.00
3	370	10000	50000	20	374.00
4	380	10000	50000	20	384.00
5	390	10000	50000	20	394.00
6	390	10000	50000	20	394.00
7	380	10000	50000	20	384.00
8	370	10000	50000	20	374.00
9	360	10000	50000	20	364.00
10	350	10000	50000	20	354.00
11	350	10000	50000	20	354.00
12	350	11000	50000	20	354.40
13	350	12000	50000	20	354.80
14	350	13000	50000	20	355.20
15	350	14000	50000	20	355.60
16	350	10000	50000	20	354.00
17	350	10000	51000	20	353.92
18	350	10000	52000	20	353.85
19	350	10000	53000	20	353.77
20	350	10000	54000	20	353.70
21	350	10000	50000	30	356.00
22	350	10000	50000	40	358.00
23	350	10000	50000	50	360.00
24	350	10000	50000	60	362.00
25	350	10000	50000	70	364.00

Chapter 2 Problem 23

Determine Cost per unit from the data supplied.

FORMULA

Direct Materials		300
Direct Labor		200
Estimated Overhead	20000	
Estimated Labor Hours	5000	
Rate per hour	4	
Labor hours	100	
Overhead		400

Total Cost		900
		=========

Please work these problems
Check your answers with the solution

Item No.	Material+ Labor	Overhead	Estimated Hours	Number of Hours	Cost Per Unit
1	400	10000	50000	20	404.00
2	410	10000	50000	20	414.00
3	420	10000	50000	20	424.00
4	430	10000	50000	20	434.00
5	440	10000	50000	20	444.00
6	450	10000	50000	20	454.00
7	440	10000	50000	20	444.00
8	430	10000	50000	20	434.00
9	420	10000	50000	20	424.00
10	410	10000	50000	20	414.00
11	400	20000	50000	20	408.00
12	400	21000	50000	20	408.40
13	400	22000	50000	20	408.80
14	400	23000	50000	20	409.20
15	400	24000	50000	20	409.60
16	400	10000	40000	20	405.00
17	400	10000	41000	20	404.88
18	400	10000	42000	20	404.76
19	400	10000	43000	20	404.65
20	400	10000	44000	20	404.55
21	400	10000	50000	40	408.00
22	400	10000	50000	50	410.00
23	400	10000	50000	60	412.00
24	400	10000	50000	70	414.00
25	400	10000	50000	80	416.00

Chapter 2 Problem 24

CH02PR24

Determine Cost per unit from the data supplied.

FORMULA

Direct Materials			150
Direct Labor			200
Estimated Overhead		10000	
Estimated Labor Dollars		5000	

SOLUTION

Direct Materials		150.00
Direct Labor		200.00
Overhead rate %	200	400.00

Total		750.00
		=========

Please work these problems
Check your answers with the solution

Item No.	Material	Overhead	Estimated Dollars	Labor	Cost Per Unit
1	150	10000	5000	200	750.00
2	160	10000	5000	200	760.00
3	170	10000	5000	200	770.00
4	180	10000	5000	200	780.00
5	190	10000	5000	200	790.00
6	150	10000	5000	200	750.00
7	140	10000	5000	200	740.00
8	130	10000	5000	200	730.00
9	120	10000	5000	200	720.00
10	110	10000	5000	200	710.00
11	350	10000	5000	200	950.00
12	350	11000	5000	200	990.00
13	350	12000	5000	200	1030.00
14	350	13000	5000	200	1070.00
15	350	14000	5000	200	1110.00
16	350	10000	5000	200	950.00
17	350	10000	6000	200	883.33
18	350	10000	7000	200	835.71
19	350	10000	8000	200	800.00
20	350	10000	9000	200	772.22
21	350	10000	50000	210	602.00
22	350	10000	50000	220	614.00
23	350	10000	50000	230	626.00
24	350	10000	50000	240	638.00
25	350	10000	50000	250	650.00

CH02PR23 Chapter 2 Problem 23

Chapter 2 Problem 25

CH02PR25

Determine total costs

FORMULA

		Per Unit	
Direct Materials		6.25	
Direct Labor		9.23	
Overhead (% of labor)	50	4.615	

Total Cost per unit		20.095	
		=========	
Number of units		10000	
Total Cost			200950

PRACTICE PROBLEMS

6.25 Direct Materials
9.23 Direct Labor
50 Overhead (% of Labor)

Item No.	Number of Units	Material	Labor	Overhead	Total Cost
1	10000	62500	92300	46150	200950
2	15000	93750	138450	69225	301425
3	20000	125000	184600	92300	401900
4	25000	156250	230750	115375	502375
5	30000	187500	276900	138450	602850
6	35000	218750	323050	161525	703325
7	40000	250000	369200	184600	803800
8	45000	281250	415350	207675	904275
9	50000	312500	461500	230750	1004750
10	55000	343750	507650	253825	1105225
11	10000	62500	92300	46150	200950
12	10000	63000	92300	46150	201450
13	10000	63500	92300	46150	201950
14	10000	64000	92300	46150	202450
15	10000	64500	92300	46150	202950
16	10000	65000	92300	46150	203450
17	10000	65500	92300	46150	203950
18	10000	66000	92300	46150	204450
19	10000	66500	92300	46150	204950
20	10000	67000	92300	46150	205450
21	100	625	923	462	2010
22	110	688	1015	508	2210
23	120	750	1108	554	2411
24	130	813	1200	600	2612
25	140	875	1292	646	2813

3 Process Costing

Condensed List of Items

Item No.		*Problems*
CH03PR01	Units Accounted for	5
CH03PR02	Units started	5
CH03PR03	Units completed	5
CH03PR04	Equivalent units—First In First Out	5
CH03PR05	Equivalent units—Average	5
CH03PR06	Equivalent units—FIFO/AVERAGE	5
CH03PR07	Unit cost—FIFO	5
CH03PR08	Unit cost—AVERAGE	5
CH03PR09	Unit cost—FIFO—AVERAGE	5
CH03PR10	Account for dollars—FIFO	5
CH03PR11	Account for dollars—AVERAGE	5
CH03PR12	Account for dollars—FIFO/AVERAGE	5
CH03PR13	Equivalent units—FIFO	5
CH03PR14	Equivalent units—AVERAGE	5
CH03PR15	Equivalent units—FIFO/AVERAGE	5
CH03PR16	Cost per unit—FIFO	5
CH03PR17	Cost per unit—AVERAGE	5

CH03PR18	Cost per unit—FIFO/AVERAGE	5
CH03PR19	Account for dollars—FIFO	5
CH03PR20	Account for dollars—AVERAGE	5
CH03PR21	Account for dollars—FIFO/AVERAGE	5
		105

SUMMARY—PROCESS COST

UNITS

CH03PR01...Account for total units
CH03PR02...Compute units started
CH03PR03...Compute units completed

DETERMINE EQUIVALENT UNITS OF PRODUCTION

	FIFO	AVERAGE	FIFO/AVE
UNITS COMPLETED	CH03PR04	CH03PR05	CH03PR06
UNITS STARTED	CH03PR13	CH03PR14	CH03PR15

COMPUTE UNIT COST

	FIFO	AVERAGE	FIFO/AVE
UNITS COMPLETED	CH03PR07	CH03PR08	CH03PR09
UNITS STARTED	CH03PR16	CH03PR17	CH03PR18

ACCOUNT FOR DOLLARS

	FIFO	AVERAGE	FIFO/AVE
UNITS COMPLETED	CH03PR10	CH03PR11	CH03PR12
UNITS STARTED	CH03PR19	CH03PR20	CH03PR21

STEPS TO COMPLETE PROCESS COST PROBLEMS

1. Account for units
2. Compute equivalent units

EUP = Equivalent Units of Production

First In First Out

Units Completed
\+ EUP – Ending Inventory
– EUP – Beginning Inventory
Equivalent Units of Production

Average

Units Completed
+ EUP – Ending Inventory
Equivalent Units of Production

3. Compute units cost
4. Account for dollars

	Ending Inventory
FIFO	Current Cost
AVERAGE	Average Cost

CH03PR01

Chapter 3 Problem 1
Account for units from data supplied.

Formula

	Work in Process - Beg	2000
+	Units Started	12000
	Units to be accounted for	14000
	Units Completed	10000
+	Work in Process - End	4000
	Units accounted for	14000

SCREEN DISPLAY

```
FACTS     FACTS     FACTS     Account for Units
                                 Units
Work in Process - Beginning       2000
Units Completed                  10000
Work in Process - End             4000

SOLUTION
                                Total   Completed   WIP-End
Work in Process - Beginning      2000
Started                         12000
Total                           14000     10000      4000
```

CELL CONTENT

	A	B	C	D	E	F
1	FACTS	FACTS	FACTS	Account f	or Units	
2				Units		
3	Work in P	rocess -	Beginning	2000		
4	Units Com	pleted		10000		
5	Work in P	rocess -	End	4000		
6						
7	SOLUTION					
8				Total	Completed	WIP-End
9	Work in P	rocess -	Beginning	+D3		
10	Started			+D4-D3+D5		
11	Total			+D9+D10	+D4	+D5

CH03PR02

Chapter 3 Problem 2
Determine units started from the data supplied.

Formula

	Units Completed	10000
+	Work in Process - End	4000
-	Work in Process - Beg	2000
	Units Started	12000

SCREEN DISPLAY

```
FACTS   Given:      Units completed
        Determine:  Units started
   Units                      Units
    10000 Units Completed
     4000 Work in Process  - End
     2000 Work in Process  - Beg
SOLUTION
                      Total  Completed  WIP-End
         WIP-Beg       2000
         Started      12000
         Total        14000    10000     4000
```

CELL CONTENT

	A	B	C	D	E
1	FACTS G	iven:	Units c	ompleted	
2	D	etermine:	Units s	tarted	
3	Units			Units	
4	10000	Units Co	mpleted		
5	4000	Work in	Process	- End	
6	2000	Work in	Process	- Beg	
7	SOLUTION				
8			Total	Completed	WIP-End
9		WIP-Beg	+A6		
10		Started	+A4+A5-A6		
11		Total	+C9+C10	+A4	+A5
12					

CH03PR03

Chapter 3 Problem 3

Determine units completed from data supplied.

FORMULA

	Work in Process - Beg	2000
+	Units Started	12000
-	Work in Process - End	4000
	Units Completed	10000

SCREEN DISPLAY

```
FACTS   Given:        Units Started
        Determine:    Units Completed
   Units                    Units
    10000 Units Started
     4000 Work in Process  - End
     2000 Work in Process  - Beg
SOLUTION
                    Total  Completed  WIP-End
         WIP-Beg     2000
         Started    10000
         Total      12000     8000      4000
```

CELL CONTENT

	A		B	C	D	E
1	FACTS	G	iven:	Units	Started	
2		D	etermine:	Units	Completed	
3	Units				Units	
4	10000		Units St	arted		
5	4000		Work in	Process	- End	
6	2000		Work in	Process	- Beg	
7	SOLUTION					
8				Total	Completed	WIP-End
9			WIP-Beg	+A6		
10			Started	+A4		
11			Total	+C9+C10	+C9+C10-A5	+A5

CH03PR04

Chapter 3 Problem 4
Determine Equivalent Units - First In First Out

Formula

Units	Per Cent Complete			Equiv. Units
10000	100		Units Completed	10000
4000	50	+	Work in Process - End	2000
2000	40	-	Work in Process - Beg	800
			Total Equivalent Units	11200

SCREEN DISPLAY

```
            FACTS     FIFO      Equivalent Units
   Units                      %  complete
    10000Completed
     2000WIP - Beg                    40
     4000WIP - End                    50
SOLUTION                  Units
Units Completed           10000              10000
WIP - End                  4000       50      2000
Total Units               14000
                                             12000
WIP - Beg                  2000       40       800
Equivalent Units                             11200
```

CELL CONTENT

	A	B	C	D	E
1		FACTS	FIFO	Equivalen	t Units
2	Units		%	complete	
3	10000	Completed			
4	2000	WIP - Beg		40	
5	4000	WIP - End		50	
6	SOLUTION		Units		
7	Units Com	pleted	+A3		+A3
8	WIP - End		+A5	+D5	+C8*(D8*.01)
9	Total Uni	ts	+C7+C8		
10					+E7+E8
11	WIP - Beg		+A4	+D4	+C11*(D11*.01)
12	Equivalen	t Units			+E10-E11

CH03PR05

Chapter 3 Problem 5
Determine Equivalent Units - Average

Formula

Units	Per Cent Complete		Equiv. Units
10000	100	Units Completed	10000
4000	50 +	Work in Process - End	2000
		Total Equivalent Units	12000
2000	40	Work in Process - Beg	

SCREEN DISPLAY

```
        FACTS     AVERAGE  Equivalent Units
   Units                    % complete
    10000Completed
     4000WIP - End                 50
     2000WIP - Beg                 40
SOLUTION
Units Completed        10000              10000
WIP - End               4000       50      2000
Total Units            14000
WIP - Beg               2000
Equivalent Units                          12000
```

CELL CONTENT

	A	B	C	D	E
1		FACTS	AVERAGE	Equivalen	t Units
2	Units		%	complete	
3	10000	Completed			
4	4000	WIP - End		50	
5	2000	WIP - Beg		40	
6	SOLUTION				
7	Units Com	pleted	+A3		+A3
8	WIP - End		+A4	+D4	+C8*(D8*.01)
9	Total Uni	ts	+C7+C8		
10	WIP - Beg		+A5		
11	Equivalen	t Units			+E7+E8

CH03PR06

Chapter 3 Problem 6
Determine Equivalent Units - FIFO/AVERAGE
FORMULA

Units	Per Cent Complete		Equiv. Units AVE.	FIFO
10000	100	Units Complete	10000	10000
4000	50	+ WIP - End	2000	2000
2000	40	+ WIP - Beg		800
		Equiv. Units	12000	11200

SCREEN DISPLAY

FACTS	Equivalent Units - FIFO - AVERAGE				
	Units	% complete			
Completed	10000				
WIP - End	4000	50			
WIP - Beg	2000	40			
SOLUTION		Units		Average	FIFO
Completed		10000		10000	10000
WIP - End		4000	50	2000	2000
Total Units		14000			
WIP - Beg		2000	40		800
Equivalent Units				12000	11200

CELL CONTENT

	A	B	C	D	E	F
1	FACTS	Equivalen	t Units -	FIFO -	AVERAGE	
2		Units	% complet	e		
3	Completed	10000				
4	WIP - End	4000	50			
5	WIP - Beg	2000	40			
6	SOLUTION		Units		Average	FIFO
7	Completed		+B3		+B3	+B3
8	WIP - End		+B4	+C4	+C8*(D8*.0 1)	+C8*(D8*.0 1)
9	Total Uni	ts	+C7+C8			
10						
11	WIP - Beg		+B5	+C5		+C11*(D11* .01)
12	Equivalen	t Units			+E7+E8	+F7+F8-F11

CH03PR07

Chapter 3 Problem 7

Compute Unit Cost - FIFO

Formula	Units	% Complete	
Complete			8000
+ WIP - End	4000	50	2000
- WIP - Beg	2000	40	800
Equivalent Units			9200
Costs added this period			25000
Cost per unit - FIFO			2.717391

SCREEN DISPLAY

```
FACTS     FACTS     FACTS       FIFO      FIFO
 Dollars     Units % Complete
     5000      2000        40 Work in process-Beginning
    25000     10000          Started
               4000        50 Work in process-End
SOLUTION Determine Unit Cost First in first out
Cost added this month                        25000
Units Completed                   8000
 + WIP End equivalent             2000
 - WIP Beg. equivalent             800
Total Equivalent units                        9200
Current cost per unit                      2.717391
```

CELL CONTENT

	A	B	C	D	E	F
1	FACTS	FACTS	FACTS	FIFO	FIFO	
2	Dollars	Units	% Complet	e		
3	5000	2000	40	Work in	process-B	eginning
4	25000	10000		Started		
5		4000	50	Work in	process-E	nd
6	SOLUTION	Determine	Unit Cos	t First i	n first o	ut
7	Cost adde	d this mo	nth		+A4	
8	Units Com	pleted		+B3+B4-B5		
9	+ WIP En	d equival	ent	+B5*(C5*.0 1)		
10	- WIP Be	g. equiva	lent	+B3*(C3*.0 1)		
11	Total Equ	ivalent u	nits		+D8+D9-D10	
12	Current c	ost per u	nit		+A4/E11	

CH03PR08

```
          Chapter 3 Problem 8
      Compute Unit Cost - AVERAGE
   Formula             Units     % Complete
          Complete                              8000
        + WIP - End       4000          50      2000
            Equivalent Units                   10000
          Costs added this period              25000
          WIP - Beg                             5000
          Total Costs                          30000
          Cost per unit - FIFO                  3.00
```

SCREEN DISPLAY

```
FACTS     FACTS     FACTS     Average  Average
 Dollars     Units % Complete
    5000      2000        40 Work in process-Beginning
   25000     10000          Started
              4000        50 Work in process-End
SOLUTION Determine Unit Cost Average
Total Costs                                 30000
Units Completed                     8000
 + WIP End equivalent               2000
 - WIP Beg. equivalent               800
Total Equivalent units                      10000
Average cost per unit                           3
```

CELL CONTENT

	A	B	C	D	E	F
1	FACTS	FACTS	FACTS	Average	Average	
2	Dollars	Units	% Complet	e		
3	5000	2000	40	Work in	process-B	eginning
4	25000	10000		Started		
5		4000	50	Work in	process-E	nd
6	SOLUTION	Determine	Unit Cos	t Average		
7	Total Cos	ts			+A3+A4	
8	Units Com	pleted		+B3+B4-B5		
9	+ WIP En	d equival	ent	+B5*(C5*.01)		
10	- WIP Be	g. equiva	lent	+B3*(C3*.01)		
11	Total Equ	ivalent u	nits		+D8+D9	
12	Average c	ost per u	nit		(A3+A4)/E11	

```
CH03PR09
                 Chapter 3 Problem 9
                 Compute Unit Costs - FIFO - AVERAGE
         Formula
                          Units  % Complete     FIFO   AVERAGE
                 Completed                       8000      8000
               + WIP - End      4000        50   2000      2000
               - WIP - Beg      2000        40    800
                 Equivalent Units                9200     10000
                 WIP - Beg               5000
                 Costs Added            25000
                 Costs                          25000     30000
                 Cost per unit - AVERAGE         2.72      3.00
```

SCREEN DISPLAY

```
FACTS    Cost Per Unit       FIFO   AVERAGE
 Dollars    Units % Complete
    5000      2000         40 Work in process-Beginning
   25000     10000           Started
              4000         50 Work in process-End
SOLUTION Determine Unit Cost             FIFO   Average
Costs                                   25000     30000
Units Completed                   8000
 + WIP End equivalent             2000
 - WIP Beg. equivalent             800
Total Equivalent units                   9200     10000
Cost per unit                            2.72      3.00
```

CELL CONTENT

	A	B	C	D	E	F
1	FACTS	Cost Per	Unit	FIFO	AVERAGE	CH03PR09
2	Dollars	Units	% Complet e			
3	5000	2000	40	Work in	process-B	eginning
4	25000	10000		Started		
5		4000	50	Work in	process-E	nd
6	SOLUTION	Determine	Unit Cos t		FIFO	Average
7	Costs				+A4	+A3+A4
8	Units Com	pleted		+B3+B4-B5		
9	+ WIP En	d equival	ent	+B5*(C5*.01)		
10	- WIP Be	g. equiva	lent	+B3*(C3*.01)		
11	Total Equ	ivalent u	nits		+D8+D9-D10	+E11+D10
12	Cost per	unit			+A4/E11	+F7/F11

SCREEN DISPLAY

CH03PR10

```
FACTS     FACTS     FACTS      FIFO     FIFO
 Dollars     Units % Complete
    5000      4000        50 Work in process-End
   25000     10000           Completed
              2000        40 Work in process-Beg
SOLUTION Determine Unit Cost First in first out
Costs added                      25000
Units Completed          10000
 + WIP End    EUP         2000
 - WIP Beg    EUP          800
Total EUP                        11200
Current cost per unit             2.23
```

SCREEN DISPLAY

```
SOLUTION FIFO Account for dollars - FIFO
                    Total Completed  W/P-End
W/P Beg              5000     5000
Added               25000    20536     4464

Total               30000    25536     4464
```

CELL CONTENT

	A	B	C	D	E	F
1	FACTS	FACTS	FACTS	FIFO	FIFO	
2	Dollars	Units	% Complet	e		
3	5000	4000	50	Work in	process-E	nd
4	25000	10000		Complete	d	
5		2000	40	Work in	process-B	eg
6	SOLUTION	Determine	Unit Cos	t First i	n first o	ut
7	Costs add	ed		+A4		
8	Units Com	pleted	+B4			
9	+ WIP En	d EUP	+B3*(C3*.01)			
10	- WIP Be	g EUP	+B5*(C5*.01)			
11	Total EUP			+C8+C9-C10		
12	Current c	ost per u	nit	+D7/D11		
13	SOLUTION	FIFO Acco	unt for d	ollars -	FIFO	
14			Total	Completed	W/P-End	
15	W/P Beg		+A3	+C15		
16	Added		+A4	+C16-(+C9 *D12)	+C9*D12	
17						
18	Total		+C15+C16	+D15+D16	+E16	

CH03PR11

SCREEN DISPLAY

```
FACTS     FACTS     FACTS     AVERAGE   AVERAGE
 Dollars     Units % Complete
    25000     10000           Completed
     5000      4000        50 Work in process-End
               2000        40 Work in process-Beg
SOLUTION Determine Unit Cost AVERAGE AVERAGE
Total Costs                       30000
Units Completed         10000
 + WIP End EUP           2000

Total Equivalent units            12000
        cost per unit              2.50
```

SCREEN DISPLAY

```
SOLUTION FIFO Account for dollars - AVERAGE
                     Total Completed  WIP-End
W/P Beg                5000
Added                 25000

Total                 30000     25000     5000
```

CELL CONTENT

	A	B	C	D	E	F
1	FACTS	FACTS	FACTS	AVERAGE	AVERAGE	
2	Dollars	Units	% Complet	e		
3	25000	10000		Complete	d	
4	5000	4000	50	Work in	process-E	nd
5		2000	40	Work in	process-B	eg
6	SOLUTION	Determine	Unit Cos	t AVERAGE	AVERAGE	
7	Total Cos	ts		+A3+A4		
8	Units Com	pleted	+B3			
9	+ WIP En	d EUP	+B4*(C4*.01)			
10						
11	Total Equ	ivalent u	nits	+C8+C9		
12	c	ost per u	nit	+D7/D11		
13	SOLUTION	FIFO Acco	unt for d	ollars -	AVERAGE	
14			Total	Completed	WIP-End	
15	W/P Beg		+A4			
16	Added		+A3			
17						
18	Total		+C15+C16	+C8*D12	+C9*D12	

CH03PR12

SCREEN DISPLAY

```
FACTS     FACTS     FACTS       FIFO    AVERAGE
 Dollars    Units % Complete
    25000     10000        50 Completed
     5000      4000        50 Work in process-End
               2000        40 Work in process-Beg
SOLUTION Determine Unit Cost AVERAGE    FIFO
Total Costs                    30000     25000
Units Completed         10000
 + WIP End EUP           2000
 - WIP Beg EUP            800
Total Equivalent units         12000     11200
Cost per unit                   2.50      2.23
```

SCREEN DISPLAY

```
SOLUTION        Account for dollars
                       Total
WIP Beg         $        5000
Added           $       25000
Total           $       30000
                                 AVERAGE     FIFO
Completed                 $       25000     25536
WIP-END    WIP-Beg        $        5000      4464
Total                     $       30000     30000
```

CELL CONTENT

	A	B	C	D	E	F
1	FACTS	FACTS	FACTS	FIFO	AVERAGE	
2	Dollars	Units	% Complet	e		
3	25000	10000		Complete	d	
4	5000	4000	50	Work in	process-E	nd
5		2000	40	Work in	process-B	eg
6	SOLUTION	Determine	Unit Cos	t AVERAGE	FIFO	
7	Total Cos	ts		+A3+A4	+A3	
8	Units Com	pleted	+B3			
9	+ WIP En	d EUP	+B4*(C4*.01)			
10	- WIP Be	g EUP	+B5*C5*.01			
11	Total Equ	ivalent u	nits	+C8+C9	+C8+C9-C10	
12	Cost per	unit		+D7/D11	+E7/E11	
13	SOLUTION	Acco	unt for d	ollars		
14			Total			
15	WIP Beg	$	+A4			
16	Added	$	+A3			
17	Total	$	+C15+C16			
18				AVERAGE	FIFO	
19	Completed		$	+C8*D12	+C17-(+C9 *E12)	
20	WIP-END	WIP-Beg	$	+C9*D12	/FI+C9*E12	
21	Total		$	+D19+D20	+E19+E20	

CH03PR13

Formula	Total Units		Units	% Comp	Equiv. Units
		Chapter 3 Problem 13			
		Determine Equivalent Units - FIFO			
WIP - Beg	2000	Complete	10000		10000
STARTED	12000	+WIP-End	4000	50	2000
WIP - End	4000	-WIP-Beg	2000	40	800
Completed	10000				11200

SCREEN DISPLAY

FACTS	FIFO	Equivalent Units	
Units		% complete	
12000Started			
2000WIP - Beg		40	
4000WIP - End		50	
SOLUTION	Units		
Units Completed	10000		10000
WIP - End	4000	50	2000
Total Units	14000		
			12000
WIP - Beg	2000	40	800
Equivalent Units			11200

CELL CONTENT

	A	B	C	D	E
1		FACTS	FIFO	Equivalen	t Units
2	Units		%	complete	
3	12000	Started			
4	2000	WIP - Beg		40	
5	4000	WIP - End		50	
6	SOLUTION		Units		
7	Units Com	pleted	+A4+A3-A5		+C7
8	WIP - End		+A5	+D5	+C8*(D8*.0 1)
9	Total Uni	ts	+C7+C8		
10					+E7+E8
11	WIP - Beg		+A4	+D4	+C11*(D11* .01)
12	Equivalen	t Units			+E10-E11

CH03PR14

Formula	Total Units	Chapter 3 Problem 14 Determine Equivalent Units - AVERAGE	Units	% Comp	Equiv. Units
WIP - Beg	2000	Complete	10000		10000
STARTED	12000	+WIP-End	4000	50	2000
WIP - End	4000	-WIP-Beg	2000	40	
Completed	10000				12000

SCREEN DISPLAY

	FACTS	AVERAGE	Equivalent Units	
Units			% complete	
12000	Started			
4000	WIP - End		50	
2000	WIP - Beg		40	
SOLUTION				
Units Completed		10000		10000
WIP - End		4000	50	2000
Total Units		14000		
WIP - Beg		2000		
Equivalent Units				12000

CELL CONTENT

	A	B	C	D	E
1		FACTS	AVERAGE	Equivalen	t Units
2	Units		%	complete	
3	12000	Started			
4	4000	WIP - End		50	
5	2000	WIP - Beg		40	
6	SOLUTION				
7	Units Com	pleted	+A5+A3-A4		+C7
8	WIP - End		+A4	+D4	+C8*(D8*.0 1)
9	Total Uni	ts	+C7+C8		
10	WIP - Beg		+A5		
11	Equivalen	t Units			+E7+E8

CH03PR15

Formula	Total Units		% Comp	Equiv. Units AVERAGE	FIFO
		Chapter 3 Problem 15			
		Determine Equivalent Units - FIFO - AVERAGE			
WIP - Beg	2000	Complete		10000	10000
STARTED	12000	+WIP-End	50	2000	2000
WIP - End	4000	-WIP-Beg	40		800
Completed	10000	Equivalent Units		12000	11200

SCREEN DISPLAY

FACTS	Equivalent Units -	FIFO - AVERAGE			
	Units	% complete			
STARTED	12000				
WIP - End	4000	50			
WIP - Beg	2000	40			
SOLUTION		Units		Average	FIFO
Completed		10000		10000	10000
WIP - End		4000	50	2000	2000
Total Units		14000			
WIP - Beg		2000	40		800
Equivalent Units				12000	11200

CELL CONTENT

	A	B	C	D	E	F
1	FACTS	Equivalen	t Units -	FIFO -	AVERAGE	
2		Units	% complet	e		
3	STARTED	12000				
4	WIP - End	4000	50			
5	WIP - Beg	2000	40			
6	SOLUTION		Units		Average	FIFO
7	Completed		+B5+B3-B4		+C7	+C7
8	WIP - End		+B4	+C4	+C8*(D8*.0 1)	+C8*(D8*.0 1)
9	Total Uni	ts	+C7+C8			
10						
11	WIP - Beg		+B5	+C5		+C11*(D11* .01)
12	Equivalen	t Units			+E7+E8	+F7+F8-F11

CH03PR16

```
                Chapter 3 Problem 16
                Determine Cost per unit - FIFO
      Formula   Cost added this month                       25000
                                                  Equiv.
         Units                          % Comp     Units
          10000  STARTED
           2000+ WIP - Beg      -          40        800
           4000- WIP - End      +          50       2000
           8000 Completed       +                   8000
                 Equivalent Units                            9200
                 Cost per unit                               2.72
```

SCREEN DISPLAY

```
FACTS     FIFO      Cost Per Unit       FIFO
 Dollars     Units % Complete
    5000      2000        40 Work in process-Beginning
   25000     10000          Started
              4000        50 Work in process-End
SOLUTION Determine Unit Cost First in first out
Cost added this month                          25000
Units Completed                       8000
 + WIP End equivalent                 2000
 - WIP Beg. equivalent                 800
Total Equivalent units                          9200
Current cost per unit                       2.717391
```

CELL CONTENT

```
        A            B            C            D             E            F

1    FACTS        FIFO         Cost Per     Unit          FIFO
2     Dollars        Units     % Complet    e

3   5000         2000         40             Work in      process-B    eginning
4   25000        10000                      Started
5                4000         50             Work in      process-E    nd
6    SOLUTION     Determine     Unit Cos    t First i     n first o    ut
7    Cost adde    d this mo    nth                        +A4
8    Units Com    pleted                    +B3+B4-B5
9     + WIP En    d equival    ent          +B5*(C5*.0
                                            1)
10    - WIP Be    g. equiva    lent         +B3*(C3*.0
                                            1)
11   Total Equ    ivalent u    nits                       +D8+D9-D10
12   Current c    ost per u    nit                        +A4/E11
```

CH03PR17

```
                 Chapter 3 Problem 17
                 Determine Cost per unit - AVERAGE
        Formula            Total Costs                        30000
                                                Equiv.
           Units                     % Comp     Units
            10000  STARTED
             2000+ WIP - Beg
             4000- WIP - End     +        50         2000
             8000                                    8000
                 Equivalent Units                             10000
                 Cost per unit                                 3.00
```

SCREEN DISPLAY

```
FACTS    FACTS    FACTS
 Dollars    Units % Complete
     5000     2000       40 Work in process-Beginning
    25000    10000          Started
              4000       50 Work in process-End
SOLUTION Determine Unit Cost  Average

Total Cost                              30000
Units Completed                 8000
 + WIP End equivalent           2000
Total Equivalent units                  10000
Cost Per Unit                               3
```

CELL CONTENT

	A	B	C	D	E	F
1	FACTS	FACTS	FACTS			
2	Dollars	Units	% Complet	e		
3	5000	2000	40	Work in	process-B	eginning
4	25000	10000		Started		
5		4000	50	Work in	process-E	nd
6	SOLUTION	Determine	Unit Cos	t Averag	e	
7						
8	Total Cos	t			+A3+A4	
9	Units Com	pleted		+B3+B4-B5		
10	+ WIP En	d equival	ent	+B5*(C5*.0 1)		
11	Total Equ	ivalent u	nits		+D9+D10	
12	Cost Per	Unit			+E8/E11	

CH03PR18

```
          Chapter 3 Problem 18
          Determine Cost per unit - FIFO - AVERAGE
Formula             % Comp.    Units     FIFO  AVERAGE
          Cost added                     25000    25000
          WIP - Beg                                5000
   Units                       % CompEquiv #
    10000  STARTED
     2000+ WIP - Beg              40       800
     4000- WIP - End     +        50      2000     2000
     8000 Completed      +                8000     8000
           Equivalent Units               9200    10000
           Cost per unit                  2.72     3.00
```

SCREEN DISPLAY

```
FACTS    FACTS    FACTS      FIFO   AVERAGE
 Dollars    Units % Complete
    5000     2000       40 Work in process-Beginning
   25000    10000         Started
             4000       50 Work in process-End
SOLUTION Determine Unit Cost          FIFO   AVERAGE
Costs                                25000    30000
Units Completed                 8000
 + WIP End equivalent           2000
 - WIP Beg. equivalent           800
Total Equivalent units                9200    10000
Cost per unit                         2.72     3.00
```

CELL CONTENT

```
This is the cell content of CH3PR18/VC:                          Page 1

          A           B           C           D           E           F

  1   FACTS       FACTS       FACTS          FIFO      AVERAGE     CH03PR18
  2    Dollars       Units    % Complet   e

  3  5000        2000        40            Work in     process-B   eginning
  4  25000       10000                    Started
  5              4000        50            Work in     process-E   nd
  6   SOLUTION    Determine    Unit Cos   t              FIFO       AVERAGE
  7   Costs                                          +A4         +A3+A4
  8   Units Com   pleted                  +B3+B4-B5
  9    + WIP En   d equival   ent         +B5*(C5*.0
                                          1)
 10    - WIP Be   g. equiva   lent        +B3*(C3*.0
                                          1)
 11   Total Equ   ivalent u   nits                   +D8+D9-D10  +D8+D9
 12   Cost per    unit                                  +A4/E11     +F7/F11
```

CH03PR19

SCREEN DISPLAY

```
FACTS     FACTS     FACTS        FIFO      FIFO
 Dollars    Units % Complete
    5000      2000         40 Work in process-Beginning
   25000     10000            Started
              4000         50 Work in process-End
SOLUTION Determine Unit Cost First in first out
Cost added this month             25000
Units Completed          8000
 + WIP End EUP           2000
 - WIP Beg EUP            800
Total Equivalent units             9200
Current cost per unit              2.72
```

SCREEN DISPLAY

```
SOLUTION FIFO Account for dollars - FIFO
                          Total Completed  W/P-End
W/P Beg                    5000     5000
Added                     25000    19565     5435

Total                     30000    24565     5435
```

CELL CONTENT

	A	B	C	D	E	F
1	FACTS	FACTS	FACTS	FIFO	FIFO	CH03PR19
2	Dollars	Units	% Complet	e		
3	5000	2000	40	Work in	process-B	eginning
4	25000	10000		Started		
5		4000	50	Work in	process-E	nd
6	SOLUTION	Determine	Unit Cos	t First i	n first o	ut
7	Cost adde	d this mo	nth	+A4		
8	Units Com	pleted	+B3+B4-B5			
9	+ WIP En	d EUP	+B5*(C5*.0 1)			
10	- WIP Be	g EUP	+B3*(C3*.0 1)			
11	Total Equ	ivalent u	nits	+C8+C9-C10		
12	Current c	ost per u	nit	+D7/D11		
13	SOLUTION	FIFO Acco	unt for d	ollars -	FIFO	
14			Total	Completed	W/P-End	
15	W/P Beg	$	+A3	+C15		
16	Added	$	+A4	I+C16-(+ C9*D12)	+C9*D12	
17						
18	Total	$	+C15+C16	+D15+D16	+E16	

SCREEN DISPLAY

CH03PR20

```
FACTS     FACTS     FACTS     AVERAGE   AVERAGE
 Dollars     Units % Complete
    25000    10000          Started
     5000     4000       50 Work in process-End
              2000       40 Work in process-Beg
SOLUTION Determine Unit Cost AVERAGE AVERAGE
Total Costs                    30000
Units Completed         8000
 + WIP End EUP          2000

Total Equivalent units         10000
Cost per unit                   3.00
```

SCREEN DISPLAY

```
SOLUTION      Account for dollars - AVERAGE
                     Total Completed  WIP-End
W/P Beg               5000
Added                25000

Total                30000    24000      6000
```

CELL CONTENT

	A	B	C	D	E	F
1	FACTS	FACTS	FACTS	AVERAGE	AVERAGE	
2	Dollars	Units	% Complet	e		
3	25000	10000		Started		
4	5000	4000	50	Work in	process-E	nd
5		2000	40	Work in	process-B	eg
6	SOLUTION	Determine	Unit Cos	t AVERAGE	AVERAGE	
7	Total Cos	ts		+A3+A4		
8	Units Com	pleted	+B3+B5-B4			
9	+ WIP En	d EUP	+B4*(C4*.0 1)			
10						
11	Total Equ	ivalent u	nits	+C8+C9		
12	Cost per	unit		+D7/D11		
13	SOLUTION	FIFO Acco	unt for d	ollars -	AVERAGE	
14			Total	Completed	WIP-End	
15	W/P Beg		+A4			
16	Added		+A3			
17						
18	Total		+C15+C16	+C8*D12	+C9*D12	

CH03PR21

SCREEN DISPLAY

```
FACTS   Account for Dollars  FIFO   AVERAGE
 Dollars    Units % Complete
    25000    10000          Started
              4000       50 Work in process-End
     5000     2000       40 Work in process-Beginning
SOLUTION Determine Unit Cost         FIFO       AVERAGE
Costs                                   25000     30000
Units Completed                     8000
 + WIP End equivalent               2000
 - WIP Beg. equivalent               800
Total Equivalent units                   9200     10000
Cost Per Unit                            2.72      3.00
```

SCREEN DISPLAY

```
SOLUTION       Account for dollars -     FIFO    AVERAGE
                      Total
WIP Beg                5000
Added                 25000
Total                 30000

Completed                               24565     24000
WIP-End                                  5435      6000
Total                                   30000     30000
```

CELL CONTENT

	A	B	C	D	E	F
1	FACTS A	ccount fo	r Dollars	FIFO	AVERAGE	
2	Dollars	Units	% Complet	e		
3	25000	10000		Started		
4		4000	50	Work in	process-E	nd
5	5000	2000	40	Work in	process-B	eginning
6	SOLUTION	Determine	Unit Cos	t	FIFO	AVERAGE
7	Costs				+A3	+A3+A5
8	Units Com	pleted		+B3+B5-B4		
9	+ WIP En	d equival	ent	+B4*C4*.01		
10	- WIP Be	g. equiva	lent	+B5*(C5*.0 1)		
11	Total Equ	ivalent u	nits		+D8+D9-D10	+D8+D9
12	Cost Per	Unit			+E7/E11	+F7/F11
13	SOLUTION	Acco	unt for d	ollars -	FIFO	AVERAGE
14			Total			
15	WIP Beg		+A5			
16	Added		+A3			
17	Total		+C15+C16			
18						
19	Completed				+C17-(+ D10*E12)	+D8*F12
20	WIP-End				+D9*E12	+D9*F12
21	Total				+E19+E20	+F19+F20

PRACTICE PROBLEMS

Problem 1

Formula

Account for units from data supplied.

	Work in Process - Beg	2000
+	Units Started	12000
	Units to be accounted for	14000
	Units Completed	10000
+	Work in Process - End	4000
	Units accounted for	14000

Item No.

1	2000	10000	4000	14000	12000
2	3000	10000	3000	13000	10000
3	4000	10000	2000	12000	8000
4	5000	10000	1000	11000	6000
5	6000	10000	0	10000	4000

Problem 2

Determine units started from data supplied.

FORMULA

	Units completed	10000
+	Work in Process - End	4000
-	Work in Process - Beg	2000
	Units started	12000

Item No.	Units Completed	WIP-End	WIP-Beg	Started
1	10000	4000	2000	12000
2	12000	4000	2000	14000
3	14000	4000	2000	16000
4	16000	4000	2000	18000
5	18000	4000	2000	20000

Problem 3

Determine units completed from data supplied.

FORMULA

	Work in Process - Beg	2000
+	Units Started	12000
-	Work in Process - End	4000
	Units Completed	10000

Item No.	Units Started	WIP-End	WIP-Beg	Completed
1	10000	4000	2000	8000
2	11000	4000	2000	9000
3	13000	4000	2000	11000
4	15000	4000	2000	13000
5	17000	4000	2000	15000

PRACTICE PROBLEMS Chapter 3

Problem 4

Determine Equivalent Units - First In First Out

Formula

Units	Per Cent Complete		Equiv. Units
10000	100	Units Completed	10000
4000	50 +	Work in Process - End	2000
2000	40 -	Work in Process - Beg	800
		Total Equivalent Units	11200

FIRST IN FIRST OUT

Completed	10000
End WIP	4000
Beg. WIP	2000

Item No.	% of completion End WIP	Beg. WIP	Equiv. #
1	50	40	11200
2	52	42	11240
3	54	44	11280
4	56	46	11320
5	58	48	11360

Problem 5 PRACTICE PRACTICE PRACTICE PRACTICE PRACTICE PRACTICE

Determine Equivalent Units - Average

Formula

Units	Per Cent Complete		Equiv. Units
10000	100	Units Completed	10000
4000	50 +	Work in Process - End	2000
		Total Equivalent Units	12000
2000	40	Work in Process - Beg	

AVERAGE

Completed	10000
End WIP	4000
Beg. WIP	2000

Item No.	% of completion End WIP	Beg. WIP	Equiv. #
1	50	40	12000
2	52	42	12080
3	54	44	12160
4	56	46	12240
5	58	48	12320

Please work these problems
Check your answers with the solution

Problem 6

Determine Equivalent Units - FIFO/AVERAGE
FORMULA

Units	Per Cent Complete		Equiv. Units AVE.	Equiv. Units FIFO
10000	100	Units Complete	10000	10000
4000	50	+ WIP - End	2000	2000
2000	40	+ WIP - Beg		800
		Equiv. Units	12000	11200

Units Completed	10000
Work in Process - End	4000
Work in Process - Beginning	2000

Item No.	WIP-End	WIP-Beg	Equivalent Units FIFO	Equivalent Units AVERAGE
1	50	40	12000	11200
2	52	42	12080	11240
3	54	44	12160	11280
4	56	46	12240	11320
5	58	48	12320	11360

PRACTICE PRACTICE PRACTICE PRACTICE PRACTICE PRACTICE

Problem 7

Compute Unit Cost - FIFO

Formula	Units	% Complete	
Complete			8000
+ WIP - End	4000	50	2000
- WIP - Beg	2000	40	800
Equivalent Units			9200
Costs added this period			25000
Cost per unit - FIFO			2.717391

Dollars	Units	% Complete	
5000	2000	40	WIP - Beginning
25000	10000		Started
	4000	50	WIP - End

Item No.	Work in Process Beg.	Work in Process End	Completed	FIFO EUP	Unit Cost
1	40	50	8000	9200	2.72
2	42	52	8000	8000	3.13
3	44	54	8000	7000	3.57
4	46	56	8000	8000	3.13
5	48	58	8000	10000	2.50

Please work these problems.
Compare your results with the solution.

Problem 8

Compute Unit Cost - AVERAGE

Formula	Units	% Complete	
Complete			8000
+ WIP - End	4000	50	2000
Equivalent Units			10000
Costs added this period			25000
WIP - Beg			5000
Total Costs			30000
Cost per unit - FIFO			3.00

Dollars	Units	% Complete	
5000	2000	40	WIP - Beginning
25000	10000		Started
	4000	50	WIP - End

Item No.	Work in Process % of complete Beg.	End	Completed	Average EUP	Unit Cost
1	40	50	8000	10000	3.00
2	42	52	8000	10080	2.98
3	44	54	8000	10160	2.95
4	46	56	8000	10240	2.93
5	48	58	8000	10320	2.91

Problem 9 PRACTICE PRACTICE PRACTICE PRACTICE PRACTICE PRACTICE

Compute Unit Costs - FIFO - AVERAGE

Formula	Units	% Complete	FIFO	AVERAGE
Completed			8000	8000
+ WIP - End	4000	50	2000	2000
- WIP - Beg	2000	40	800	
Equivalent Units			9200	10000
WIP - Beg		5000		
Costs Added		25000		
Costs			25000	30000
Cost per unit - AVERAGE			2.72	3.00

Dollars	Units	% Complete	
5000	2000	40	WIP - Beginning
25000	10000		Started
	4000	50	WIP - End
	8000		Completed

Item No.	Work in Process Beg.	End	FIFO EUP	FIFO CPU	Average EUP	Average CPU
1	40	50	9200	2.72	10000	3.00
2	42	52	9240	2.71	10080	2.98
3	44	54	9280	2.69	10160	2.95
4	46	56	9320	2.68	10240	2.93
5	48	58	9360	2.67	10320	2.91

PRACTICE PROBLEMS

Chapter 3

Problem 10

Formula

Account for Dollars - FIFO

	Units	% Comp.	FIFO	
WIP - Beg			5000	
Current Costs			25000	30000
Equivalent Units			11200	
Cost per unit			2.23	
WIP - End	4000	50	2.23	4464
Completed				25536
Total Costs				30000

5000 WIP-Beg $

Units

8000 Started
4000 WIP-End
2000 WIP-Beg
10000 Completed

Item No.	Dollars Added	% Complete Work in Process Beg.	End	First in First out WIP-End	Completed
1	25000	40	50	4464	25536
2	26000	40	50	4643	26357
3	27000	40	50	4821	27179
4	28000	40	50	5000	28000
5	29000	40	50	5179	28821

Problem 11 PRACTICE PRACTICE PRACTICE PRACTICE PRACTICE PRACTICE

Formula

Account for Dollars - AVERAGE

	Units	% Comp.	AVERAGE	
WIP - Beg			5000	
Current Costs			25000	30000
Equivalent Units			12000	
Cost per unit			2.50	
WIP - End	4000	50	2.50	5000
Completed	10000		2.50	25000
Total Costs				30000

8000 Started
4000 WIP-End
2000 WIP-Beg
10000 Completed

Item No.	Total Dollars	% Complete Work in Process Beg.	End	Average Equiv. Units	Dollars Completed	WIP-End
1	30000	40	50	12000	25000	5000
2	35000	40	50	12000	29167	5833
3	40000	40	50	12000	33333	6667
4	45000	40	50	12000	37500	7500
5	50000	40	50	12000	41667	8333

Problem 12

Account for dollars - AVE/FIFO

Formula			AVERAGE		FIFO	
	To be acctd for					
	WIP - Beg		$ 5000		$ 5000	
	Current Costs		25000		25000	
	Equivalent Units		12000		11200	
	Cost per unit		2.50	*	2.23	**
	Accounted for as follows:					
% Complete		Units	AVERAGE		FIFO	
50	WIP - End	4000	5000		4460	**
	Costs		25000	*	25540	
	Total		30000		30000	

Dollars

25000	Costs added
5000	WIP-Beg $

Units

8000	Started
4000	WIP-End
2000	WIP-Beg
10000	Completed

	% Complete Work in Process		First in First out		Average	
Item No.	Beg.	End	WIP-End	Completed	WIP-End	Completed
1	40	50	4464	25536	5000	25000
2	42	50	4480	25520	5000	25000
3	44	50	4496	25504	5000	25000
4	46	50	4513	25487	5000	25000
5	48	50	4529	25471	5000	25000

Problem 13 PRACTICE PRACTICE PRACTICE PRACTICE

Determine Equivalent Units - FIFO

Formula	Total Units		Units	% Comp	Equiv. Units
WIP - Beg	2000	Complete	10000		10000
STARTED	12000	+WIP-End	4000	50	2000
WIP - End	4000	-WIP-Beg	2000	40	800
Completed	10000				11200

FIRST IN FIRST OUT

Started	12000
End WIP	4000
Beg. WIP	2000
Completed	10000

	% of completion		
Item No.	End WIP	Beg. WIP	Equiv. #
1	50	40	11200
2	52	42	11240
3	54	44	11280
4	56	46	11320
5	58	48	11360

Please work these problems.
Compare your results with the solution.

Problem 14

Determine Equivalent Units - AVERAGE

Formula	Total Units		Units	% Comp	Equiv. Units
WIP - Beg	2000	Complete	10000		10000
STARTED	12000	+WIP-End	4000	50	2000
WIP - End	4000	-WIP-Beg	2000	40	
Completed	10000				12000

AVERAGE

Started	12000
End WIP	4000
Beg. WIP	2000
Completed	10000

	% of completion		
Item No.	End WIP	Beg. WIP	Equiv. #
1	50	40	12000
2	52	42	12080
3	54	44	12160
4	56	46	12240
5	58	48	12320

Please work these problems.
Compare your results with the solution.

Problem 15

Determine Equivalent Units - FIFO - AVERAGE

Formula	Total Units		% Comp	Equiv. Units AVERAGE	FIFO
WIP - Beg	2000	Complete		10000	10000
STARTED	12000	+WIP-End	50	2000	2000
WIP - End	4000	-WIP-Beg	40		800
Completed	10000	Equivalent Units		12000	11200

Units Started	12000
Work in Process - End	4000
Work in Process - Beginning	2000
Units Completed	10000

			Equivalent Units	
Item No.	WIP-End	WIP-Beg	FIFO	AVERAGE
1	50	40	12000	11200
2	52	42	12080	11240
3	54	44	12160	11280
4	56	46	12240	11320
5	58	48	12320	11360

Problem 16

Determine Cost per unit - FIFO

Formula	Cost added this month				25000
Units			% Comp	Equiv. Units	
10000	STARTED				
2000+	WIP - Beg	-	40	800	
4000-	WIP - End	+	50	2000	
8000	Completed	+		8000	
	Equivalent Units				9200
	Cost per unit				2.72

Dollars	Units	% Complete	
5000	2000	40	WIP - Beginning
25000	10000		Started
	4000	50	WIP - End

Item No.	Work in Process Beg.	End	Completed	First In First Out EUP	CPU
1	40	50	8000	9200	2.72
2	42	52	8000	8000	3.13
3	44	54	8000	7000	3.57
4	46	56	8000	8000	3.13
5	48	58	8000	10000	2.50

Problem 17 PRACTICE PRACTICE PRACTICE PRACTICE PRACTICE PRACTICE

Determine Cost per unit - AVERAGE

Formula	Total Costs				30000
Units			% Comp	Equiv. Units	
10000	STARTED				
2000+	WIP - Beg				
4000-	WIP - End	+	50	2000	
8000				8000	
	Equivalent Units				10000
	Cost per unit				3.00

Dollars	Units	
5000	2000	WP Beginning
25000	10000	Started
	4000	WP End

Item No.	Work in Process % of Completion Beg.	End	Units Completed	EUP Average	Unit Cost
1	40	50	8000	10000	3.00
2	42	52	8000	10080	2.98
3	44	54	8000	10160	2.95
4	46	56	8000	10240	2.93
5	48	58	8000	10320	2.91

Problem 18

Determine Cost per unit - FIFO - AVERAGE

Formula		% Comp.	Units	FIFO	AVERAGE
Cost added				25000	25000
WIP - Beg					5000
Units			% Comp	Equiv #	
10000 STARTED					
2000+ WIP - Beg			40	800	
4000- WIP - End	+		50	2000	2000
8000 Completed	+			8000	8000
Equivalent Units				9200	10000
Cost per unit				2.72	3.00

Dollars	Units		
25000	10000	Started	Started
	4000	WIP - End	
5000	2000	WIP - Beginning	
	8000	Completed	

	Work in Process		FIFO		AVERAGE	
Item No.	Beg.	End	EUP	CPU	EUP	CPU
1	40	50	11200	2.23	12000	2.50
2	42	52	11240	2.22	12080	2.48
3	44	54	11280	2.22	12160	2.47
4	46	56	11320	2.21	12240	2.45
5	48	58	11360	2.20	12320	2.44

Please work these problems.
Compare your results with the solution.

Problem 19

Account for Dollars - FIFO

Formula					
Costs added this period			25000		
Equivalent Units				9200	
Cost per unit				2.72	
WIP - Beg			5000		
To be accounted for					30000
	Units	% Comp.	Per Unit		
WIP - End	4000	50	2.72	5435	
Completed				24565	
Accounted for					30000

5000 $ WIP-Beg

Units	
10000	Started
2000	WIP-Beg
4000	WIP-End
8000	Completed

	Dollars	% Complete			First In - First Out	
	Added	Work in Process				
Item No.		Beg.	End	EUP	WIP-End	Completed
1	25000	40	50	9200	5435	24565
2	26000	40	50	9200	5652	25348
3	27000	40	50	9200	5870	26130
4	28000	40	50	9200	6087	26913
5	29000	40	50	9200	6304	27696

Problem 20

Account for Dollars - AVERAGE

Formula					
WIP - Beg			5000		
Costs added this period			25000		
Equivalent Units				10000	
Cost per unit				3.00	
To be accounted for					30000
	Units	% Comp.	Per Unit		
WIP - End	4000	50	3.00	6000	
Completed	8000		3.00	24000	
Accounted for					30000

10000 Started
4000 WIP-End
2000 WIP-Beg
8000 Completed

	Total	% Complete		Average		
	Dollars	Work in Process		Equiv.	Dollars	
Item No.		Beg.	End	Units	Completed	WIP-End
1	30000	40	50	10000	24000	6000
2	35000	40	50	10000	28000	7000
3	40000	40	50	10000	32000	8000
4	45000	40	50	10000	36000	9000
5	50000	40	50	10000	40000	10000

Problem 21 PRACTICE PRACTICE PRACTICE PRACTICE PRACTICE PRACTICE

				FIFO	AVERAGE
Formula					
Costs				25000	30000
Equivalent Units				9200	10000
Cost Per Unit				2.72	3.00
WIP-Beg			$	5000	5000
Added This Period				25000	25000
To be accounted for			$	30000	30000
	Units	% Comp.			
WIP-End	4000	50		5435	6000
Completed	8000			24565	24000
Accounted for				30000	30000

5000 $ WIP Beg $
Units
10000 Started
2000 WIP-Beg
4000 WIP-End
8000 Completed

	Dollars	% Complete		First in First out		AVERAGE	
	Added	Work in Process					
Item No.		Beg.	End	WIP-End	Completed	WIP-End	Completed
1	25000	40	50	5435	24565	6000	24000
2	26000	40	50	5652	25348	6200	24800
3	27000	40	50	5870	26130	6400	25600
4	28000	40	50	6087	26913	6600	26400
5	29000	40	50	6304	27696	6800	27200

CHAPTER 3

SUMMARY - PROCESS COST

STEPS TO COMPLETE PROCESS COST PROBLEMS

1. Account for units
2. Compute equivalent units

   EUP = Equivalent Units of Production

   First In First Out

   Units Completed
   + EUP - Ending Inventory
   - EUP - Beginning Inventory
   Equivalent Units of Production

   Average

   Units Completed
   + EUP - Ending Inventory
   Equivalent Units of Production
3. Compute unit cost
4. Account for dollars

	Ending Inventory
FIFO	Current Cost
AVERAGE	Average Cost

UNITS

CH03PR01 ... Account for total units
CH03PR02 ... Compute units started
CH03PR03 ... Compute units completed

DETERMINE EQUIVALENT UNITS OF PRODUCTION

	FIFO	AVERAGE	FIFO/AVE
UNITS COMPLETED	CH03PR04	CH03PR05	CH03PR06
UNITS STARTED	CH03PR13	CH03PR14	CH03PR15

COMPUTE UNIT COST

	FIFO	AVERAGE	FIFO/AVE
UNITS COMPLETED	CH03PR07	CH03PR08	CH03PR09
UNITS STARTED	CH03PR16	CH03PR17	CH03PR18

ACCOUNT FOR DOLLARS

	FIFO	AVERAGE	FIFO/AVE
UNITS COMPLETED	CH03PR10	CH03PR11	CH03PR12
UNITS STARTED	CH03PR19	CH03PR20	CH03PR21

4 Cost Behavior

Condensed List of Items

Item No.		*Problems*
CH04PR01	Variable expense—V.E. %	25
CH04PR02	Variable expense—V.E. per unit	25
CH04PR03	Variable expense—Fixed expense	25
CH04PR04	Fixed expense	25
CH04PR05	High-low—Fixed expense	25
CH04PR06	High-low—V.E. rate and fixed	25
CH04PR07	High-low—Variable rate	25
CH04PR08	Least squares	
CH04PR09	Least squares	
CH04PR10	Formula (y = a + bx)	25
	Total	200

HOW TO USE THE MATERIAL IN THIS CHAPTER

The way to learn about spreadsheets is to work with them on a computer. The instructions in this chapter will help you if you input them in a computer and observe the results of changes in the FACTS. One of the advantages of the use of spreadsheets is that it is not necessary to have a background in computer science to use them. After you have selected the item in this chapter that you desire to work, follow these procedures.

Input the CELL CONTENT of the item into your computer exactly as we have indicated.

In order to make certain that you have copied the CELL CONTENT, we have provided you with a number of items that you may use to check your work. Change the FACTS of the item that you pressed in your computer with the data that we have supplied.

Compare your SOLUTION with the SOLUTION that we have provided. If they are the same, save the project.

Input your own FACTS and observe the changes in the SOLUTION. You may focus on the concepts in the problem without the tedium of arithmetical computations. You have the opportunity to work an infinite number of problems and the computer will make the computations. You may observe trends and the impact of the changes of the FACTS on the SOLUTION.

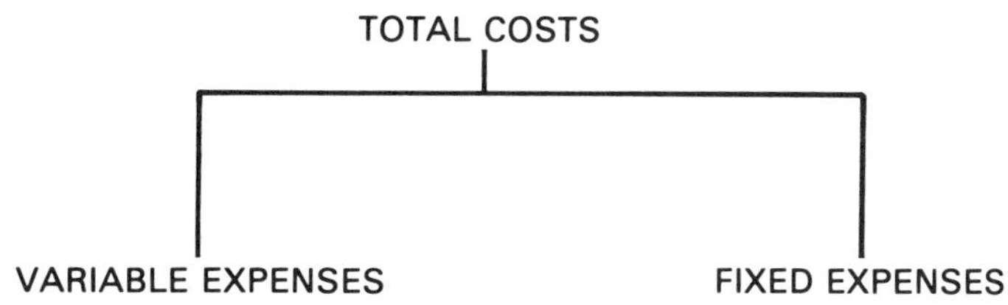
TOTAL COSTS
VARIABLE EXPENSES
FIXED EXPENSES

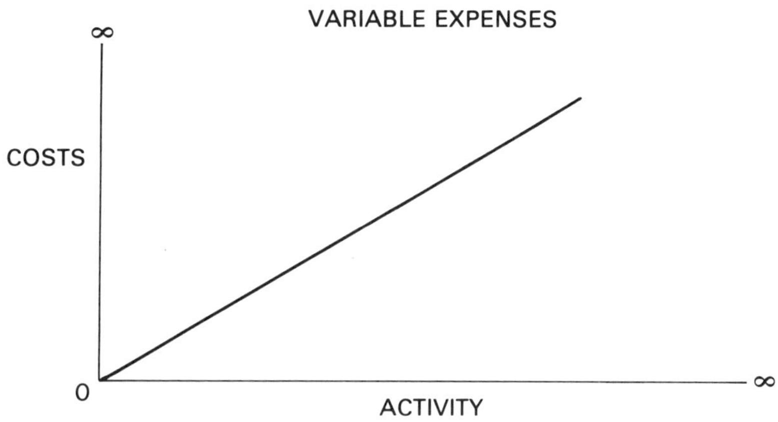
VARIABLE EXPENSES
∞
COSTS
0
ACTIVITY
∞

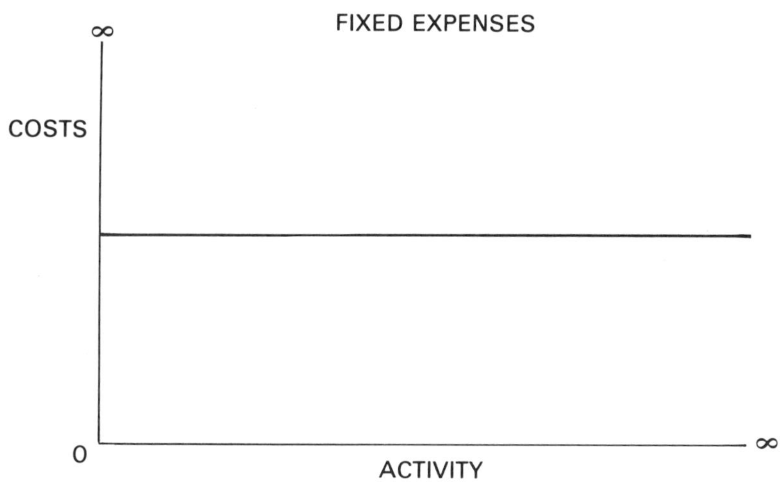
FIXED EXPENSES
∞
COSTS
0
ACTIVITY
∞

CH04PR01

Chapter 4 Problem 1

Compute Amount of Variable expense using amount of sales and variable expense percent.

SCREEN DISPLAY

```
                    FACTS

     10000 Sales $
        80 Variable Expense %

SOLUTION           SOLUTION

Variable Exp.  $        8000
```

CELL CONTENT

	A	B	C	D
1	FACTS		FACTS	
2				
3	10000	Sales $	Units	
4	80	Variable	Expense	%
5				
6	SOLUTION		SOLUTION	
7				
8	Variable	Exp. $	+A3*(A4*.01)	

CH04PR02

Chapter 4 Problem 2

Compute Amount of Variable expense using units of sales and amount of variable expense per unit.

SCREEN DISPLAY

```
FACTS                 FACTS

      5000 Sales - Units
        10 V.E. $ - Per Unit

SOLUTION              SOLUTION

Variable Exp.  $       50000
```

CELL CONTENT

	A	B	C
1	FACTS		FACTS
2			
3	5000	Sales -	Units
4	10	V.E. $ -	Per Unit
5			
6	SOLUTION		SOLUTION
7			
8	Variable	'Exp. $	+A3*A4

CH04PR03

Chapter 4 Problem 3

Given:
  Sales, Fixed Expense and Net Income
Compute:
  Amount of Variable expense and
  variable expense percent.

SCREEN DISPLAY

```
  FACTS                FACTS

   100000 Sales - Dollars

    30000 Fixed Expense $
    10000 Net Income
SOLUTION             SOLUTION

Variable Expense $     60000
Variable Expense %        60
```

CELL CONTENT

	A	B	C
1	FACTS		FACTS
2			
3	100000	Sales -	Dollars
4			
5	30000	Fixed Ex	pense $
6	10000	Net Inco	me
7	SOLUTION		SOLUTION
8			
9	Variable	Expense $	+A3-A5-A6
10	Variable	Expense %	(+C9/A3)* 100

CH04PR04

Chapter 4 Problem 4

Given:
  Units manufactured
  Fixed expense dollars
Compute:
 Fixed expense per unit

SCREEN DISPLAY

```
      FACTS                FACTS

         8000 Manufactured - Units
        30000 Fixed Expense -  Dollars

    SOLUTION             SOLUTION
                             Fixed Expense
                          Dollars  Per Unit
    Fixed Expense            30000     3.75
```

CELL CONTENT

	A	B	C	D
1	FACTS		FACTS	
2				
3	8000	Manufact	ured - Un	its
4	30000	Fixed Ex	pense -	Dollars
5				
6	SOLUTION		SOLUTION	
7			Fixed	Expense
8			Dollars	Per Unit
9	Fixed Exp	ense	+A4	+A4/A3

CH04PR05

Chapter 4 Problem 5

Given:		Units	Dollars
	High	10000	30000
	Low	5000	30000

Compute:
Variable rate per unit
Fixed expense dollars

SCREEN DISPLAY

```
FACTS               FACTS

                       Units  Dollars
          High         10000    30000
          Low           5000    30000
SOLUTION            SOLUTION
                      Units   Dollars Variable     Fixed
          High         10000    30000        0     30000
          Low           5000    30000        0     30000
          Diff.         5000        0
Variable Rate Per Unit              0    F.E =     30000
```

CELL CONTENT

	A	B	C	D	E	F
1	FACTS		FACTS			
2						
3			Units	Dollars		
4		High	10000	30000		
5		Low	5000	30000		
6	SOLUTION		SOLUTION			
7			Units	Dollars	Variable	Fixed
8		High	+C4	+D4	+C8*D11	+D8-E8
9		Low	+C5	+D5	+C9*D11	+D9-E9
10		Diff.	+C8-C9	+D8-D9		
11	Variable	Rate Per	Unit	+D10/C10	F.E =	+F9

CH04PR06

Chapter 4 Problem 6

```
Given:                  Units  Dollars
         High           10000    30000
         Low             5000    30000
Compute:
 Variable rate per unit
 Fixed expense dollars
```

SCREEN DISPLAY

```
FACTS                FACTS

                         Units  Dollars
         High            20000    30000
         Low              5000    15000
SOLUTION             SOLUTION
                        Units   Dollars Variable     Fixed
         High            20000    30000    20000     10000
         Low              5000    15000     5000     10000
                         15000    15000
Variable Rate Per Unit             1.00 F.E.         10000
```

CELL CONTENT

	A	B	C	D	E	F
1	FACTS		FACTS			
2						
3			Units	Dollars		
4		High	10000	30000		
5		Low	5000	15000		
6	SOLUTION		SOLUTION			
7			Units	Dollars	Variable	Fixed
8		High	+C4	+D4	+C8*D11	+D8-E8
9		Low	+C5	30000	+C9*D11	+D9-E9
10			+C8-C9	+D8-D9		
11	Variable	Rate Per	Unit	+D10/C10	F.E.	+F9

CH04PR07

Chapter 4 Problem 7

Given:		Units	Dollars
	High	10000	30000
	Low	5000	30000

Compute:
Variable rate per unit
Fixed expense dollars

SCREEN DISPLAY

FACTS		FACTS			
		Units	Dollars		
	High	8000	1000		
	Low	5000	700		
SOLUTION		SOLUTION			
		Units	Dollars	Variable	Fixed
	High	8000	1000	800	200
	Low	5000	700	500	200
		3000	300		
Variable	Rate Per	Unit	.1		

CELL CONTENT

	A	B	C	D	E	F
1	FACTS		FACTS			
2						
3			Units	Dollars		
4		High	8000	1000		
5		Low	5000	700		
6	SOLUTION		SOLUTION			
7			Units	Dollars	Variable	Fixed
8		High	+C4	+D4	+C8*D11	+D8-E8
9		Low	+C5	+D5	+C9*D11	+D9-E9
10			+C8-C9	+D8-D9		
11	Variable	Rate Per	Unit	+D10/C10		

CH04PR08

SCREEN DISPLAY

FACTS		12	Number of items	
	Units	Dollars		
	X	Y	XY	X2
January	17	5500	93500	289
February	19	5800	110200	361
March	25	7000	175000	625
April	22	6500	143000	484
May	18	5600	100800	324
June	15	4900	73500	225
Totals	116	35300	696000	2308

SCREEN DISPLAY

SOLUTION					
			696000	116	2308
			35300	12	116
Multiply by		12	8352000	1392	27696
		22	776600	264	2552
	Difference		7575400	1128	25144
				Variable rate	301.2806
				Fixed expense	5.554489

CELL CONTENT

	A	B	C	D	E	F
1	FACTS		12	Number o	f items	
2		Units	Dollars			
3		X	Y	XY	X2	
4	January	17	3000+2500	+B4*C4	+B4*B4	
5	February	19	5800	+B5*C5	+B5*B5	
6	March	25	7000	+B6*C6	+B6*B6	
7	April	22	6500	+B7*C7	+B7*B7	
8	May	18	5600	+B8*C8	+B8*B8	
9	June	15	4900	+B9*C9	+B9*B9	
10	Totals	@SUM(B4... B9	@SUM(C4... C9	@SUM(D4... D9	@SUM(E4... E9	
11						
12						
13	SOLUTION					
14				+D10	+B10	+E10
15				+C10	+C1	+B10
16	Multiply	by	+C1	+D14*C16	+E14*C16	+F14*C16
17			+B7	+D15*C17	+E15*C17	+F15*C17
18						
19		D	ifference	+D16-D17	+E16-E17	+F16-F17
20				Vari	able rate	+D19/F19
21				Fixe	d expense	+D14-(F14* F20)/E14

CH04PR09

SCREEN DISPLAY

FACTS			12 Number of items		CH04PR09
	Units	Dollars			
	X	Y	XY	X2	
January	23	5500	126500	529	
February	28	5800	162400	784	
March	33	7000	231000	1089	
April	38	6500	247000	1444	
May	43	5600	240800	1849	
June	48	4900	235200	2304	
Totals	213	35300	1242900	7999	

SCREEN DISPLAY

SOLUTION				
		1242900	213	7999
		35300	12	213
Multiply by	12	14914800	2556	95988
	38	1341400	456	8094
	Difference	13573400	2100	87894
			Variable rate	154.4292
			Fixed expense	35.77859

CELL CONTENT

	A	B	C	D	E	F
1	FACTS		12	Number o	f items	
2		Units	Dollars			
3		X	Y	XY	X2	
4	January	23	3000+2500	+B4*C4	+B4*B4	
5	February	+B4+5	5800	+B5*C5	+B5*B5	
6	March	+B5+5	7000	+B6*C6	+B6*B6	
7	April	+B6+5	6500	+B7*C7	+B7*B7	
8	May	+B7+5	5600	+B8*C8	+B8*B8	
9	June	+B8+5	4900	+B9*C9	+B9*B9	
10	Totals	@SUM(B4... B9	@SUM(C4... C9	@SUM(D4... D9	@SUM(E4... E9	
11						
12	SOLUTION					
13				+D10	+B10	+E10
14				+C10	+C1	+B10
15	Multiply	by	+C1	+D13*C15	+E13*C15	+F13*C15
16			+B7	+D14*C16	+E14*C16	+F14*C16
17						
18		D	ifference	+D15-D16	+E15-E16	+F15-F16
19				Vari	able rate	+D18/F18
20				Fixe	d expense	+D13-(F13*F19)/E13

CH04PR10

Chapter 4 Problem 10

Given:
a = Fixed expense
b = Variable rate per unit
x = Number of units
Compute:
y = amount of expense

SCREEN DISPLAY

FACTS	FACTS	FACTS	FACTS	FACTS
	Fixed	a =	154.4292	
	Variable	b =	35.77859	
	Units	x =	10.00	
SOLUTION		SOLUTION		SOLUTION
y	=	a	+	bx
512.2151		154.4292		357.7859

CELL CONTENT

	A	B	C	D	E
1	FACTS	FACTS	FACTS	FACTS	FACTS
2					
3		Fixed	a =	154.4292	
4		Variable	b =	35.77859	
5		Units	x =	10	
6	SOLUTION		SOLUTION		SOLUTION
7	y	=	a	+	bx
8	+C8+E8		+D3		+D4*D5

Chapter 4 Problem 1

CH04PR01

Compute Amount of Variable expense using amount of sales and variable expense percent.

PRACTICE PROBLEMS

PRACTICE PRACTICE PRACTICE PRACTICE PRACTICE PRACTICE

Please work these problems.
Compare your results with the solution.

Item No.	Sales Dollars	Variable %	V. E. Dollars
1	10000	80	8000
2	15000	80	12000
3	20000	80	16000
4	25000	80	20000
5	30000	80	24000
6	10000	82	8200
7	10000	84	8400
8	10000	86	8600
9	10000	88	8800
10	10000	90	9000
11	9500	80	7600
12	9000	80	7200
13	8500	80	6800
14	8000	80	6400
15	7500	80	6000
16	10000	78	7800
17	10000	76	7600
18	10000	74	7400
19	10000	72	7200
20	10000	70	7000
21	10000	80	8000
22	11000	78	8580
23	12000	76	9120
24	13000	74	9620
25	14000	72	10080

CH04PR02

Chapter 4 Problem 2

Compute Amount of Variable expense
using units of sales and amount of
variable expense per unit.

PRACTICE PRACTICE PRACTICE PRACTICE PRACTICE PRACTICE

PRACTICE PROBLEMS

Please work these problems.
Compare your results with the solution.

Item No.	Sales Units	V.E. Per Unit	V. E. Dollars
1	5000	8	40000
2	10000	8	80000
3	15000	8	120000
4	20000	8	160000
5	25000	8	200000
6	10000	10	100000
7	10000	12	120000
8	10000	14	140000
9	10000	16	160000
10	10000	18	180000
11	9500	8	76000
12	9000	8	72000
13	8500	8	68000
14	8000	8	64000
15	7500	8	60000
16	10000	8	80000
17	10000	6	60000
18	10000	4	40000
19	10000	2	20000
20	10000	0	0
21	10000	8	80000
22	11000	6	66000
23	12000	4	48000
24	13000	2	26000
25	14000	0	0

PRACTICE PROBLEMS

PRACTICE PROBLEMS

PRACTICE PRACTICE PRACTICE PRACTICE PRACTICE PRACTICE

Given:
Sales, Fixed Expense and Net Income
Compute:
Amount of Variable expense and
variable expense percent.

Please work these problems.
Compare your results with the solution.

Item No.	Sales Dollars	F.E. Dollars	Net Income	Variable Expense Dollars	Variable Expense Per Cent
1	100000	30000	10000	60000	60
2	105000	35000	15000	55000	52
3	110000	40000	20000	50000	45
4	115000	45000	25000	45000	39
5	120000	50000	30000	40000	33
6	100000	52000	32000	16000	16
7	100000	54000	34000	12000	12
8	100000	56000	36000	8000	8
9	100000	58000	38000	4000	4
10	100000	60000	40000	0	0
11	99500	18000	20000	61500	62
12	99000	18000	20000	61000	62
13	98500	18000	20000	60500	61
14	98000	18000	20000	60000	61
15	97500	18000	20000	59500	61
16	100000	18200	20200	61600	62
17	100000	18400	20400	61200	61
18	100000	18600	20600	60800	61
19	100000	18800	20800	60400	60
20	100000	19000	21000	60000	60
21	10000	800	800	8400	84
22	11000	600	600	9800	89
23	12000	400	400	11200	93
24	13000	200	200	12600	97
25	14000	0	0	14000	100

CH04PR04

Chapter 4 Problem 4

PRACTICE PROBLEMS

Given:
  Units manufactured
  Fixed expense dollars
Compute:
 Fixed expense per unit

Please work these problems.
Compare your results with the solution.

	Fixed Expense		
Item No.	Dollars	Units	Per Unit
1	30000	8000	3.75
2	35000	8000	4.38
3	40000	8000	5.00
4	45000	8000	5.63
5	50000	8000	6.25
6	30000	8000	3.75
7	25000	8000	3.13
8	20000	8000	2.50
9	15000	8000	1.88
10	10000	8000	1.25
11	30000	8000	3.75
12	30000	9000	3.33
13	30000	10000	3.00
14	30000	11000	2.73
15	30000	12000	2.50
16	30000	8000	3.75
17	30000	7000	4.29
18	30000	6000	5.00
19	30000	5000	6.00
20	30000	4000	7.50
21	30000	8000	3.75
22	31000	8275	3.75
23	32000	8525	3.75
24	33000	8800	3.75
25	34000	9075	3.75

CH04PR05

Chapter 4 Problem 5

PRACTICE PROBLEMS

		Units	Dollars
Given:			
	High	10000	30000
	Low	5000	30000

Compute:
Variable rate per unit
Fixed expense dollars

Please work these problems.
Compare your results with the solution.

	Units		Dollars			
Item No.	High	Low	High	Low	Variable	Fixed
1	10000	5000	30000	30000	0	30000
2	11000	5000	30000	30000	0	30000
3	12000	5000	30000	30000	0	30000
4	13000	5000	30000	30000	0	30000
5	14000	5000	30000	30000	0	30000
6	10000	5000	29000	29000	0	29000
7	10000	6000	28000	28000	0	28000
8	10000	7000	27000	27000	0	27000
9	10000	8000	26000	26000	0	26000
10	10000	9000	25000	25000	0	25000
11	10000	9500	400	400	0	400
12	9500	10000	410	410	0	410
13	9000	10500	420	420	0	420
14	8500	11000	430	430	0	430
15	8000	11500	440	440	0	440
16	10000	5000	3400	3400	0	3400
17	9500	5500	3500	3500	0	3500
18	9000	6000	3600	3600	0	3600
19	8500	6500	3700	3700	0	3700
20	8000	7000	3800	3800	0	3800
21	10000	5000	3900	3900	0	3900
22	10000	4950	4000	4000	0	4000
23	10000	4900	4100	4100	0	4100
24	10000	4850	4200	4200	0	4200
25	10000	4800	4300	4300	0	4300

PRACTICE PROBLEMS PRACTICE PROBLEMS

PRACTICE PRACTICE PRACTICE PRACTICE PRACTICE PRACTICE

Given:		Units	Dollars
	High	10000	30000
	Low	5000	30000

Compute:
Variable rate per unit
Fixed expense dollars

Please work these problems.
Compare your results with the solution.

Item No.	Units High	Units Low	Dollars High	Dollars Low	Variable Per Unit	Fixed
1	20000	5000	30000	15000	1.00	10000
2	20500	5000	30000	15000	0.97	10161
3	21000	5000	30000	15000	0.94	10313
4	21500	5000	30000	15000	0.91	10455
5	22000	5000	30000	15000	0.88	10588
6	19500	5000	30000	15000	1.03	9828
7	20000	5000	30000	15000	1.00	10000
8	20500	5000	30000	15000	0.97	10161
9	21000	5000	30000	15000	0.94	10313
10	21500	5000	30000	15000	0.91	10455
11	20000	6000	30000	15000	1.07	8571
12	20000	7000	30000	15000	1.15	6923
13	20000	8000	30000	15000	1.25	5000
14	20000	9000	30000	15000	1.36	2727
15	20000	10000	30000	15000	1.50	0
16	20000	4500	30000	15000	0.97	10645
17	20000	5500	30000	15000	1.03	9310
18	20000	6500	30000	15000	1.11	7778
19	20000	7500	30000	15000	1.20	6000
20	20000	8500	30000	15000	1.30	3913
21	20000	5000	29000	16000	0.87	11667
22	20000	5000	28000	17000	0.73	13333
23	20000	5000	27000	18000	0.60	15000
24	20000	5000	26000	19000	0.47	16667
25	20000	5000	25000	20000	0.33	18333

CH04PR07

Chapter 4 Problem 7

PRACTICE PRACTICE PRACTICE PRACTICE PRACTICE PRACTICE

PRACTICE PROBLEMS PRACTICE PROBLEMS

Given:		Units	Dollars
	High	10000	30000
	Low	5000	30000

Compute:
Variable rate per unit
Fixed expense dollars

Please work these problems.
Compare your results with the solution.

Item No.	Units High	Units Low	Dollars High	Dollars Low	Variable	Fixed
1	8000	5000	1000	700	0.10	200
2	9000	5000	1000	700	0.08	325
3	10000	5000	1000	700	0.06	400
4	11000	5000	1000	700	0.05	450
5	12000	5000	1000	700	0.04	486
6	8000	5500	1000	700	0.12	40
7	8000	3000	2000	1000	0.20	400
8	8000	4000	1000	700	0.08	400
9	8000	5000	1000	700	0.10	200
10	8000	6000	1000	800	0.10	200
11	8000	5000	1100	800	0.10	300
12	8000	5000	1200	800	0.13	133
13	8000	5000	1300	900	0.13	233
14	8000	5000	1400	900	0.17	67
15	8000	5000	1500	1000	0.17	167
16	8000	5000	1000	900	0.03	733
17	8000	5000	1000	950	0.02	867
18	8000	5000	1000	1000	0.00	1000
19	8000	5000	800	500	0.10	0
20	8000	5000	400	250	0.05	0
21	8000	5000	1000	700	0.10	200
22	8000	5000	1000	750	0.08	333
23	8000	5000	1000	800	0.07	467
24	8000	5000	1000	850	0.05	600
25	8000	5000	1000	900	0.03	733

Chapter 4 Problem 10

CH04PR10

PRACTICE PRACTICE PRACTICE PRACTICE PRACTICE PRACTICE

PRACTICE PROBLEMS PRACTICE PROBLEMS

Given:
a = Fixed expense
b = Variable rate per unit
x = Number of units
Compute:
y = amount of expense

Please work these problems.
Compare your results with the solution.

Item No.	a	b	x	y
1	154.4292	35.77859	10	512.2151
2	48	50	10	548
3	58	50	10	558
4	68	50	10	568
5	78	50	10	578
6	45.78	50	12	645.78
7	58.12	50	14	758.12
8	70.46	50	16	870.46
9	82.80	50	18	982.8
10	95.14	50	20	1095.14
11	8	5	10	58
12	11	5	10	61
13	14	5	10	64
14	17	5	10	67
15	20	5	10	70
16	120	75	20	1620
17	130	75	20	1630
18	140	75	20	1640
19	150	75	20	1650
20	160	75	20	1660
21	50	20	20	450
22	50	25	20	550
23	50	30	20	650
24	50	35	20	750
25	50	40	20	850

5 Break-even Sales

Condensed List of Items

Item No.	Given	Compute	*Problems*
CH05PR01	Variable expense % Fixed expense	Break-even sales dollars	5
CH05PR02	Variable expense $ Fixed expense	Break-even sales dollars	5
CH05PR03	S. P. per unit V. E. per unit Fixed expenses	Break-even sales dollars	5
CH05PR04	S. P. per unit V. E. per unit Fixed expenses	Break-even sales dollars Break-even sales units	5
CH05PR05	S. P. per unit V.E. % Fixed expenses Desired profit	Break-even sales dollars Break-even sales units Sales for desired profit	5
CH05PR06	V.E. $ Fixed expenses S. P. per unit	Break-even sales dollars Break-even sales units	5

CH05PR07	V.E. % Fixed expenses S. P. per unit Proposed sales—units	Break-even sales dollars Proposed sales	5
CH05PR08	V.E. $ Fixed expenses S. P. per unit Proposed sales—units	Break-even sales dollars Break-even sales units Proposed sales dollars Proposed sales units	5
CH05PR09	V.E. % B.E. Sales $	Fixed expenses	5
CH05PR10	V.E. $ V.E. $	Fixed expenses	5
CH05PR11	V.E. % Fixed expenses B.E. Sales units	B.E. Sales $ S. P. per unit	5
CH05PR12	V.E. % Fixed expenses S. P. per unit	B.E. Sales dollars B.E. Sales units	5
CH05PR13	Sales Variable expenses Profit	Fixed expenses B.E. Sales dollars	5
CH05PR14	Sales Variable expenses Profit S. P. per unit	Fixed expenses B.E. Sales dollars B.E. Sales units	25
CH05PR15	Desired profit Sales—units Sales—dollars Expenses	V.E.—per unit Fixed expenses S.P.—per unit B. E.—dollars & units Sales—desired profit dollars & units	—
CH05PR16	V.E. % Fixed expenses S.P.—per unit Volume	V. E. $ Contribution Margin Income	25
	Total		115

BREAKEVEN SALES

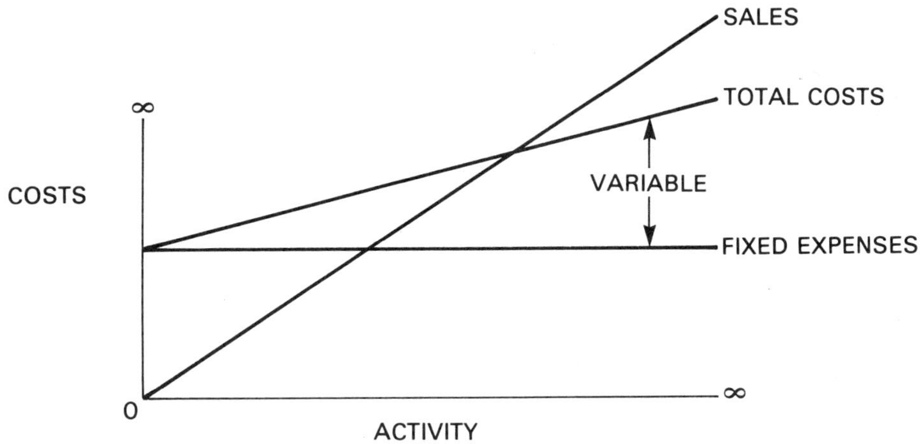

Increase in	Effect On Breakeven Sales
Variable Expense	Increase
Fixed Expense	Increase
Selling Price	Decrease
Decrease in	
Variable Expense	Decrease
Fixed Expense	Increase
Selling Price	Increase

EFFECT OF COSTS ON BREAKEVEN SALES

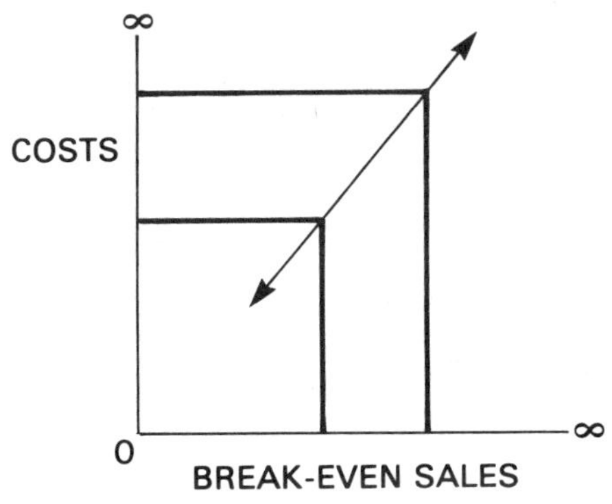

EFFECT OF SELLING PRICE ON BREAKEVEN SALES

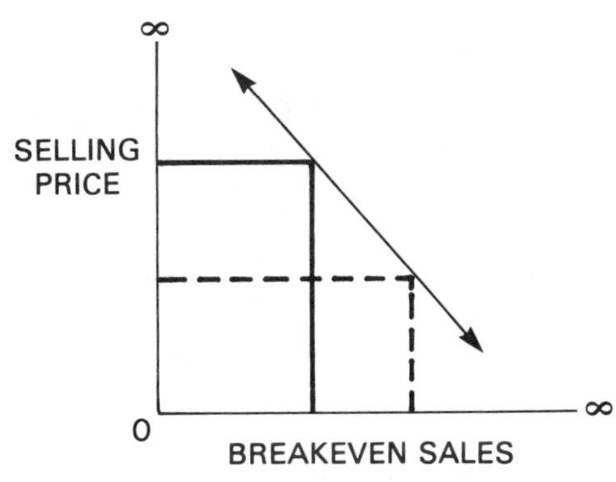

Relationships

Increase

	V.E. % +	V.E. $ +	F.E. +	SP per # +
BES $	+	+	+	−
BES #	+	+	+	−
COGS	+	+	+	N.E.
CM	−	−	−	+
Profit	−	−	−	+
CPU	+	+	+	N.E.

Decrease

	V.E. %	V.E. $	F.E.	SP per #
BES $	−	−	−	+
BES #	−	−	−	+
COGS	−	−	−	N.E.
CM	+	+	+	−
Profit	+	+	+	−
CPU	−	−	−	N.E.

LEGEND

+	increase
−	decrease
N.E.	no effect
V.E. %	Variable expense per cent
V.E. $	Variable expense dollars
F.E.	Fixed expense
SP per #	Selling price per unit
BES $	Break-even sales dollars
BES #	Break-even sales units
COGS	Cost of goods sold
CM	Contribution Margin
Profit	Profit
CPU	Cost per unit

Chapter 5
Condensed List of Items

Filename		Problems
CH05PR01	Break-even sales No. 1	5
CH05PR02	Break-even sales No. 2	5
CH05PR03	Break-even sales No. 3	5
CH05PR04	Break-even sales No. 4	5
CH05PR05	Break-even sales No. 5	5
CH05PR06	Break-even sales No. 6	5
CH05PR07	Break-even sales No. 7	5
CH05PR08	Break-even sales No. 8	5
CH05PR09	Break-even sales No. 9	5
CH05PR10	Break-even sales No. 10	5
CH05PR11	Break-even sales No. 11	5
CH05PR12	Break-even sales No. 12	5
CH05PR13	Break-even sales No. 13	5
CH05PR14	Break-even sales No. 14	25
CH05PR15	Break-even sales No. 15	---
CH05PR16	Contribution Margin	25
	Total	115

CH05PR01

Chapter 5 Problem 1

Given:
   Variable Expense %
   Fixed Expenses
Required
   Compute break-even sales

SCREEN DISPLAY

FACTS	FACTS	FACTS	
	VARIABLE EXPENSES	80 %	
	FIXED	10000	
SOLUTION	SOLUTION	SOLUTION	
		Break-Even Sales	50000

CELL CONTENT

	A	B	C	D	E	F
1	FACTS		FACTS		FACTS	
2						
3			VARIABLE	EXPENSES	80	%
4			FIXED		10000	
5						
6						
7						
8						
9	SOLUTION		SOLUTION		SOLUTION	
10						
11				Break-Eve	n Sales	+E4/(1-(E3 *.01)

CH05PR02

Chapter 5 Problem 2

```
Given:
   Variable Expense   $
   Fixed Expenses
Required
   Compute break-even sales
```

SCREEN DISPLAY

```
  FACTS              FACTS              FACTS

                   Variable Expense $      8000
                   Fixed Expense          10000



SOLUTION           SOLUTION           SOLUTION

                            Break-Even Sales       18000
```

CELL CONTENT

	A	B	C	D	E	F
1	FACTS		FACTS		FACTS	
2						
3			VARIABLE	EXPENSES$	8000	
4			FIXED		10000	
5						
6						
7						
8						
9	SOLUTION		SOLUTION		SOLUTION	
10						
11				Break-Eve	n Sales	+E3+E4

CH05PR03

```
                    Chapter 5 Problem 3
        Given:
           Selling Price - per unit
           Variable expense - per unit
           Fixed expense
        Required
           Compute break-even sales
```

SCREEN DISPLAY

```
   FACTS               FACTS                FACTS
                 Per Unit
Selling Price - per unit          10
V.E. - per unit                    8
Fixed expenses                 10000



SOLUTION           SOLUTION            SOLUTION

                            Break-Even Sales       50000
```

CELL CONTENT

	A	B	C	D	E	F
1	FACTS		FACTS		FACTS	
2		Per	Unit			
3	Selling P	rice - pe	r unit	10		
4	V.E. - pe	r unit		8		
5	Fixed exp	enses		10000		
6						
7						
8						
9	SOLUTION		SOLUTION		SOLUTION	
10						
11				Break-Eve	n Sales	+D5/(1-(D4 /D3))

CH05PR04

```
                Chapter 5 Problem 4
          Given:
             Selling Price - per unit
             Variable expense - per unit
             Fixed expense
          Required
             Compute break-even sales dollars
             Compute break-even sales units
```

SCREEN DISPLAY

```
    FACTS              FACTS                FACTS
                  Per Unit
 Selling Price - per unit          10
 V.E. - per unit                    8
 Fixed expenses                 10000



 SOLUTION            SOLUTION             SOLUTION

                              Break-Even Sales $     50000
                              BES - Units             5000
```

CELL CONTENT

	A	B	C	D	E	F
1	FACTS		FACTS		FACTS	
2		Per	Unit			
3	Selling P	rice - pe	r unit	10		
4	V.E. - pe	r unit		8		
5	Fixed exp	enses		10000		
6					/F$	
7						
8						
9	SOLUTION		SOLUTION		SOLUTION	
10						
11				Break-Eve	n Sales $	+D5/(1-(D4 /D3))
12				BES - Uni	ts	+F11/D3

CH05PR05

Chapter 5 Problem 5

Given:

- Selling Price - per unit
- Variable expense %
- Fixed expense
- Desired profit

Required

- Compute break-even sales dollars
- Compute break-even sales units
- Compute sales for desired profit

SCREEN DISPLAY

```
   FACTS               FACTS                FACTS
               Per Unit
 Selling Price - per unit          10
 Variable Expense %                80
 Fixed expenses                  8000
 Desired Profit                  2000
 SOLUTION           SOLUTION                     Sales
                             Break-Even     $     40000
                             Break-Even Units      4000
                        Sales for desired profit   50000
```

CELL CONTENT

	A	B	C	D	E	F
1	FACTS		FACTS		FACTS	
2		Per	Unit			
3	Selling P	rice - pe	r unit	10		
4	Variable	Expense %		80		
5	Fixed exp	enses		8000		
6	Desired P	rofit		2000		
7						
8	SOLUTION		SOLUTION			Sales
9				Break-Eve	n $	+D5/(1-(D4 *.01))
10				Break-Eve	n Units	+F9/D3
11		S	ales for	desired p	rofit	(+D5+D6)/(1-(D4*.01)

CH05PR06

```
              Chapter 5 Problem 6
Given:
   Variable expense   $
   Fixed expense
   Selling Price - per unit
Required
   Compute break-even sales dollars
   Compute break-even sales units
```

SCREEN DISPLAY

```
FACTS                 FACTS                 FACTS

Variable Expense $                    8000
Fixed expenses                        8000
S.P. per unit                           10

SOLUTION              SOLUTION                        Sales

                                Break-Even      $      16000
                                Break-Even - Units      1600
```

CELL CONTENT

	A	B	C	D	E	F
1	FACTS		FACTS		FACTS	
2						
3	Variable	Expense $		8000		
4	Fixed exp	enses		8000		
5	S.P. per	unit		10		
6						
7	SOLUTION		SOLUTION			Sales
8						
9				Break-Eve	n $	+D3+D4
10				Break-Eve	n - Units	+F9/D5

CH05PR07

Chapter 5 Problem 7

Given:
- Variable expense %
- Fixed expenses
- Selling Price - per unit
- Proposed sales - units

Required
- Compute break-even sales dollars
- Compute break-even sales units
- Compute proposed sales dollars
- Compute proposed sales units

SCREEN DISPLAY

FACTS		FACTS		FACTS
Variable Expense %			80	
Fixed expenses			8000	
S.P. per unit			10	
Proposed sales - units			5000	
			Sales	
SOLUTION			Dollars	Units
	Break-Even	$	40000	4000
	Proposed sales		50000	5000

CELL CONTENT

	A	B	C	D	E	F
1	FACTS		FACTS		FACTS	
2						
3	Variable	Expense %		80		
4	Fixed exp	enses		8000		
5	S.P. per	unit		10		
6	Proposed	sales -	units	5000		
7						
8					Sales	
9	SOLUTION			Dollars	Units	
10		Break-Eve	n $	+D4/(1-(D3 *.01)	+D10/D5	
11		Proposed	sales	+D6*D5	+D11/D5	

CH05PR08

Chapter 5 Problem 8

Given:
- Variable expense $
- Fixed expenses
- Selling Price - per unit
- Proposed sales - units

Required
- Compute break-even sales dollars
- Compute break-even sales units
- Compute proposed sales dollars
- Compute proposed sales units

SCREEN DISPLAY

```
     FACTS                FACTS                FACTS

  Variable Expense $                 8000
  Fixed expenses                     8000
  S.P. per unit                        10
  Proposed sales -  units            2000

                                          Sales
  SOLUTION                      Dollars    Units
           Break-Even     $       16000     1600
           Proposed sales         20000     2000
```

CELL CONTENT

	A	B	C	D	E
1	FACTS		FACTS		FACTS
2					
3	Variable	Expense $		8000	
4	Fixed exp	enses		8000	
5	S.P. per	unit		10	
6	Proposed	sales -	units	2000	
7					
8					Sales
9	SOLUTION			Dollars	Units
10		Break-Eve	n $	+D3+D4	+D10/D5
11		Proposed	sales	+D6*D5	+D11/D5

CH05PR09

Chapter 5 Problem 9

```
Given:
   Variable expense   %
   Break-even sales
Required
   Fixed Expenses
```

SCREEN DISPLAY

```
   FACTS               FACTS               FACTS

 Variable Expense %                  80
 Break-even sales                 50000



 SOLUTION
          Fixed Expenses          10000
```

CELL CONTENT

	A	B	C	D
1	FACTS		FACTS	
2				
3	Variable	Expense %		80
4	Break-eve	n sales		50000
5				
6				
7				
8				
9	SOLUTION			
10		Fixed Exp	enses	+D4-((D3*.01)*D4)

CH05PR10

Chapter 5 Problem 10

Given:
   Variable expense $
   Break-even sales
Required
   Compute fixed expenses

SCREEN DISPLAY

FACTS	FACTS	
Variable Expense $		40000
Break-even sales		50000
SOLUTION		
	Fixed Expenses	10000

CELL CONTENT

	A	B	C	D
1	FACTS		FACTS	
2				
3	Variable	Expense $		40000
4	Break-eve	n sales		50000
5				
6				
7				
8				
9	SOLUTION			
10		Fixed Exp	enses	+D4-D3

CH05PR11

Chapter 5 Problem 11

Given:
- Variable expense %
- Fixed expenses
- Break-even units

Required
- Compute
  - Break-even sales
  - Selling price per unit

SCREEN DISPLAY

```
      FACTS                FACTS                FACTS

  Variable Expense %                    80
  Fixed Expenses                     10000
  Break-Even - units                  1000


  SOLUTION
                     Break-even sales       50000
                     S.P. Per Unit             50
```

CELL CONTENT

	A	B	C	D	E
1	FACTS		FACTS		FACTS
2					
3	Variable	Expense %		80	
4	Fixed Exp	enses		10000	
5	Break-Eve	n - units		1000	
6					
7					
8	SOLUTION				
9			Break-eve	n sales	+D4/(1-(D3 *.01)
10			S.P. Per	Unit	+E9/D5

CH05PR12

```
                Chapter 5 Problem 12
           Given:
              Variable expense   %
              Fixed expenses
              Selling Price per unit
           Required
              Compute
                Break-even sales dollars
                Break-even sales units
```

SCREEN DISPLAY

```
     FACTS                  FACTS                 FACTS

  Variable Expense %                    80
  Fixed Expenses                     10000
  Selling Price per unit                10


  SOLUTION
                      Break-even sales       50000
                      Number of Units         5000
```

CELL CONTENT

	A	B	C	D	E
1	FACTS		FACTS		FACTS
2					
3	Variable	Expense %		80	
4	Fixed Exp	enses		10000	
5	Selling P	rice per	unit	10	
6					
7					
8	SOLUTION				
9			Break-eve	n sales	+D4/(1-(D3 *.01)
10			Number of	Units	+E9/D5

CH05PR13

```
                Chapter 5 Problem 13
      Given:
         Sales
         Variable expense  $
         Profit
      Required
         Compute
            Fixed Expense
            Break-even sales dollars
```

SCREEN DISPLAY

```
   FACTS               FACTS                FACTS
Sales                             60000
Variable Expense                  48000
Profit                             2000



SOLUTION
                  Fixed Expense           10000
                  Break-even sales        50000
```

CELL CONTENT

	A	B	C	D	E
1	FACTS		FACTS		FACTS
2	Sales			60000	
3	Variable	Expense		48000	
4	Profit			2000	
5					
6					
7					
8	SOLUTION				
9			Fixed Exp	ense	+D2-D3-D4
10			Break-eve	n sales	+E9/(1-(D3 /D2

CH05PR14

```
                Chapter 5 Problem 14
        Given:
           Sales
           Variable expense  $
           Profit
           Selling Price Per Unit
        Required
           Compute
              Fixed Expense
              Break-even sales dollars
              Break-even sales units
```

SCREEN DISPLAY

```
   FACTS              FACTS              FACTS
Sales                           60000
Variable Expense                48000
Profit                           2000
S.P. Per Unit                      10


SOLUTION
                   Fixed Expense          10000
                   Break-even sales $     50000
                   Break-even sales        5000 units
```

CELL CONTENT

	A	B	C	D	E	F
1	FACTS		FACTS		FACTS	
2	Sales			60000		
3	Variable	Expense		48000		
4	Profit			2000		
5	S.P. Per	Unit		10		
6						
7						
8	SOLUTION					
9			Fixed Exp	ense	+D2-D3-D4	
10			Break-eve	n sales $	+E9/(1-(D3 /D2	
11			Break-eve	n sales	+E10/D5	units

CH05PR15

SCREEN DISPLAY

FACTS	FACTS	
Desired Profit	10000	
	Year 1	Year 2
Units Sold	5000	8000
Sales Revenue	65000	104000
Expenses	75000	90000

SCREEN DISPLAY

SOLUTION	Year 1	Year 2	Change
Units Sold	5000	8000	3000
Sales Revenue	65000	104000	39000
Expenses	75000	90000	15000
V.E. Per Unit			5.00
Fixed Expense $			50000
S.P. per unit			13
Break-even		Dollars	81250
Break-even		Units	6250
Sales at desired profit		Dollars	97500
		Units	7500

CELL CONTENT

	A	B	C	D	E
1	FACTS		FACTS		
2	Desired P	rofit	10000		
3			Year 1	Year 2	
4	Units Sol	d	5000	8000	
5	Sales Rev	enue	65000	104000	
6	Expenses		75000	90000	
7					
13	SOLUTION		Year 1	Year 2	Change
14	Units Sol	d	+C4	+D4	+D14-C14
15	Sales Rev	enue	65000	104000	+D15-C15
16	Expenses		75000	90000	+D16-C16
17	V.E. Per	Unit			+E16/E14
18	Fixed Exp	ense $			+D16-(D14*E 17)
19	S.P. per	unit			+E15/E14
20	Break-eve	n		Dollars	+E18/(1- (E17/E19)
21	Break-eve	n		Units	+E20/E19
22	Sales at	desired p	rofit	Dollars	+E18+C2/ (1-(E17/E19
23				Units	+E22/E19

CH05PR16

Chapter 5 Problem 16

Given:
- Variable expense %
- Fixed expense
- Selling price per unit
- Volume (units)

Required
- Sales
- Variable expense $
- Contribution Margin
- Income

SCREEN DISPLAY

FACTS		FACTS		
Var. Exp		60 %		
Fixed Exp		35000		
Sales per unit		250		
Volume		400	425	
SOLUTION				Diff.
	Sales	100000	106250	6250
	Var. Exp	60000	63750	3750
	C.M.	40000	42500	2500
	Fixed	35000	35000	0
	Income	5000	7500	2500

CELL CONTENT

	A	B	C	D	E
1	FACTS		FACTS		
2	Var. Exp		60	%	
3	Fixed Exp		35000		
4	Sales per	unit	250		
5	Volume		400	425	
6	SOLUTION				Diff.
7		Sales	+C5*C4	+D5*C4	+D7-C7
8		Var. Exp	+C7*(C2*.0 1)	+D7*(C2*.0 1)	+E7*(C2*.0 1)
9		C.M.	+C7-C8	+D7-D8	+E7-E8
10		Fixed	+C3	+C3	0
11		Income	+C9-C10	+D9-D10	+E9-E10
12					

PRACTICE PROBLEMS

Chapter 5

Problem 1

Given:
Variable Expense %
Fixed Expenses
Required
Compute break-even sales

Item #	VAR %	Fixed	Break-Evn
1	80	10000	50000
2	82	10000	55556
3	84	10000	62500
4	86	10000	71429
5	88	10000	83333

PRACTICE PRACTICE PRACTICE PRACTICE PRACTICE PRACTICE

Problem 2

Given:
Variable Expense $
Fixed Expenses
Required
Compute break-even sales

Item No.	V.E. $	F.E. $	B.E.S.
1	8000	10000	18000
2	8000	12000	20000
3	8000	14000	22000
4	8000	16000	24000
5	8000	18000	26000

Problem 3 PRACTICE PRACTICE PRACTICE PRACTICE PRACTICE PRACTICE

Given:
Selling Price - per unit
Variable expense - per unit
Fixed expense
Required
Compute break-even sales

Item No.	Per Unit S.P.	V.E.	F.E.	B.E.S.
1	10	8	10000	50000
2	11	8	10000	36667
3	12	8	10000	30000
4	13	8	10000	26000
5	14	8	10000	23333

Problem 4
PRACTICE PRACTICE PRACTICE PRACTICE PRACTICE PRACTICE

Given:
Selling Price - per unit
Variable expense - per unit
Fixed expense
Required
Compute break-even sales dollars
Compute break-even sales units

Item No.	Per Unit S.P	V.E.	F.E	B.E.S. $	Unit
1	10	8	10000	50000	5000
2	11	8	10000	36667	3333
3	12	8	10000	30000	2500
4	13	8	10000	26000	2000
5	14	8	10000	23333	1667

Problem 5	Prob. 5a	Prob. 5b	Prob. 5c	Prob. 5d
Given:				
Selling Price - per unit	10	11	12	13
Variable expense %	80	80	80	80
Fixed expense	8000	8000	8000	8000
Desired profit	2000	3000	4000	5000
Compute				
Break-even sales dollars	40000	40000	40000	40000
Break-even sales units	4000	3636	3333	3077
Sales for desired profit	50000	55000	60000	65000

PRACTICE PRACTICE PRACTICE PRACTICE PRACTICE PRACTICE PRACTICE PRACTICE

Problem 6	Prob. 6a	Prob. 6b	Prob. 6c	Prob. 6d
Given:				
Variable expense $	8000	10000	12000	14000
Fixed expense	8000	8000	8000	8000
Selling Price - per unit	10	12	14	16
Compute				
Break-even sales dollars	16000	18000	20000	22000
Break-even sales units	1600	1500	1429	1375

PRACTICE PRACTICE PRACTICE PRACTICE PRACTICE PRACTICE PRACTICE PRACTICE

Problem 7	Prob.7a	Prob.7b	Prob.7c	Prob.7d
Given:				
Variable expense %	80	80	80	80
Fixed expense	8000	8000	8000	8000
Selling Price - per unit	10	12	14	16
Proposed sales - units	5000	5000	5000	5000
Compute				
Break-even sales dollars	40000	40000	40000	40000
Break-even sales units	4000	3333	2857	2500
Proposed sales dollars	50000	60000	70000	80000
Proposed sales units				

PRACTICE PRACTICE PRACTICE PRACTICE PRACTICE PRACTICE PRACTICE PRACTICE

Problem 8	Prob. 8a	Prob. 8b	Prob. 8c	Prob. 8d
Given:				
Variable expense $	8000	8000	8000	8000
Fixed expense	8000	8000	8000	8000
Selling Price - per unit	10	12	14	16
Proposed sales - units	5000	5000	5000	5000
Compute				
Break-even sales dollars	16000	16000	16000	16000
Break-even sales units	1600	1333	1143	1000
Proposed sales dollars	50000	60000	70000	80000
Proposed sales units				

PRACTICE PRACTICE PRACTICE PRACTICE PRACTICE PRACTICE PRACTICE PRACTICE

Chapter 5 PRACTICE PROBLEMS

Problem 9

Given:
- Variable expense %
- Break-even sales

Required
- Fixed Expenses

Item No.	V.E.%	B.E.S	F.E
1	80	50000	10000
2	82	50000	9000
3	84	50000	8000
4	86	50000	7000
5	88	50000	6000

Problem 10

Given:
- Variable expense $
- Break-even sales

Required
- Compute fixed expenses

Item No.	V.E. $	B.E.S	F.E
1	40000	50000	10000
2	40500	50000	9500
3	41000	50000	9000
4	41500	50000	8500
5	42000	50000	8000

Problem 11 PRACTICE PRACTICE PRACTICE PRACTICE PRACTICE PRACTICE

Given:
- Variable expense %
- Fixed expenses
- Break-even units

Required
- Compute
  - Break-even sales
  - Selling price per unit

Item			Break-even		S.P.
No.	V.E. %	F.E.	Dolla	Units	Per #
1	80	10000	50000	1000	50.00
2	82	10000	55556	1500	37.04
3	84	10000	62500	2000	31.25
4	86	10000	71429	2500	28.57
5	88	10000	83333	3000	27.78

Problem 12

Given:
- Variable expense %
- Fixed expenses
- Selling Price per unit

Required
- Compute
  - Break-even sales dollars
  - Break-even sales units

Item			S.P.	Break-even	
No.	V.E. %	F.E.	Per #	$	Units
1	80	10000	10	50000	5000
2	82	10000	12	55556	4630
3	84	10000	14	62500	4464
4	86	10000	16	71429	4464
5	88	10000	18	83333	4630

Problem 13 PRACTICE PRACTICE PRACTICE PRACTICE PRACTICE PRACTICE

Given:
- Sales
- Variable expense $
- Profit

Required
- Compute
  - Fixed Expense
  - Break-even sales dollars

Item No.	Sales	V.E.$	Prof	Fixed Exp.	B.E.S
1	60000	48000	2000	10000	50000
2	62000	48000	2000	12000	53143
3	64000	48000	2000	14000	56000
4	66000	48000	2000	16000	58667
5	68000	48000	2000	18000	61200

CH05PR14

Chapter 5 Problem 14

Given:
- Sales
- Variable expense $
- Profit
- Selling Price Per Unit

Required
- Compute
  - Fixed Expense
  - Break-even sales dollars
  - Break-even sales units

Sales 60000

Item No.	V.E.	Profit	S.P. Per unit	F.E.	B. E. Units
1	48000	2000	10	10000	5000
2	50000	2000	10	8000	4800
3	52000	2000	10	6000	4500
4	54000	2000	10	4000	4000
5	56000	2000	10	2000	3000
6	48000	2100	10	9900	4950
7	48000	2200	10	9800	4900
8	48000	2300	10	9700	4850
9	48000	2400	10	9600	4800
10	48000	2500	10	9500	4750
11	48000	2000	12	10000	4167
12	48000	2000	14	10000	3571
13	48000	2000	16	10000	3125
14	48000	2000	18	10000	2778
15	48000	2000	20	10000	2500
16	47000	1900	10	11100	5123
17	46000	1800	10	12200	5229
18	45000	1700	10	13300	5320
19	44000	1600	10	14400	5400
20	43000	1500	10	15500	5471
21	48000	2000	12	10000	4167
22	48500	2200	14	9300	3466
23	49000	2400	16	8600	2932
24	49500	2600	18	7900	2508
25	50000	2800	20	7200	2160

CH05PR16

Chapter 5 Problem 16

Given:
- Variable expense %
- Fixed expense
- Selling price per unit
- Volume (units)

Required
- Sales
- Variable expense $
- Contribution Margin
- Income

	Variable	Sales	Volume Units		Change in
Item No.	Exp. %	Per Unit	Present	Proposed	Income
1	60	250	400	425	2500
2	65	260	400	425	2275
3	70	270	400	425	2025
4	75	280	400	425	1750
5	80	290	400	425	1450
6	60	250	410	425	1500
7	60	250	420	425	500
8	60	250	430	425	-500
9	60	250	440	425	-1500
10	60	250	450	425	-2500
11	60	250	400	435	3500
12	60	250	400	445	4500
13	60	250	400	455	5500
14	60	250	400	465	6500
15	60	250	400	475	7500
16	60	250	400	485	8500
17	60	250	400	495	9500
18	60	250	400	505	10500
19	60	250	400	515	11500
20	60	250	400	525	12500
21	60	250	400	535	13500
22	60	250	400	545	14500
23	60	250	400	555	15500
24	60	250	400	565	16500
25	60	250	400	575	17500

6 Segments Absorption and Direct Costing

Condensed List of Items

Item No.		*Problems*
CH06PR01	Segments by division	___
CH06PR02	Segments by division	___
CH06PR03	Segments by products	___
CH06PR04	Segments by products	___
CH06PR05	Segments by one product line	___
CH06PR06	Segments by one product line	___
CH06PR07	Costing Absorption and direct	25
CH06PR08	Costing Absorption and direct	25
CH06PR09	Costing Absorption and direct	25
CH06PR10	Direct Costing	___
CH06PR11	Absorption Costing	___
CH06PR12	Costing Absorption and direct	___
CH06PR13	Costing Absorption and direct	25
CH06PR14	Costing Absorption and direct	25
CH06PR15	Costing Absorption and direct	25
	Total	150

DIRECT COSTING VS ABSORPTION COSTING

The difference between direct costing and absorption costing is the handling of FIXED overhead cost.

Absorption costing determines the cost of inventory using each element of cost including direct materials, direct labor, variable manufacturing overhead and all of FIXED manufacturing overhead costs. This means that the FIXED manufacturing overhead costs are allocated between cost of sales and inventory. The effect of this is that the FIXED costs allocated to inventory are deferred to a subsequent period.

Direct costing values inventory only with VARIABLE manufacturing costs. The cost of the inventory includes direct materials, direct labor and direct variable manufacturing overhead. The total amount of FIXED manufacturing costs are charged to the period in which they are incurred.

	COST METHOD	
INVENTORY VALUATION	*ABSORPTION*	*DIRECT*
DIRECT MATERIALS	YES	YES
DIRECT LABOR	YES	YES
OVERHEAD-VARIABLE	YES	YES
OVERHEAD-FIXED	YES	NO

DISTRIBUTION OF FIXED COSTS FOR PERIOD

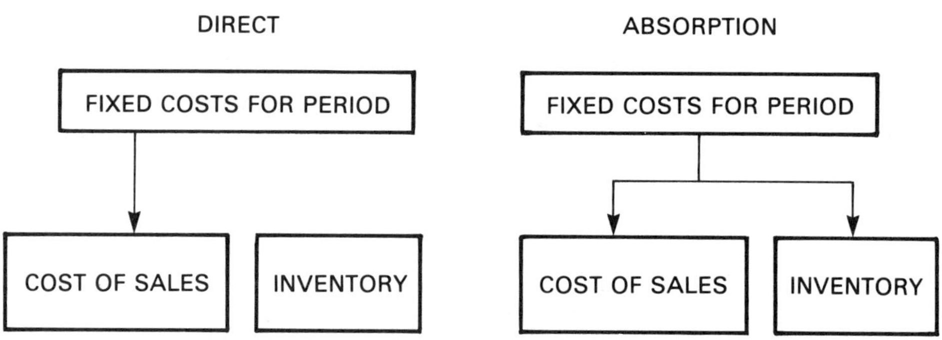

DIRECT COSTING VS ABSORPTION COSTING EFFECT OF INVENTORY ON NET INCOME

Direct costing will not be effected by the quantity of production that is included in the inventory. All of the FIXED overhead costs will be charged to the period in which it is incurred. The cost of the inventory will include only the variable items.

Absorption costing will be effected by production that is included in the inventory. With this costing method, a portion of FIXED overhead costs will be included in inventory. This means that some of the FIXED overhead costs of this period are deferred to a subsequent period. As ending inventory increases, the amount of net income is increased. Conversely as ending inventory decreases, the amount of net income is decreased. There is an inverse relationship between beginning inventory and net income. As beginning inventory is decreased, net income is increased. If beginning inventory is increased, net income is decreased.

ABSORPTION COSTING

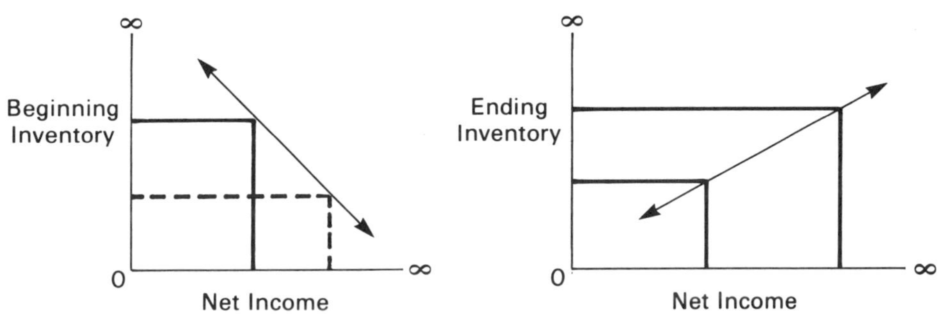

DIRECT COSTING

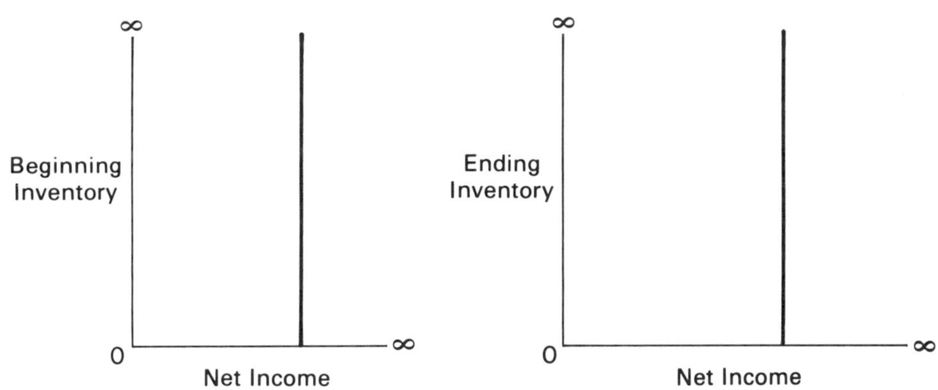

PER UNIT

	UNITS PRODUCED	
	INCREASE	DECREASE
Fixed	Decrease	Increase
Variable	Constant	Constant

TOTAL COSTS

	UNITS PRODUCED	
	INCREASE	DECREASE
Fixed	Constant	Constant
Variable	Increase	Decrease

The cost of the units produced will be effected by the number of units that are produced.

The VARIABLE manufacturing costs per unit will remain constant within the relevant range of activity. The total costs will change as the number of units produced is changed. If the number of units produced is increased, the total VARIABLE costs will increase. If the number of units produced is decreased, the total VARIABLE costs will decrease.

The total FIXED manufacturing costs will remain constant within the relevant range of activity. The FIXED manufacturing costs per unit will be influenced by the units produced. If the units produced are increased, the FIXED costs per unit will decrease. If the units produced are decreased, the FIXED costs per unit will increase.

VARIABLE MANUFACTURING COSTS

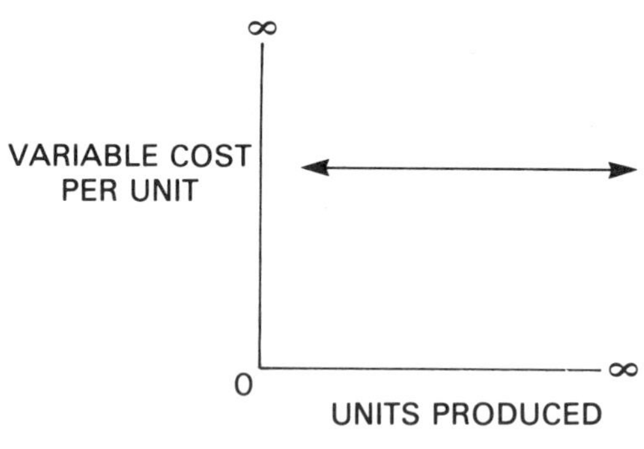

FIXED MANUFACTURING COSTS

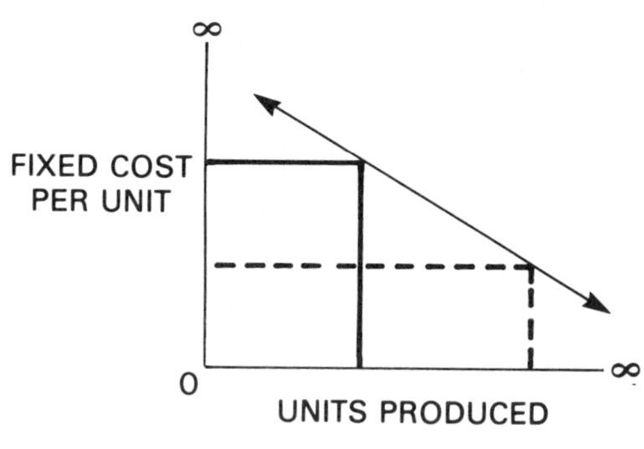

SCREEN DISPLAY

CH06PR01

```
Segments by divisions
FACTS                FACTS              FACTS
                           Division Division
                               1        2
Sales                        300000   200000
Variable COGS                    .4       .3
Variable Other                   .1       .1
Direct Fixed                  90000    80000
Common fixed              25000
```

SCREEN DISPLAY

```
SOLUTION            SOLUTION
                    Division Division  Total
                       1        2      company
Sales                300000   200000   500000
Variable COGS        120000    60000   180000
Variable Other        30000    20000    50000
Contrib. Margin      150000   120000   270000
Direct fixed          90000    80000   170000
Segment margin        60000    40000   100000
Common fixed                            25000
Net income                              75000
```

CELL CONTENT

	A	B	C	D	E
1	Segments	by divisi	ons		
2	FACTS		FACTS		FACTS
3				Division	Division
4				1	2
5	Sales			300000	200000
6	Variable	COGS		.4	.3
7	Variable	Other		.1	.1
8	Direct Fi	xed		90000	80000
9	Common fi	xed	25000		
10					
11					
12					
13	SOLUTION		SOLUTION		
14			Division	Division	Total
15			1	2	company
16	Sales		+D5	+E5	+C16+D16
17	Variable	COGS	+D5*D6	+E5*E6	+C17+D17
18	Variable	Other	+D7*D5	+E7*E5	+C18+D18
19	Contrib.	Margin	+C16-C17-C 18	+D16-D17-D 18	+C19+D19
20	Direct fi	xed	+D8	+E8	+C20+D20
21	Segment m	argin	+C19-C20	+D19-D20	+E19-E20
22	Common fi	xed			+C9
23	Net incom	e			+E21-E22

SCREEN DISPLAY

CH06PR02

```
Segments by divisions
FACTS               FACTS               FACTS
                              Division Division
                                 1        2
Sales                            50000    50000
Variable COGS                       .5       .3
Variable Other                      .1      .15
Direct Fixed                      5000     6000
Common fixed                2500
```

SCREEN DISPLAY

```
SOLUTION            SOLUTION
                    Division Division  Total
                       1        2      company
Sales                  50000    50000   100000
Variable COGS          25000    15000    40000
Variable Other          5000     7500    12500
Contrib. Margin        20000    27500    47500
Direct fixed            5000     6000    11000
Segment margin         15000    21500    36500
Common fixed                              2500
Net income                               34000
```

CELL CONTENT

	A	B	C	D	E
1	Segments	by divisi	ons		
2	FACTS		FACTS		FACTS
3				Division	Division
4				1	2
5	Sales			50000	50000
6	Variable	COGS		.5	.3
7	Variable	Other		.1	.15
8	Direct Fi	xed		5000	6000
9	Common fi	xed	2500		
10					
11					
12					
13	SOLUTION		SOLUTION		
14			Division	Division	Total
15			1	2	company
16	Sales		+D5	+E5	+C16+D16
17	Variable	COGS	+D5*D6	+E5*E6	+C17+D17
18	Variable	Other	+D7*D5	+E7*E5	+C18+D18
19	Contrib.	Margin	+C16-C17-C 18	+D16-D17-D 18	+C19+D19
20	Direct fi	xed	+D8	+E8	+C20+D20
21	Segment m	argin	+C19-C20	+D19-D20	+E19-E20
22	Common fi	xed			+C9
23	Net incom	e			+E21-E22

CH06PR03

SCREEN DISPLAY

```
Segments by products
FACTS                  FACTS                FACTS
                       Product  Product
                          1        2
Sales                    75000   125000
Variable COGS              .25       .3
Variable Other             .05      .12
Direct Fixed             30000    40000
Com fixed     10000
```

SCREEN DISPLAY

```
SOLUTION               SOLUTION
                       Product  Product  Division
                          1        2
Sales                    75000   125000    200000
Variable COGS            18750    37500     56250
Variable Other            3750    15000     18750
Contrib. Margin          52500    72500    125000
Direct fixed             30000    40000     70000
Segment margin           22500    32500     55000
Common fixed                                10000
Net income                                  45000
```

CELL CONTENT

	A	B	C	D	E
1	Segments	by produc	ts		
2	FACTS		FACTS		FACTS
3			Product	Product	Division
4			1	2	2
5	Sales		75000	125000	
6	Variable	COGS	.25	.3	
7	Variable	Other	.05	.12	
8	Direct Fi	xed	30000	40000	
9	Com fixed	10000			
10					
11					
12					
13	SOLUTION		SOLUTION		
14			Product	Product	Division
15			1	2	company
16	Sales		+C5	+D5	+C16+D16
17	Variable	COGS	+C6*C5	+D6*D16	+C17+D17
18	Variable	Other	+C7*C5	+D7*D16	+C18+D18
19	Contrib.	Margin	+C16-C17-C 18	+D16-D17-D 18	+C19+D19
20	Direct fi	xed	+C8	+D8	+C20+D20
21	Segment m	argin	+C19-C20	+D19-D20	+E19-E20
22	Common fi	xed			+B9
23	Net incom	e			+E21-E22

SCREEN DISPLAY

CH06PR04

Segments by products				
FACTS		FACTS		FACTS
		Product	Product	
		1	2	
Sales		85000	60000	
Variable COGS		.4	.25	
Variable Other		.1	.05	
Direct Fixed		25000	30000	
Com fixed	15000			

SCREEN DISPLAY

SOLUTION	SOLUTION		
	Product	Product	Division
	1	2	
Sales	85000	60000	145000
Variable COGS	34000	15000	49000
Variable Other	8500	3000	11500
Contrib. Margin	42500	42000	84500
Direct fixed	25000	30000	55000
Segment margin	17500	12000	29500
Common fixed			15000
Net income			14500

CELL CONTENT

	A	B	C	D	E
1	Segments	by produc	ts		
2	FACTS		FACTS		FACTS
3			Product	Product	Division
4			1	2	
5	Sales		85000	60000	
6	Variable	COGS	.4	.25	
7	Variable	Other	.1	.05	
8	Direct Fi	xed	25000	30000	
9	Com fixed	15000			
10					
11					
12					
13	SOLUTION		SOLUTION		
14			Product	Product	Division
15			1	2	
16	Sales		+C5	+D5	+C16+D16
17	Variable	COGS	+C6*C5	+D6*D16	+C17+D17
18	Variable	Other	+C7*C5	+D7*D16	+C18+D18
19	Contrib.	Margin	+C16-C17-C 18	+D16-D17-D 18	+C19+D19
20	Direct fi	xed	+C8	+D8	+C20+D20
21	Segment m	argin	+C19-C20	+D19-D20	+E19-E20
22	Common fi	xed			+B9
23	Net incom	e			+E21-E22

CH06PR05

SCREEN DISPLAY

Segments by one product line			
FACTS		FACTS	FACTS
		Domestic	Foreign
Sales		80000	40000
Variable COGS		.32	.32
Variable Other		.05	.4
Direct Fixed		15000	10000
Com fixed	15000		

SCREEN DISPLAY

SOLUTION	SOLUTION		
	Domestic	Foreign	Total
Sales	80000	40000	120000
Variable COGS	25600	12800	38400
Variable Other	4000	16000	20000
Contrib. Margin	50400	11200	61600
Direct fixed	15000	10000	25000
Segment margin	35400	1200	36600
Common fixed			15000
Net income			21600

CELL CONTENT

	A	B	C	D	E
1	Segments	by one pr	oduct lin	e	
2	FACTS		FACTS		FACTS
3			Domestic	Foreign	
4	Sales		80000	40000	
5	Variable	COGS	.32	.32	
6	Variable	Other	.05	.4	
7	Direct Fi	xed	15000	10000	
8	Com fixed	15000			
9					
10					
11					
12	SOLUTION		SOLUTION		
13			Domestic	Foreign	Total
14	Sales		+C4	+D4	+C14+D14
15	Variable	COGS	+C5*C4	+D5*D14	+C15+D15
16	Variable	Other	+C6*C4	+D6*D14	+C16+D16
17	Contrib.	Margin	+C14-C15-C 16	+D14-D15-D 16	+C17+D17
18	Direct fi	xed	+C7	+D7	+C18+D18
19	Segment m	argin	+C17-C18	+D17-D18	+E17-E18
20	Common fi	xed			+B8
21	Net incom	e			+E19-E20

SCREEN DISPLAY

CH06PR06

```
Segments by one product line
FACTS              FACTS              FACTS
                   Domestic Foreign
Sales                  40000   125000
Variable COGS             .4      .35
Variable Other            .1      .35
Direct Fixed           18000    20000
Com fixed    12500
```

SCREEN DISPLAY

```
SOLUTION           SOLUTION
                   Domestic Foreign    Total
Sales                  40000   125000   165000
Variable COGS          16000    43750    59750
Variable Other          4000    43750    47750
Contrib. Margin        20000    37500    57500
Direct fixed           18000    20000    38000
Segment margin          2000    17500    19500
Common fixed                             12500
Net income                                7000
```

CELL CONTENT

```
         A            B            C            D            E

 1   Segments     by one pr    oduct lin    e
 2   FACTS                     FACTS                      FACTS
 3                             Domestic     Foreign
 4   Sales                     40000        125000
 5   Variable     COGS         .4           .35
 6   Variable     Other        .1           .35
 7   Direct Fi    xed          18000        20000
 8   Com fixed    12500
 9
10
11
12   SOLUTION                  SOLUTION
13                             Domestic     Foreign        Total
14   Sales                     +C4          +D4          +C14+D14
15   Variable     COGS         +C5*C4       +D5*D14      +C15+D15
16   Variable     Other        +C6*C4       +D6*D14      +C16+D16
17   Contrib.     Margin       +C14-C15-C   +D14-D15-D   +C17+D17
                               16           16
18   Direct fi    xed          +C7          +D7          +C18+D18
19   Segment m    argin        +C17-C18     +D17-D18     +E17-E18
20   Common fi    xed                                    +B8
21   Net incom    e                                      +E19-E20
```

CH06PR07

Chapter 6 Problem 7

```
Given
  Number of units
  Variable manufacturing cost per unit
  Fixed  manufacturing cost
Compute
  Cost per unit
    Absorption costing
    Direct costing
```

SCREEN DISPLAY

```
Absorption costing
FACTS                 FACTS                 FACTS
     3000 Number of units
        8 Variable manufacturing per unit
    15000 Fixed-manufacturing
    20000 Fixed-selling and administrative
Solution              Solution
  Absorp.  Direct
        8          8 Variable costs
        5            Fixed overhead
       13          8 Cost per unit
```

CELL CONTENT

	A	B	C	D	E
1	Absorptio	n costing			
2	FACTS		FACTS		FACTS
3	3000	Number o	f units		
4	8	Variable	manufact	uring per	unit
5	15000	Fixed-ma	nufacturi	ng	
6	20000	Fixed-se	lling and	adminitr	ative
7	Solution		Solution		
8	Absorp.	Direct			
9	+A4	+A4	Variable	costs	
10	+A5/A3		Fixed ov	erhead	
11	+A9+A10	+B9	Cost per	unit	

CH06PR08

Chapter 6 Problem 8

Given
- Beginning inventory
- Units produced
- Units sold
- Sales price per unit
- Variable per unit
- Fixed overhead

Compute
- Cost per unit-absorption and direct

SCREEN DISPLAY

```
Absorption costing
FACTS                FACTS                FACTS
         0 Beginning inventory
      5000 Units produced
      4000 Units sold
        10 Sales price per unit
         4 Variable per unit
     10000 Fixed overhead

SOLUTION             SOLUTION             SOLUTION
                     Absorpt.   Direct
Cost per unit                6         4
```

CELL CONTENT

	A	B	C	D	E
1	Absorptio	n costing			
2	FACTS		FACTS		FACTS
3	0	Beginnin	g invento	ry	
4	5000	Units pr	oduced		
5	4000	Units so	ld		
6	10	Sales pr	ice per u	nit	
7	4	Variable	per unit		
8	10000	Fixed ov	erhead		
9					
10	SOLUTION		SOLUTION		SOLUTION
11			Absorpt.	Direct	
12	Cost per	unit	+A7+(A8/A4	+A7	

SCREEN DISPLAY

CH06PR09

```
Absorption costing
FACTS                FACTS                FACTS
         0 Beginning inventory
      5000 Units produced
      4000 Units sold
        10 Sales price per unit
         4 Variable per unit
     10000 Fixed manufacturing overhead
```

SCREEN DISPLAY

```
SOLUTION             SOLUTION             SOLUTION
                              Absorpt.    Direct
Cost per unit                        6         4
Inventory                         6000      4000
Sales                            40000     40000
Cost of goods manufactured       24000     16000
Difference                       16000     24000
```

CELL CONTENT

	A	B	C	D	E
1	Absorptio	n costing			
2	FACTS		FACTS		FACTS
3	0	Beginnin	g invento	ry	
4	5000	Units pr	oduced		
5	4000	Units so	ld		
6	10	Sales pr	ice per u	nit	
7	4	Variable	per unit		
8	10000	Fixed ov	erhead		
9					
10					
11					
12					
13	SOLUTION		SOLUTION		SOLUTION
14				Absorpt.	Direct
15	Cost per	unit		+A7+(A8/A4	+A7
16	Inventory			+A4-A5*D15	+A4-A5*E15
17	Sales			+A5*A6	+A5*A6
18	Cost of g	oods manu	factured	+A5*D15	+A5*A7
19	Differenc	e		+D17-D18	+E17-E18

DIRECT COSTING SCREEN DISPLAY DIRECT COSTING

CH06PR10

```
FACTS              FACTS              FACTS
       12 Sales price per unit
        5 Variable per unit
    24000 Fixed manufacturing overhead
    25000 Fixed selling and administrative
Year 1   Year 2   Year 3
        0        0     1000 Beginning inventory
     8000     8000     8000 Units produced
     8000     7000     9000 Units sold
```

SCREEN DISPLAY

```
Cost per unit              5
                  Year 1    Year 2    Year 3     Total
Ending Inventory
Units                      0      1000         0         0
Dollars                    0      5000         0         0

                  Year 1    Year 2    Year 3     Total
Sales                  96000     84000    108000    288000
Variable               40000     35000     45000    120000
Contrib. Margin        56000     49000     63000    168000
Fixed Costs            49000     49000     49000    147000
Net Income              7000         0     14000     21000
```

CELL CONTENT

	A	B	C	D	E	F
2	FACTS		FACTS		FACTS	
3	12	Sales pr	ice per u	nit		
4	5	Variable	per unit			
5	24000	Fixed ma	nufacturi	ng overhe	ad	
6	25000	Fixed se	lling and	administ	rative	
7	Year 1	Year 2	Year 3			
8	0	0	1000	Beginnin	g invento	ry
9	8000	8000	8000	Units pr	oduced	
10	8000	7000	9000	Units so	ld	
15	Cost per	unit	+A4			
16			Year 1	Year 2	Year 3	Total
17	Ending In	ventory				
18	Units		+A8+A9-A10	+B8+B9-B10	+C8+C9-C10	+A8+@SUM(A 9...C9)-@S UM(A10...C 10
19	Dollars		+C18*A4	+D18*A4	+E18*A4	+E18*A4
20						
21			Year 1	Year 2	Year 3	Total
22	Sales		+A10*A3	+B10*A3	+C10*A3	@SUM(C22.. .E22
23	Variable		+A10*A4	+B10*A4	+C10*A4	@SUM(C23.. .E23
24	Contrib.	Margin	+C22-C23	+D22-D23	+E22-E23	+F22-F23
25	Fixed Cos	ts	+A5+A6	+A5+A6	+A5+A6	@SUM(C25.. .E25
26	Net Incom	e	+C24-C25	+D24-D25	+E24-E25	+F24-F25

ABSORPTION COSTING SCREEN DISPLAY ABSORPTION COSTING

CH06PR11

```
FACTS                FACTS                FACTS
       12 Sales price per unit
        5 Variable per unit
    24000 Fixed mfd overhead
    25000 Fixed selling and administrative
Year 1   Year 2   Year 3
        0        0     1000 Beginning inventory
     8000     8000     8000 Units produced
     8000     7000     9000 Units sold
```

SCREEN DISPLAY

```
Cost per unit                 8        8        8
                  Year 1   Year 2   Year 3    Total
Ending Inventory
Units                         0     1000        0        0
Dollars                       0     5000        0        0

                  Year 1   Year 2   Year 3    Total
Sales                 96000    84000   108000   288000
Variable              64000    56000    72000   192000
Contrib. Margin       32000    28000    36000    96000
S & A                 25000    25000    25000    75000
Net Income             7000     3000    11000    21000
```

CELL CONTENT

	A	B	C	D	E	F
2	FACTS		FACTS		FACTS	
3	12	Sales pr	ice per u	nit		
4	5	Variable	per unit			
5	24000	Fixed mf	d overhea	d		
6	25000	Fixed se	lling and	administ	rative	
7	Year 1	Year 2	Year 3			
8	0	0	1000	Beginnin	g invento	ry
9	8000	8000	8000	Units pr	oduced	
10	8000	7000	9000	Units so	ld	
15	Cost per	unit	+A4+(A5/A9	+A4+(A5/B9	+A4+(A5/C9	
16			Year 1	Year 2	Year 3	Total
17	Ending In	ventory				
18	Units		+A8+A9-A10	+B8+B9-B10	+C8+C9-C10	+A8+@SUM(A 9...C9)-@S UM(A10...C 10
19	Dollars		+C18*A4	+D18*A4	+E18*A4	+E18*A4
20						
21			Year 1	Year 2	Year 3	Total
22	Sales		+A10*A3	+B10*A3	+C10*A3	@SUM(C22.. .E22
23	Variable		+A10*C15	+B10*D15	+C10*E15	@SUM(C23.. .E23
24	Contrib.	Margin	+C22-C23	+D22-D23	+E22-E23	+F22-F23
25	S & A		+A6	+A6	+A6	@SUM(C25.. .E25
26	Net Incom	e	+C24-C25	+D24-D25	+E24-E25	+F24-F25

SCREEN DISPLAY

CH06PR12

```
Absorption vs Direct Costing
FACTS              FACTS              FACTS
       12 Sales price per unit
        5 Variable per unit
    24000 Fixed manufacturing overhead
    25000 Fixed selling and administrative
Year 1   Year 2   Year 3
       0        0     1000 Beginning inventory
     8000     8000     8000 Units produced
     8000     7000     9000 Units sold
```

SCREEN DISPLAY

```
Cost per unit
Direct Costing              5
Absorption                  8
                  Year 1   Year 2   Year 3   Total
Direct-Net income    7000        0    14000   21000
Inventory diff.         0     3000    -3000       0
Absorption           7000     3000    11000   21000
```

CELL CONTENT

	A	B	C	D	E	F
1	Absorptio	n vs Dire	ct Costin	g		
2	FACTS		FACTS		FACTS	
3	12	Sales pr	ice per u	nit		
4	5	Variable	per unit			
5	24000	Fixed ma	nufacturi	ng overhe	ad	
6	25000	Fixed se	lling and	administ	rative	
7	Year 1	Year 2	Year 3			
8	0	0	1000	Beginnin	g invento	ry
9	8000	8000	8000	Units pr	oduced	
10	8000	7000	9000	Units so	ld	
11						
12						
13						
14	Cost per	unit				
15	Direct Co	sting	+A4			
16	Absorptio	n	+A4+(A5/A9			
17			Year 1	Year 2	Year 3	Total
18	Direct-Ne	t income	+A10*(A3-A 4)-A5-A6	+B10*(A3-A 4)-A5-A6	+C10*(A3-A 4)-A5-A6	@SUM(C18.. .E18
19	Inventory	diff.	(+A9-A10)* (C16-C15)	(+B9-B10)* (C16-C15)	(+C9-C10)* (C16-C15)	@SUM(C19.. .E19
20	Absorptio	n	+A10*(A3-C 16)-A6	+B10*(A3-C 16)-A6	+C10*(A3-C 16)-A6	@SUM(C20.. .E20

CH06PR13 Chapter 6 Problem 13

```
Given
   Units produced
   Units sold
   Variable cost
   Fixed cost
Compute
   Cost of Goods Sold
   Inventory
   Total cost
```

SCREEN DISPLAY

```
FACTS
    20000 Units produced
    18000 Units sold
     8.00 Variable cost
    20000 Fixed cost
SOLUTION           SOLUTION           SOLUTION
                            Absorpt.   Direct
Cost of Goods Sold     18000   162000   164000
Inventory               2000    18000    16000
Total Cost                     180000   180000
```

CELL CONTENT

	A	B	C	D	E
1	Absorptio	n vs Dire	ct costin	g	
2	FACTS				
3	20000	Units pr	oduced		
4	18000	Units so	ld		
5	8	Variable	cost		
6	20000	Fixed co	st		
7	SOLUTION		SOLUTION		SOLUTION
8				Absorpt.	Direct
9	Cost of G	oods Sold	+A4	(+A4*(A5+(A6/A3)	(+A4*A5)+A 6
10	Inventory		+A3-A4	(+C10*(A5+ (A6/A3)	+C10*A5
11	Total Cos	t		+D9+D10	+E9+E10
12					

CH06PR14

Chapter 6 Problem 14

Given
- Units produced
- Units sold
- Variable cost
- Fixed cost

Compute
- Cost of Goods Sold
- Inventory
- Total cost

SCREEN DISPLAY

```
Absorption vs Direct costing
FACTS
    10000 Units produced
     8000 Units sold
     8.00 Variable cost
    20000 Fixed cost
SOLUTION            SOLUTION            SOLUTION
                             Absorpt.    Direct
Cost of Goods Sold      8000    80000     84000
Inventory               2000    20000     16000
Total Cost                     100000    100000
```

CELL CONTENT

	A	B	C	D	E
1	Absorptio	n vs Dire	ct costin	g	
2	FACTS				
3	10000	Units pr	oduced		
4	8000	Units so	ld		
5	8	Variable	cost		
6	20000	Fixed co	st		
7	SOLUTION		SOLUTION		SOLUTION
8				Absorpt.	Direct
9	Cost of G	oods Sold	+A4	(+A4*(A5+(A6/A3)	(+A4*A5)+A 6
10	Inventory		+A3-A4	(+C10*(A5+ (A6/A3)	+C10*A5
11	Total Cos	t		+D9+D10	+E9+E10

CH06PR15

Chapter 6 Problem 15

Given
- Units produced
- Units sold
- Variable cost
- Fixed cost

Compute
- Cost of Goods Sold
- Inventory
- Total cost

SCREEN DISPLAY

```
Absorption vs Direct costing
FACTS
    10000 Units produced
     8000 Units sold
     8.00 Variable cost
    20000 Fixed cost
SOLUTION             SOLUTION             SOLUTION
                              Absorpt.    Direct
Cost of Goods Sold       8000    80000     84000
Inventory                2000    20000     16000
Total Cost                      100000    100000
```

CELL CONTENT

	A	B	C	D	E
1	Absorptio	n vs Dire	ct costin	g	
2	FACTS				
3	10000	Units pr	oduced	oduced	
4	8000	Units so	ld		
5	/F$8	Variable	cost		
6	20000	Fixed co	st		
7	SOLUTION		SOLUTION		SOLUTION
8				Absorpt.	Direct
9	Cost of G	oods Sold	+A4	(+A4*(A5+(A6/A3)	(+A4*A5)+A 6
10	Inventory		+A3-A4	(+C10*(A5+ (A6/A3)	+C10*A5
11	Total Cos	t		+D9+D10	+E9+E10

Given
- Number of units
- Variable manufacturing cost per unit
- Fixed manufacturing cost

Compute
- Cost per unit
  - Absorption costing
  - Direct costing

Please work these problems.
Compare your results with the solution.

Item No.	Number of units	Var. Mfg per unit	Fixed Mfg.	Cost per unit Absorp.	Cost per unit Direct
1	3000	8	15000	13.00	8
2	4000	8	15000	11.75	8
3	5000	8	15000	11.00	8
4	6000	8	15000	10.50	8
5	7000	8	15000	10.14	8
6	3000	9	15000	14.00	9
7	3000	10	15000	15.00	10
8	3000	11	15000	16.00	11
9	3000	12	15000	17.00	12
10	3000	13	15000	18.00	13
11	3000	8	16000	13.33	8
12	3000	8	17000	13.67	8
13	3000	8	18000	14.00	8
14	3000	8	19000	14.33	8
15	3000	8	20000	14.67	8
16	3000	9	15000	14.00	9
17	3000	10	15000	15.00	10
18	3000	11	15000	16.00	11
19	3000	12	15000	17.00	12
20	3000	13	15000	18.00	13
21	5000	10	18000	13.60	10
22	7000	12	20000	14.86	12
23	9000	14	22000	16.44	14
24	11000	16	24000	18.18	16
25	13000	18	26000	20.00	18

Chapter 6 Problem 8 PRACTICE PROBLEMS

Given
Beginning inventory
Units produced
Units sold
Sales price per unit
Variable per unit
Fixed overhead
Compute
Cost per unit-absorption and direct

PRACTICE PRACTICE PRACTICE PRACTICE PRACTICE PRACTICE

Please work these problems.
Compare your results with the solution.

0 Beginning inventory

4000 Units sold
10 Sales price per unit

Item No.	Units Produced	Variable Per Unit	Fixed Overhead	Cost per unit Absorpt.	Direct
1	5000	4	10000	6.00	4.00
2	6000	4	10000	5.67	4.00
3	7000	4	10000	5.43	4.00
4	8000	4	10000	5.25	4.00
5	9000	4	10000	5.11	4.00
6	5000	5	10000	7.00	5.00
7	5000	6	10000	8.00	6.00
8	5000	7	10000	9.00	7.00
9	5000	8	10000	10.00	8.00
10	5000	9	10000	11.00	9.00
11	5000	4	12000	6.40	4.00
12	5000	4	14000	6.80	4.00
13	5000	4	16000	7.20	4.00
14	5000	4	18000	7.60	4.00
15	5000	4	20000	8.00	4.00
16	6000	5	10000	6.67	5.00
17	7000	6	12000	7.71	6.00
18	8000	7	14000	8.75	7.00
19	9000	8	16000	9.78	8.00
20	10000	9	18000	10.80	9.00
21	4500	4	12000	6.67	4.00
22	7500	5	11000	6.47	5.00
23	7000	6	10000	7.43	6.00
24	6500	7	9000	8.38	7.00
25	6000	8	8000	9.33	8.00

Chapter 6 Problem 9

CH06PR09

PRACTICE PROBLEMS

PRACTICE PROBLEMS

Given
- Beginning inventory
- Units produced
- Units sold
- Sales price per unit
- Variable per unit
- Fixed overhead

Compute
- Cost per unit-absorption and direct
- Inventory
- Cost of goods manufactured
- Difference

Please work these problems.
Compare your results with the solution.

0 Beginning inventory
10 Sales price per unit
10000 Fixed overhead

Item No.	Units Produced	Units Sold	Variable per unit	Difference Absorp.	Difference Direct
1	5000	4000	4.00	16000.00	24000.00
2	6000	4000	4.00	17333.33	24000.00
3	7000	4000	4.00	18285.71	24000.00
4	8000	4000	4.00	19000.00	24000.00
5	9000	4000	4.00	19555.56	24000.00
6	5000	5000	4.00	20000.00	30000.00
7	5000	6000	4.00	24000.00	36000.00
8	5000	7000	4.00	28000.00	42000.00
9	5000	8000	4.00	32000.00	48000.00
10	5000	9000	4.00	36000.00	54000.00
11	5000	4000	4.00	16000.00	24000.00
12	5000	4000	4.20	15200.00	23200.00
13	5000	4000	4.40	14400.00	22400.00
14	5000	4000	4.60	13600.00	21600.00
15	5000	4000	4.80	12800.00	20800.00
16	6000	5000	4.00	21666.67	30000.00
17	7000	6000	4.00	27428.57	36000.00
18	8000	7000	4.00	33250.00	42000.00
19	9000	8000	4.00	39111.11	48000.00
20	10000	9000	4.00	45000.00	54000.00
21	11000	10000	4.00	50909.09	60000.00
22	12000	11000	4.00	56833.33	66000.00
23	13000	12000	4.00	62769.23	72000.00
24	14000	13000	4.00	68714.29	78000.00
25	15000	14000	4.00	74666.67	84000.00

Chapter 6 Problem 13

CH06PR13

PRACTICE PROBLEMS

Given
- Units produced
- Units sold
- Variable cost
- Fixed cost

Compute
- Cost of Goods Sold
- Inventory
- Total cost

PRACTICE PROBLEMS

PRACTICE PRACTICE PRACTICE PRACTICE PRACTICE PRACTICE

Please work these problems.
Compare your results with the solution.

8.00 Variable cost
20000 Fixed cost

	Units		Absorption		Direct	
Item No.	Produced	Sold	COGS	Inventory	COGS	Inventory
1	20000	18000	162000	18000	164000	16000
2	22000	18000	160364	35636	164000	32000
3	24000	18000	159000	53000	164000	48000
4	26000	18000	157846	70154	164000	64000
5	28000	18000	156857	87143	164000	80000
6	20000	20000	180000	0	180000	0
7	20000	19500	175500	4500	176000	4000
8	20000	19000	171000	9000	172000	8000
9	20000	18500	166500	13500	168000	12000
10	20000	18000	162000	18000	164000	16000
11	23000	18000	159652	44348	164000	40000
12	26000	18000	157846	70154	164000	64000
13	29000	18000	156414	95586	164000	88000
14	32000	18000	155250	120750	164000	112000
15	35000	18000	154286	145714	164000	136000
16	20000	17000	153000	27000	156000	24000
17	20000	16000	144000	36000	148000	32000
18	20000	15000	135000	45000	140000	40000
19	20000	14000	126000	54000	132000	48000
20	20000	13000	117000	63000	124000	56000
21	25000	18000	158400	61600	164000	56000
22	30000	20000	173333	86667	180000	80000
23	35000	22000	188571	111429	196000	104000
24	40000	24000	204000	136000	212000	128000
25	45000	26000	219556	160444	228000	152000

Chapter 6 Problem 14

CH06PR14

PRACTICE PROBLEMS

Given
- Units produced
- Units sold
- Variable cost
- Fixed cost

Compute
- Cost of Goods Sold
- Inventory
- Total cost

Please work these problems.
Compare your results with the solution.

10000 Units produced
8000 Units sold
2000 Inventory
20000 Fixed Cost

Item No.	Variable Cost	Absorption COGS	Absorption Inventory	Direct Cost COGS	Direct Cost Inventory
1	8	80000	20000	84000	16000
2	9	88000	22000	92000	18000
3	10	96000	24000	100000	20000
4	11	104000	26000	108000	22000
5	12	112000	28000	116000	24000
6	8	80000	20000	84000	16000
7	7	72000	18000	76000	14000
8	6	64000	16000	68000	12000
9	5	56000	14000	60000	10000
10	4	48000	12000	52000	8000
11	20	176000	44000	180000	40000
12	22	192000	48000	196000	44000
13	24	208000	52000	212000	48000
14	26	224000	56000	228000	52000
15	28	240000	60000	244000	56000
16	50	416000	104000	420000	100000
17	60	496000	124000	500000	120000
18	70	576000	144000	580000	140000
19	80	656000	164000	660000	160000
20	90	736000	184000	740000	180000
21	50	416000	104000	420000	100000
22	45	376000	94000	380000	90000
23	40	336000	84000	340000	80000
24	35	296000	74000	300000	70000
25	30	256000	64000	260000	60000

Chapter 6 Problem 15

CH06PR15

PRACTICE PROBLEMS

Given
- Units produced
- Units sold
- Variable cost
- Fixed cost

Compute
- Cost of Goods Sold
- Inventory
- Total cost

Please work these problems.
Compare your results with the solution.

10000 Units produced
8000 Units sold
2000 Inventory

Item No.	Variable Cost	Fixed Cost	Absorption COGS	Absorption Inventory	Direct Cost COGS	Direct Cost Inventory
1	8	20000	80000	20000	84000	16000
2	9	22000	89600	22400	94000	18000
3	10	24000	99200	24800	104000	20000
4	11	26000	108800	27200	114000	22000
5	12	28000	118400	29600	124000	24000
6	8	20000	80000	20000	84000	16000
7	7	18000	70400	17600	74000	14000
8	6	16000	60800	15200	64000	12000
9	5	14000	51200	12800	54000	10000
10	4	12000	41600	10400	44000	8000
11	20	10000	168000	42000	170000	40000
12	22	8000	182400	45600	184000	44000
13	24	6000	196800	49200	198000	48000
14	26	4000	211200	52800	212000	52000
15	28	2000	225600	56400	226000	56000
16	50	20000	416000	104000	420000	100000
17	60	30000	504000	126000	510000	120000
18	70	40000	592000	148000	600000	140000
19	80	50000	680000	170000	690000	160000
20	90	60000	768000	192000	780000	180000
21	50	50000	440000	110000	450000	100000
22	45	60000	408000	102000	420000	90000
23	40	70000	376000	94000	390000	80000
24	8	0	64000	16000	64000	16000
25	0	20000	16000	4000	20000	0

7 Contribution Margin

Condensed List of Items

Item No.		*Problems*
CH07PR01	Contribution margin format	5
CH07PR02	Change in income	5
CH07PR03	Change in contribution margin	5
CH07PR04	Operating leverage	5
CH07PR05	Change in income	5
CH07PR06	Change in contribution margin	5
CH07PR07	Break-even units—CM per unit	5
CH07PR08	Break-even units—CM Ratio %	5
CH07PR09	Margin safety dollars and percent	5
CH07PR10	Change in contribution margin	
CH07PR11	CM % and break-even dollars	5
CH07PR12	Average contribution margin	5
CH07PR13	Average CM and BE units	5
CH07PR14	CM and BE	5
CH07PR15	Average CM, BE units and dollars	5
CH07PR16	Average CM and BE units	5
	Total	75

TRADITIONAL FORMAT

Sales
—Cost of Goods Sold
Gross Profit
—Expenses
Net Income

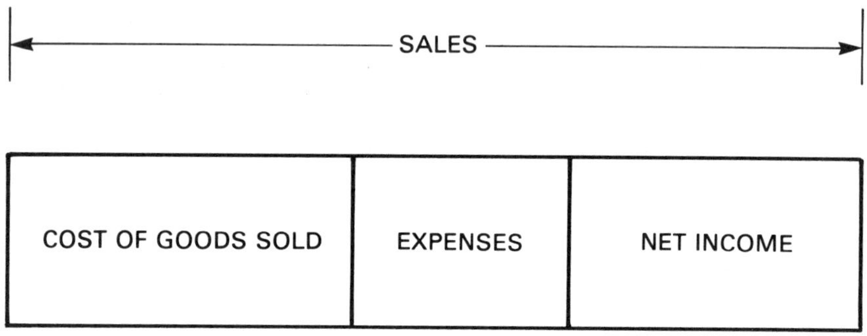

CONTRIBUTION FORMAT

Sales
—Variable Expenses
CONTRIBUTION MARGIN
—Fixed Expenses
Net Income

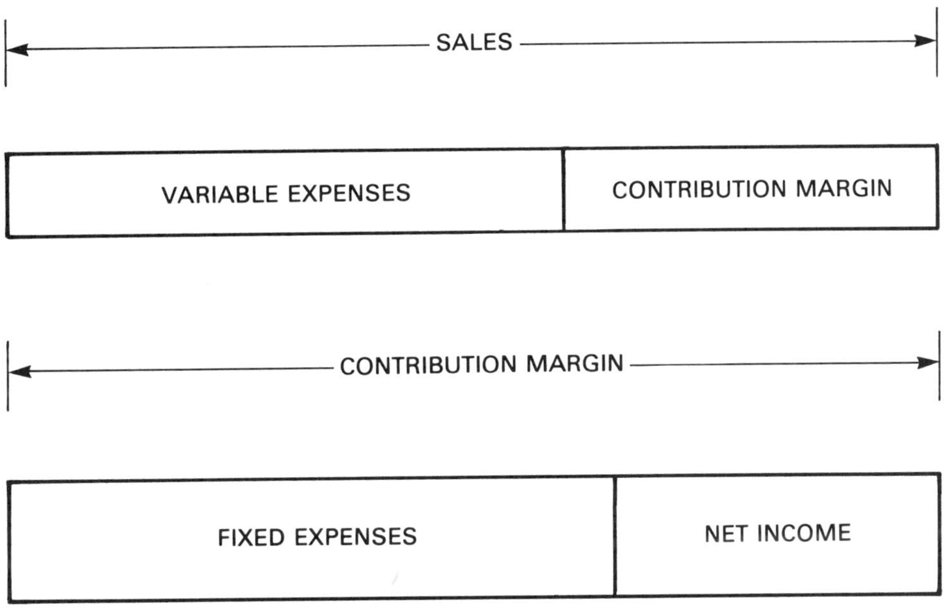

CH07PR01

Chapter 7 Problem 1

Given
- Sales
- Variable Expenses
- Fixed Expenses
- Number of Units

Compute
- Sales
- Variable Expenses
- Contribution Margin
- Fixed Expenses
- Net income

SCREEN DISPLAY

```
  FACTS                  FACTS
                        Per Unit
Sales                      250
Variable Expenses          150
Fixed Expenses           35000
Number of Units            400
SOLUTION                SOLUTION Total     Per Unit
Sales                             100000        250
Variable Expenses                  60000        150
Contribution Margin                40000        100
Fixed Expenses                     35000
Net income                          5000
```

CELL CONTENT

	A	B	C	D	E
1	FACTS		FACTS		
2			Per Unit		
3	Sales		250		
4	Variable	Expenses	150		
5	Fixed Exp	enses	35000		
6	Number of	Units	400		
7	SOLUTION		SOLUTION	Total	Per Unit
8	Sales			+C6*C3	+C3
9	Variable	Expenses		+C6*C4	+C4
10	Contribut	ion Margi	n	+D8-D9	+E8-E9
11	Fixed Exp	enses		+C5	
12	Net incom	e		+D10-D11	

CH07PR02

Chapter 7 Problem 2

Given
- CM ratio
- Sales increase
- Fixed expense increase

Compute
- Contribution Margin
- Increase in income

SCREEN DISPLAY

```
FACTS                FACTS

CM ratio                   40 %
Changes
Sales increase          30000
F.E. increase           10000

SOLUTION
                   30000        40     12000
                                       10000
          Increase in income            2000
```

CELL CONTENT

	A	B	C	D
1	FACTS		FACTS	
2				
3	CM ratio		40	%
4	Changes			
5	Sales inc	rease	30000	
6	F.E. incr	ease	10000	
7				
8	SOLUTION			
9		+C5	+C3	+B9*(C9*.0 1)
10				+C6
11		Increase	in income	+D9-D10

CH07PR03 Chapter 7 Problem 3

```
Given
   Proposed
     Volume
     Contribution Margin per unit
   Present
     Volume
     Contribution Margin per unit
Compute
   Proposed CM
   Present  CM
   Change in CM
```

SCREEN DISPLAY

```
FACTS                 FACTS
          Proposed   Present
Volume         350       400
CM per #       125       100


SOLUTION              SOLUTION
Proposed CM             43750
Present  CM             40000
Change in CM             3750
```

CELL CONTENT

	A	B	C
1	FACTS		FACTS
2		Proposed	Present
3	Volume	350	400
4	CM per #	125	100
5			
6			
7	SOLUTION		SOLUTION
8	Proposed	CM	+B3*B4
9	Present	CM	+C3*C4
10	Change in	CM	+C8-C9

CH07PR04

Chapter 7 Problem 4

```
Given
   C.M.
   Net Inc.
Compute
   Operating Leverage
```

SCREEN DISPLAY

```
FACTS                  FACTS

                          A Co.    B Co.
C.M.                       40000    70000
Net Inc.                   10000    10000

SOLUTION               SOLUTION

Operating Leverage
                       A Co.           4.00
                       B Co.           7.00
```

CELL CONTENT

	A	B	C	D
1	FACTS		FACTS	
2				
3			A Co.	B Co.
4	C.M.		40000	70000
5	Net Inc.		10000	10000
6				
7	SOLUTION		SOLUTION	
8				
9	Operating	Leverage		
10			A Co.	+C4/C5
11			B Co.	+D4/D5

CH07PR05

Chapter 7 Problem 5

```
Given
   Sales - per unit
   Variable expense
   Proposed
    Change in F.E.
    Increase in sales
Compute
   Change in C.M.
   Change in F.E
   Change in Income
```

SCREEN DISPLAY

```
FACTS                  FACTS

Sales - per unit          250
Variable expense          150
Proposed
 Change in F.E.         10000
 Increase in sales      30000
SOLUTION              SOLUTION
Change in C.M.                     12000
Change in F.E                      10000
Change in Income                    2000
```

CELL CONTENT

	A	B	C	D
1	FACTS		FACTS	
2				
3	Sales - p	er unit	250	
4	Variable	expense	150	
5	Proposed			
6	Change i	n F.E.	10000	
7	Increase	in sales	30000	
8	SOLUTION		SOLUTION	
9	Change in	C.M.		+C7*(1-(C4 /C3)
10	Change in	F.E		+C6
11	Change in	Income		+D9-D10
12				

CH07PR06

Chapter 7 Problem 6

Given
- Proposed units
- Proposed Contribution margin
- Present units
- Present Contribution margin

Compute
- Proposed C.M.
- Present C.M.
- Change in C.M.

SCREEN DISPLAY

FACTS	FACTS	
	Units	C.M.
Proposed	350	125
Present	400	100
SOLUTION	SOLUTION	
Proposed C.M.		43750
Present C.M.		40000
Change in C.M.		3750

CELL CONTENT

	A	B	C	D
1	FACTS		FACTS	
2			Units	C.M.
3	Proposed		350	125
4	Present		400	100
5				
6	SOLUTION		SOLUTION	
7				
8	Proposed	C.M.		+C3*D3
9	Present	C.M.		+C4*D4
10	Change in	C.M.		+D8-D9
11				
12				

CH07PR07

Chapter 7 Problem 7

```
Given
   Fixed Expense
   CM-Per Unit
Compute

   Break-even-units
```

SCREEN DISPLAY

```
FACTS                  FACTS

Fixed Expense              35000
CM-Per Unit                  100


SOLUTION               SOLUTION

Break-even                   350 units
```

CELL CONTENT

	A	B	C	D
1	FACTS		FACTS	
2				
3	Fixed Exp	ense	35000	
4	CM-Per Un	it	100	
5				
6				
7	SOLUTION		SOLUTION	
8				
9	Break-eve	n	+C3/C4	units

CH07PR08

Chapter 7 Problem 8

Given
Fixed Expense
CM-Ratio %

Compute
Break-even-units

SCREEN DISPLAY

FACTS		FACTS	
Fixed Expense		35000	
CM-Ratio %		40	
SOLUTION		SOLUTION	
Break-even	$	87500	units

CELL CONTENT

	A	B	C	D
1	FACTS		FACTS	
2				
3	Fixed Exp	ense	35000	
4	CM-Ratio	%	40	
5				
6				
7	SOLUTION		SOLUTION	
8				
9	Break-eve	n $	+C3/(C4*.01)	units

CH07PR09

Chapter 7 Problem 9

Given	
Sales	200000
Break-even sales	160000
Compute	
Margin safety $	40000
Margin safety %	20

SCREEN DISPLAY

FACTS	FACTS
Sales	200000
Break-even sales	160000
SOLUTION	SOLUTION
Margin safety $	40000
Margin safety %	20

CELL CONTENT

	A	B	C
1	FACTS		FACTS
2			
3	Sales		200000
4	Break-eve	n sales	160000
5			
6			
7	SOLUTION		SOLUTION
8			
9	Margin sa	fety $	+C3-C4
10	Margin sa	fety %	(+C9/C3)*1 00

CH07PR10   Chapter 10 Problem 10

```
Given     Volume      Present and Proposed
          Salaries    Present and Proposed
          C M         Present and Proposed
Compute   Proposed C.M.
          Present  C.M.
          Change in CM
          Change in salaries
          Change in income
```

SCREEN DISPLAY

```
FACTS              FACTS
           Present              Proposed
Volume         400 Units              15 %
Salaries      6000 Per Mth            15
C M            100 Per unit           85
SOLUTION           SOLUTION
Proposed C.M.          39100
Present  C.M.          40000
Change in CM            -900
Change in salaries      6000
Change in income        5100
```

CELL CONTENT

	A	B	C	D	E
1	FACTS		FACTS		
2		Present		Proposed	
3	Volume	400	Units	15	%
4	Salaries	6000	Per Mth	15	
5	C M	100	Per unit	85	
6	SOLUTION		SOLUTION		
7	Proposed		+B3*(1+(D3 *.01))*D5		
8	Present		+B3*B5		
9	Change in	CM	+C7-C8		
10	Change in	salaries	+B4		
11	Increase	in income	+C9+C10		

CH07PR11

Chapter 7 Problem 11

Given	Product A
	Sales and Variable Expenses
	Product A
	Sales and Variable Expenses
Compute	Contribution margin %
	Break-even dollars

SCREEN DISPLAY

FACTS	FACTS		
	Sales	V.E.	
A	80000	60000	
B	20000	10000	
F. E.			27000
SOLUTION		SOLUTION	
	Sales	V.E.	Total
Total	100000	70000	0.70
C.M. %			30
Break-even dollars			90000

CELL CONTENT

	A	B	C	D
1	FACTS	FACTS		
2				
3		Sales	V.E.	
4	A	80000	60000	
5	B	20000	10000	
6	F. E.			27000
7	SOLUTION		SOLUTION	
8		Sales	V.E.	Total
9	Total	+B4+B5	+C4+C5	(+C4+C5)/(B4+B5)
10	C.M. %			((+B9-C9)/ B9)*100
11	Break-eve	n dollars		+D6/(D10*. 01)

Chapter 7 Problem 12

CH07PR12

Given		Year 1	Year 2
	Product X	CM Per #	Units Sold
	Product Y	CM Per #	Units Sold
Compute			
	Product X	CM	CM
	Product Y	CM	CM
	Average CM		

SCREEN DISPLAY

```
SALES MIX  FACTS    FACTS
         CM Per #       Units Sold
                   Year 1   Year 2
Product X        5   1000     2000
Product Y        3   3000     2000
Solution Solution Solution
Contrib. Margin    Year 1   Year 2
         Product X   5000    10000
         Product Y   9000     6000
         Total      14000    16000
       Average CM     3.5        4
```

CELL CONTENT

	A	B	C	D
1	SALES MIX	FACTS	FACTS	
2		CM Per #	Un	its Sold
3			Year 1	Year 2
4	Product X	5	1000	2000
5	Product Y	3	3000	2000
6	Solution	Solution	Solution	
7	Contrib.	Margin	Year 1	Year 2
8		Product X	+C4*B4	+D4*B4
9		Product Y	+C5*B5	+D5*B5
10		Total	+C8+C9	+D8+D9
11	Av	erage CM	+C10/(C4+C5	+D10/(D4+D5

Chapter 7 Problem 13

CH07PR13

	Prod X		Prod Y	
Given	Year 1	Year 2	Year 1	Year 2
	FE	FE	FE	FE
	# sold	# sold	# sold	# sold
	CM Per #	CM Per #	CM Per #	CM Per #
Compute	Prod X		Prod Y	
	Year 1	Year 2	Year 1	Year 2
	CM	CM	CM	CM

SCREEN DISPLAY

SALES MIX	FACTS	FACTS		
F.E. =	27000	Units Sold		
	CM Per #	Year 1	Year 2	
Product X	3	1000	2000	
Product Y	6	3000	9000	
Solution	Solution	Solution		
Contrib.	Margin	Year 1	Year 2	Total
	Product X	3000	6000	9000
	Product Y	18000	54000	72000
	Total	21000	60000	81000
	Average CM	5.25	5.45	5.40
Break-even units				5000

CELL CONTENT

	A	B	C	D	E
1	SALES MIX	FACTS	FACTS		
2	F.E. =	27000	Un	its Sold	
3		CM Per #	Year 1	Year 2	
4	Product X	3	1000	2000	
5	Product Y	6	3000	9000	
6	Solution	Solution	Solution		
7	Contrib.	Margin	Year 1	Year 2	Total
8		Product X	+C4*B4	+D4*B4	+C8+D8
9		Product Y	+C5*B5	+D5*B5	+C9+D9
10		Total	+C8+C9	+D8+D9	+C10+D10
11	Av	erage CM	+C10/(C 4+C5	+D10/(D 4+D5	+E10/(C 4+C5+D4+D5)
12	Break-eve	n units			+B2/E11

CH07PR14

Chapter 7 Problem 14

Given		Units	Per Unit	
	Product X	Sold	C.M.	
	Product Y	Sold	C.M.	
	C.M. %			
Compute	Total C.M.			Sales
	Total Units			V. E.
	Average C. M.			C.M.
	Break-even-dollars			F.E.
	Break-even-units			Profit

SCREEN DISPLAY

```
FACTS                     C.M.
        Units Sold Per Unit
Product X      1000        5
Product Y      3000        3
C.M. %                    30
Solution                    Solution
                                         B. E.
Total C.M.               14000  Sales     46667
Total Units               4000  V. E.     32667
Average  C. M.             3.5  C.M.      14000
Break-even-dollars       46667  F.E.      14000
Break-even-units         13333  Profit        0
```

CELL CONTENT

	A	B	C	D	E
1	FACTS		C.M.		
2	U	nits Sold	Per Unit		
3	Product X	1000	5		
4	Product Y	3000	3		
5	C.M. %		30		
6	Solution			Solution	
7					B. E.
8	Total C.M	.	(B3*C3)+(B 4*C4)	Sales	+C11
9	Total Uni	ts	+B3+B4	V. E.	+C11-C8
10	Average	C. M.	+C8/C9	C.M.	+E8-E9
11	Break-eve	n-dollars	+C8/(C5 *.01)	F.E.	+E10
12	Break-eve	n-units	+C11/C10	Profit	+E10-E11

Chapter 7 Problem 15

CH07PR15

Given	Product X	# Sold CM Per #		
	Product Y	# Sold CM Per #		
		F.E.	C.M. %	
Compute	Total C.M.		Sales	B. E.
	Average C. M.		V. E.	
	Break-even-dollars		C. M.	
	Break-even units			

SCREEN DISPLAY

FACTS	FACTS	C.M.	FACTS	FACTS
	# Sold	Per #		
Product X	2000	10		
Product Y	4000	30		
27000	F.E.	30	C.M. %	
Solution			Solution	B. E.
Total C.M.		140000	Sales	90000
Average C. M.		23	V. E.	63000
Break-even-dollars		90000	C. M.	27000
Break-even units		1157		
	X	386	10	3857
	Y	771	30	23143

CELL CONTENT

	A	B	C	D	E
1	FACTS	FACTS	C.M.	FACTS	FACTS
2		# Sold	Per #		
3	Product X	2000	10		
4	Product Y	4000	30		
5	27000	F.E.	30	C.M. %	
6	Solution			Solution	B. E.
7	Total C.M	.	(B3*C3)+(B 4*C4)	Sales	+C9
8	Average	C. M.	+C7/(B3 +B4)	V. E.	+E7-A5
9	Break-eve	n-dollars	+A5/(C5 *.01)	C. M.	+A5
10	Break-eve	n units	+A5/C8		
11		X	(B3/(B3 +B4)*C10	10	+C11*D11
12		Y	(B4/(B4 +B3)*C10	30	+C12*D12

Chapter 7 Problem 16

CH07PR16

			Year 1	Year 2	
Given	Product X CM Per #		Units Sold		
	Product Y CM Per #		Units Sold		
	F.E. =	27000	C.M. = %	30	
Compute	Contribution Marg.				
		Product X	Year 1	Year 2	Total
		Product Y	Year 1	Year 2	Total
		Total	Year 1	Year 2	Total
		Average CM	Year 1	Year 2	Total
	Break-even units				Total

SCREEN DISPLAY

FACTS	FACTS	Units Sold		
	CM Per #	Year 1	Year 2	
Product X	3	1000	4000	
Product Y	5	1000	3500	
F.E. =	27000	C.M. = %	30	
Solution		Solution		Solution
Contribution Marg.		Year 1	Year 2	Total
	Product X	3000	12000	15000
	Product Y	5000	17500	22500
	Total	8000	29500	37500
	Average CM	4.00	3.93	3.95
Break-even units				6840

CELL CONTENT

	A	B	C	D	E
1	FACTS	FACTS	Un	its Sold	
2		CM Per #	Year 1	Year 2	
3	Product X	3	1000	4000	
4	Product Y	5	1000	3500	
5	F.E. =	27000	C.M. = %	30	
6	Solution		Solution		Solution
7	Contribut	ion Marg.	Year 1	Year 2	Total
8		Product X	+C3*B3	+D3*B3	+C8+D8
9		Product Y	+C4*B4	+D4*B4	+C9+D9
10		Total	+C8+C9	+D8+D9	+C10+D10
11	Av	erage CM	+C10/(C 3+C4	+D10/(D 3+D4	+E10/(C 3+C4+D3+D4)
12	Break-eve	n units			+B5/E11

Chapter 7 PRACTICE PROBLEMS

Please work these problems.
Compare your results with the solution.

Problem 1

Given
- Sales
- Variable Expenses
- Fixed Expenses
- Number of Units

Compute
- Sales
- Variable Expenses
- Contribution Margin
- Fixed Expenses
- Net income

Item No.	Per # Sales	F.E.	V.E.	Number of #	Cont. Margin	Net Inc.
1	250	35000	150	400	40000	5000
2	260	35000	150	400	44000	9000
3	270	35000	150	400	48000	13000
4	280	35000	150	400	52000	17000
5	290	35000	150	400	56000	21000

Problem 2

Given
- CM ratio
- Sales increase
- Fixed expense increase

Compute
- Contribution Margin
- Increase in income

Item No.	CM ratio	Changes Sales	F.E.	Inc.
1	40	30000	10000	2000
2	42	30000	10000	2600
3	44	30000	10000	3200
4	46	30000	10000	3800
5	48	30000	10000	4400

PRACTICE PRACTICE PRACTICE PRACTICE PRACTICE PRACTICE

Problem 3

Given
- Proposed
  - Volume
  - Contribution Margin per unit
- Present
  - Volume
  - Contribution Margin per unit

Compute
- Proposed CM
- Present CM
- Change in CM

Item No.	Present Vol.	CM #	Proposed Vol.	CM #	Change CM
1	400	100	350	125	3750
2	410	100	350	125	2750
3	420	100	350	125	1750
4	430	100	350	125	750
5	440	100	350	125	-250

Problem 4

Given
- C.M.
- Net Inc.

Compute
- Operating Leverage

Item No.	C.M.	Net Inc.	Oper. Lev.
1	40000	10000	4.00
2	50000	10000	5.00
3	60000	10000	6.00
4	70000	10000	7.00
5	80000	10000	8.00

Chapter 7 PRACTICE PROBLEMS

Please work these problems.

Problem 5

Given
- Sales - per unit
- Variable expense
- Proposed
  - Change in F.E.
  - Increase in sales

Compute
- Change in C.M.
- Change in F.E
- Change in Income

Item No.	Per Unit Sales	V.E.	Proposed F.E	Sales	Change Inc.
1	250	150	10000	30000	2000
2	260	150	10000	30000	2692
3	270	150	10000	30000	3333
4	280	150	10000	30000	3929
5	290	150	10000	30000	4483

Problem 6 PRACTICE PRACTICE PRACTICE PRACTICE PRACTICE PRACTICE

Given
- Proposed units
- Proposed Contribution margin
- Present units
- Present Contribution margin

Compute
- Proposed C.M.
- Present C.M.
- Change in C.M.

Item No.	Proposed Units	C.M.	Present Units	C.M.	Change C.M.
1	350	125	400	100	3750
2	360	125	400	100	5000
3	370	125	400	100	6250
4	380	125	400	100	7500
5	390	125	400	100	8750

Problem 7

Given
- Fixed Expense
- CM-Per Unit

Compute
- Break-even-units

Item No.	F.E.	C..M Per #	B.E. Units
1	35000	100	350
2	36000	100	360
3	37000	100	370
4	38000	100	380
5	39000	100	390

Problem 8 PRACTICE PRACTICE PRACTICE PRACTICE PRACTICE PRACTICE

Given
- Fixed Expense
- CM-Ratio %

Compute
- Break-even-units

Item No.	F.E.	C.M. Ratio	B.E. Units
1	35000	40	87500
2	36000	40	90000
3	37000	40	92500
4	38000	40	95000
5	39000	40	97500

Please work these problems.

Problem 9

Given
Sales 200000
Break-even sales 160000

Compute
Margin safety $ 40000
Margin safety % 20

Item No.	Sales	B.E.S	Margin $	Safety %
1	200000	160000	40000	20
2	210000	160000	50000	24
3	220000	160000	60000	27
4	230000	160000	70000	30
5	240000	160000	80000	33

Problem 11 PRACTICE PRACTICE PRACTICE PRACTICE PRACTICE PRACTICE

Given Product A
Sales and Variable Expenses
Product A
Sales and Variable Expenses
Compute Contribution margin %
Break-even dollars

Total Sales 10000
Fixed 2700

Item	Product A Sales %	V.E. %	Product B Sale %	V.E. %	BES
1	0.80	.75	0.20	0.50	9000
2	0.82	.77	0.18	0.52	9818
3	0.84	.79	0.16	0.54	10800
4	0.86	.81	0.14	0.56	12000
5	0.88	.83	0.12	0.58	13500

Problem 12 PRACTICE PRACTICE PRACTICE PRACTICE PRACTICE PRACTICE

Given	Year 1	Year 2
Product X	CM Per #	Units Sold
Product Y	CM Per #	Units Sold
Compute		
Product X	CM	CM
Product Y	CM	CM
Average CM		

Item No.	Product X CM #	Units	Product Y CM #	Units	Ave. C.M.
1	5	1000	3	3000	3.50
2	6	1000	3	3000	3.75
3	7	1000	3	3000	4.00
4	8	1000	3	3000	4.25
5	9	1000	3	3000	4.50

Please work these problems.
Compare your results with the solution.

Problem 13

	Prod X		Prod Y	
Given	Year 1	Year 2	Year 1	Year 2
	FE	FE	FE	FE
	# sold	# sold	# sold	# sold
	CM Per #	CM Per #	CM Per #	CM Per #
Compute	Prod X		Prod Y	
	Year 1	Year 2	Year 1	Year 2
	CM	CM	CM	CM

Item No.	Product X Unit	C.M	Product Y Unit	C.M	Ave. C.M
1	1000	3	3000	6	5.25
2	1100	3	3000	6	5.20
3	1200	3	3000	6	5.14
4	1300	3	3000	6	5.09
5	1400	3	3000	6	5.05

PRACTICE PRACTICE PRACTICE PRACTICE PRACTICE PRACTICE

Problem 14

		Units	Per Unit	
Given	Product X	Sold	C.M.	
	Product Y	Sold	C.M.	
	C.M. %			
Compute	Total C.M.			Sales
	Total Units			V. E.
	Average C. M.			C.M.
	Break-even-dollars			F.E.
	Break-even-units			Profit

Contr.Mar % 30
Fixed Exp. 14000

Item	Product X Quant	CM #	Product Y Quant	CM #	Ave. C.M.	Break-even $	Units
1	1000	5.00	3000	3.00	3.50	46667	13333
2	1200	5.00	3000	3.00	3.57	50000	14000
3	1400	5.00	3000	3.00	3.64	53333	14667
4	1600	5.00	3000	3.00	3.70	56667	15333
5	1800	5.00	3000	3.00	3.75	60000	16000

Please work these problems.
Compare your results with the solution.

Problem 15

Given

Product X # Sold CM Per #
Product Y # Sold CM Per #
F.E.

Compute Total C.M.
Average C. M.
Break-even-dollars
Break-even units

C.M. % Sales / V. E. / C. M. B. E.

27000 Fixed expense
30 CM %
10 Contribution Margin Product A
30 Contribution Margin Product B

Item	Units sold Product		Ave	B R E A K E V E N Total		Product	
No.	A	B	CM	$	Units	A	B
1	2000	4000	23.33	90000	1157	386	771
2	2500	4000	22.31	90000	1210	466	745
3	3000	4000	21.43	90000	1260	540	720
4	3500	4000	20.67	90000	1306	610	697
5	4000	4000	20.00	90000	1350	675	675

Problem 16 PRACTICE PRACTICE PRACTICE PRACTICE PRACTICE PRACTICE

Given Product X CM Per # (Year 1 Year 2 Units Sold)
Product Y CM Per # Units Sold
F.E. = 27000 C.M. = % 30

Compute Contribution Marg.
Product X Year 1 Year 2 Total
Product Y Year 1 Year 2 Total
Total Year 1 Year 2 Total
Average CM Year 1 Year 2 Total
Break-even units Total

Fixed Exp. 27000
Prod X units 1000
Prod Y units 1000

Item	Product X CM #	Y CM #	Cont. Marg Total	Ave	B.E. Units
1	3.00	5.00	8000	4.00	6750
2	4.00	5.00	9000	4.50	6000
3	5.00	5.00	10000	5.00	5400
4	6.00	5.00	11000	5.50	4909
5	7.00	5.00	12000	6.00	4500

8 Budgets

Condensed List of Items

Item No.		*Problems*
CH08PR01	Sales budget	25
CH08PR02	Production budget	25
CH08PR03	Cash budget	25
CH08PR04	Direct materials budget	25
CH08PR05	Direct labor budget	25
CH08PR06	Overhead budget	25
CH08PR07	Economic order quantity	25
CH08PR08	Economic production run	25
CH08PR09	Safety stock	25
	Total	225

Chapter 8 Problem 1

CH08PR01

Given
- Projected Sales
- Selling Price
- Collection-period of sale %
- Collection-following period %

Compute
- Sales
- Collection-period of sale
- Collection-following period
- Collection-total

SCREEN DISPLAY

```
FACTS     SALES Budget            Period
                              1        2        3
Projected Sales            1000     2000     3000
Selling Price                50       50       50
Collection
Period of sale               75 %
Following period             25 %
SOLUTION               Period 1  Period 2 Period 3
Sales                     50000   100000   150000
Period of sale            37500    75000   112500
Following period                   12500    25000
Total collected           37500    87500   137500
```

CELL CONTENT

	A	B	C	D	E
1	FACTS	SALES Bud	get	Period	
2			1	2	3
3	Projected	Sales	1000	2000	3000
4	Selling P	rice	50	50	50
5	Collectio	n			
6	Period of	sale	75	%	
7	Following	period	25	%	
8	SOLUTION		Period 1	Period 2	Period 3
9	Sales		+C3*C4	+D3*D4	+E3*E4
10	Period of	sale	+C9*C6*.01	+D9*C6*.01	+E9*C6*.01
11	Following	period		+C9*C7*.01	+D9*C7*.01
12	Total col	lected	+C10+C11	+D10+D11	+E10+E11

Chapter 8 Problem 2

Given
Expected Sales
Finished Goods - End
Finished Goods - Beginning
Compute
Units to be produced

SCREEN DISPLAY

FACTS	Production Budget FACTS		
	Period		
	1	2	3
Expected sales	1000	1500	2000
Fin. Goods - End	150	200	150
Fin. Goods - Beg	100	200	300
SOLUTION			
Expected sales	1000	1500	2000
+ Fin. Goods - End	150	200	150
Required	1150	1700	2150
- Fin. Goods - Beg	100	150	200
To be produced	1050	1550	1950

CELL CONTENT

	A	B	C	D	E
1	FACTS	Productio	n Budget	FACTS	
2				Period	
3			1	2	3
4	Expected	sales	1000	1500	2000
5	Fin. Goo	ds - End	150	200	150
6	Fin. Goo	ds - Beg	100	200	300
7	SOLUTION				
8	Expected	sales	1000	1500	2000
9	+ Fin. Go	ods - End	150	200	150
10	Required		+C8+C9	+D8+D9	+E8+E9
11	- Fin. Go	ods - Beg	100	150	200
12	To be pro	duced	+C10-C11	+D10-D11	+E10-E11

CH08PR03

Chapter 8 Problem 3

Given
Cash-Balance- Beginning
Receipts
Disbursements
Compute
Cash-Balance- End

SCREEN DISPLAY

FACTS	Cash Budget	FACTS Period		
		1	2	3
Beg. Bal		12000	10000	10350
Receipts		55000	75000	85000
Disbursements		38000	67000	78000
Solution				
Beg. Bal		12000	10000	10350
Receipts		55000	75000	85000
Total Available		67000	85000	95350
Disbursements		38000	67000	78000
End Bal.		29000	18000	17350

CELL CONTENT

	A	B	C	D	E
1	FACTS	Cash Budg	et	FACTS	
2				Period	
3			1	2	3
4	Beg. Bal		12000	10000	10350
5	Receipts		55000	75000	85000
6	Disbursem	ents	38000	67000	78000
7	Solution				
8	Beg. Bal		12000	10000	10350
9	Receipts		55000	75000	85000
10	Total Ava	ilable	+C8+C9	+D8+D9	+E8+E9
11	Disbursem	ents	38000	67000	78000
12	End Bal.		+C10-C11	+D10-D11	+E10-E11

CH08PR04

Chapter 8 Problem 4

Given
- Units to be produced
- Direct material-per unit
- Desired ending inventory
- Beginning inventory

Compute
- Purchases
- Ending inventory

SCREEN DISPLAY

```
FACTS     Direct materials budget     FACTS
                              Period
                            1          2          34
Units-production         1000       1500        2000
DM Per unit                 2
Desired  End Inv         2300       2000        1500
Beginning Inv.           1000
SOLUTION
Beginning Inv.           1000       2300        2000
Production               2000       3000        4000
Purchases                 700       3300        4500
Ending Inventory         2300       2000        1500
```

CELL CONTENT

	A	B	C	D	E
1	FACTS	Direct ma	terials b	udget	FACTS
2				Period	
3			1	2	34
4	Units-pro	duction	1000	1500	2000
5	DM Per un	it	2		
6	Desired	End Inv	2300	2000	1500
7	Beginning	Inv.	1000		
8	SOLUTION				
9	Beginning	Inv.	+C7	+C12	+D12
10	Productio	n	+C4*C5	+D4*C5	+E4*C5
11	Purchases		+C9+C10-C6	+D9+D10-D6	+E9+E10-E6
12	Ending In	ventory	+C9+C10-C1	+D9+D10-D1	+E9+E10-E1

Chapter 8 Problem 5

CH08PR05

```
Given
   To be produced
   DL Hrs per  unit
   DL  $  per  unit
Compute
   Total Hours
   DL  $  per  unit
   Total Cost
```

SCREEN DISPLAY

```
FACTS     Direct Labor Budget          FACTS
                            PERIOD
                              1        2        3
To be produced              1000     2000     3000
DL Hrs per  unit               5
DL  $  per  unit               4
SOLUTION
Total Hours                 5000    10000    15000
DL  $  per  unit               4        4        4
Total Cost                 20000    40000    60000
```

CELL CONTENT

	A	B	C	D	E
1	FACTS	Direct La	bor Budge	t	FACTS
2				PERIOD	
3			1	2	3
4	To be pro	duced	1000	2000	3000
5	DL Hrs pe	r unit	5		
6	DL $ pe	r unit	4		
7	SOLUTION				
8	Total Hou	rs	+C4*C5	+D4*C5	+E4*C5
9	DL $ pe	r unit	4	4	4
10	Total Cos	t	+C8*C9	+D8*D9	+E8*E9

CH08PR06

Chapter 8 Problem 6

Given
- Budgeted DL Hours
- Variable OH Rate
- Fixed OH

Compute
- Variable Overhead
- Fixed Overhead
- Total

SCREEN DISPLAY

FACTS Overhead Budget	FACTS		
	PERIOD		
	1	2	3
Budgeted DL Hours	5250	7750	9750
Variable OH Rate	2		
Fixed OH	15000		
SOLUTION			
Variable Overhead	10500	15500	19500
Fixed Overhead	15000	15000	15000
Total	25500	30500	34500

CELL CONTENT

	A	B	C	D	E
1	FACTS	Overhead	Budget	FACTS	
2				PERIOD	
3			1	2	3
4	Budgeted	DL Hours	5250	7750	9750
5	Variable	OH Rate	2		
6	Fixed OH		15000		
7	SOLUTION				
8	Variable	Overhead	+C4*C5	+D4*C5	+E4*C5
9	Fixed Ove	rhead	+C6	+C6	+C6
10	Total		+C8+C9	+D8+D9	+E8+E9

CH08PR07

Chapter 8 Problem 7

```
Given
        Annual quantity used in units
        Cost of placing one order
        annual cost of carrying one unit
Compute
        Economic order quantity
```

SCREEN DISPLAY

```
FACTS                 FACTS
Compute Economic order quantity

     3000 Annual quantity used in units
       10 Cost of placing one order
       .8 annual cost of carrying one unit

Solution

Economic order quantity           274
```

CELL CONTENT

	A	B	C	D	E
1	FACTS		FACTS		
2	Compute E	conomic o	rder quan	tity	
3					
4	3000	Annual q	uantity u	sed in un	its
5	10	Cost of	placing o	ne order	
6	.8	annual c	ost of ca	rrying on	e unit
7					
8	Solution				
9					
10	Economic	order qua	ntity	@SQRT((2*A4*A5/A6)	

Chapter 8 Problem 8

```
Given
    units produced each year
    setup costs to change production
    annual cost of carrying one unit
Compute
    Economic production run
```

SCREEN DISPLAY

```
FACTS               FACTS
Compute   Economic production run

    15000 units produced each year
      150 setup costs to change production
        2 annual cost of carrying one unit

SOLUTION            SOLUTION

Economic production run         1500
```

CELL CONTENT

	A	B	C	D	E
1	FACTS		FACTS		
2	Compute	Economic	productio	n run	
3					
4	15000	units pr	oduced ea	ch year	
5	150	setup co	sts to ch	ange prod	uction
6	2	annual c	ost of ca	rrying on	e unit
7					
8	SOLUTION		SOLUTION		
9					
10	Economic	productio	n run	@SQRT((2*A4*A5/A6)	

Chapter 8 Problem 9

CH08PR09

Given
- Maximum expected usage per week
- Average usage per week
- Lead time (weeks)

Compute
- Maximum expected usage per week
- Average usage per week
- Excess
- Lead time (weeks)
- Safety Stock

SCREEN DISPLAY

```
FACTS                 FACTS
Compute reorder point
       65 Maximum expected usage per week
       50 Average usage per week
        3 Lead time (weeks)

SOLUTION              SOLUTION
       65 Maximum expected usage per week
       50 Average usage per week
       15 Excess
        3 Lead time (weeks)
       45 Safety Stock
```

CELL CONTENT

	A	B	C	D	E
1	FACTS		FACTS		
2	Compute r	eorder po	int		
3	65	Maximum	expected	usage per	week
4	50	Average	usage per	week	
5	3	Lead tim	e (weeks)		
6					
7	SOLUTION		SOLUTION		
8	65	Maximum	expected	usage per	week
9	50	Average	usage per	week	
10	+A8-A9	Excess			
11	3	Lead tim	e (weeks)		
12	+A10*A11	Safety S	tock		

Given
- Projected Sales
- Selling Price
- Collection-period of sale %
- Collection-following period %

Compute
- Sales
- Collection-period of sale
- Collection-following period
- Collection-total

Please work these problems.
Compare your results with the solution.

50000 Period 1
100000 Period 2
150000 Period 3

	Collection		Collection		
Item No.	Period of Sale	Next Month	Period 1	2	3
1	75	25	37500	87500	137500
2	80	20	40000	90000	140000
3	82	18	41000	91000	141000
4	84	16	42000	92000	142000
5	86	14	43000	93000	143000
6	75	25	37500	87500	137500
7	73	27	36500	86500	136500
8	71	29	35500	85500	135500
9	69	31	34500	84500	134500
10	67	33	33500	83500	133500
11	75	25	37500	87500	137500
12	78	22	39000	89000	139000
13	81	19	40500	90500	140500
14	84	16	42000	92000	142000
15	87	13	43500	93500	143500
16	75	25	37500	87500	137500
17	71	29	35500	85500	135500
18	67	33	33500	83500	133500
19	63	37	31500	81500	131500
20	59	41	29500	79500	129500
21	75	25	37500	87500	137500
22	74	26	37000	87000	137000
23	73	27	36500	86500	136500
24	72	28	36000	86000	136000
25	71	29	35500	85500	135500

CH08PR02

Chapter 8 Problem 2

PRACTICE PROBLEMS

PRACTICE PROBLEMS

Given
  Expected Sales
    Finished Goods - End
    Finished Goods - Beginning
Compute
    Units to be produced

PRACTICE PRACTICE PRACTICE PRACTICE PRACTICE PRACTICE

Please work these problems.
Compare your results with the solution.

Item No.	Expected Sales	Finished Goods End	Beg	To Be Produced
1	1000	150	100	1050
2	2000	150	100	2050
3	3000	150	100	3050
4	4000	150	100	4050
5	5000	150	100	5050
6	1000	150	100	1050
7	900	150	100	950
8	800	150	100	850
9	700	150	100	750
10	600	150	100	650
11	1000	200	100	1100
12	1000	250	100	1150
13	1000	300	100	1200
14	1000	350	100	1250
15	1000	400	100	1300
16	1000	150	100	1050
17	1000	140	100	1040
18	1000	130	100	1030
19	1000	120	100	1020
20	1000	110	100	1010
21	1000	150	150	1000
22	1000	150	200	950
23	1000	150	250	900
24	1000	150	300	850
25	1000	150	350	800

CH08PR03

Chapter 8 Problem 3

PRACTICE PROBLEMS

PRACTICE PROBLEMS

PRACTICE PRACTICE PRACTICE PRACTICE PRACTICE PRACTICE

Given
Cash-Balance- Beginning
Receipts
Disbursements
Compute
Cash-Balance- End

Please work these problems.
Compare your results with the solution.

Item No.	Beg. Bal.	Receipts	Disburse.	End Bal
1	12000	55000	38000	29000
2	13000	55000	38000	30000
3	14000	55000	38000	31000
4	15000	55000	38000	32000
5	16000	55000	38000	33000
6	12000	55000	38000	29000
7	11000	55000	38000	28000
8	10000	55000	38000	27000
9	9000	55000	38000	26000
10	8000	55000	38000	25000
11	12000	55000	38000	29000
12	12000	56000	38000	30000
13	12000	57000	38000	31000
14	12000	58000	38000	32000
15	12000	59000	38000	33000
16	12000	55000	38000	29000
17	12000	54000	38000	28000
18	12000	53000	38000	27000
19	12000	52000	38000	26000
20	12000	51000	38000	25000
21	12000	55000	38000	29000
22	12000	55000	39000	28000
23	12000	55000	40000	27000
24	12000	55000	41000	26000
25	12000	55000	42000	25000

CH08PR04

Chapter 8 Problem 4

PRACTICE PROBLEMS PRACTICE PROBLEMS

PRACTICE PRACTICE PRACTICE PRACTICE PRACTICE PRACTICE

Given
- Units to be produced
- Direct material-per unit
- Desired ending inventory
- Beginning inventory

Compute
- Purchases
- Ending inventory

Please work these problems.
Compare your results with the solution.

Item No.	Beg. Inv.	Prod	Purch	End Inv
1	1000	2000	700	2300
2	1200	2000	700	2500
3	1400	2000	700	2700
4	1600	2000	700	2900
5	1800	2000	700	3100
6	1000	2000	700	2300
7	1000	2200	700	2500
8	1000	2400	700	2700
9	1000	2600	700	2900
10	1000	2800	700	3100
11	1000	2000	700	2300
12	1000	2000	900	2100
13	1000	2000	1100	1900
14	1000	2000	1300	1700
15	1000	2000	1500	1500
16	1000	2000	700	2300
17	800	2000	700	2100
18	600	2000	700	1900
19	400	2000	700	1700
20	200	2000	700	1500
21	1000	2000	700	2300
22	1000	1800	700	2100
23	1000	1600	700	1900
24	1000	1400	700	1700
25	1000	1200	700	1500

PRACTICE PRACTICE PRACTICE PRACTICE PRACTICE PRACTICE

Given
   To be produced
   DL Hrs per unit
   DL $ per unit
Compute
   Total Hours
   DL $ per unit
   Total Cost

Please work these problems.
Compare your results with the solution.

Item No.	Total Hours	DL $ per Unit	Total Cost
1	5000	4	20000
2	6000	4	24000
3	7000	4	28000
4	8000	4	32000
5	9000	4	36000
6	5000	4	20000
7	4900	4	19600
8	4800	4	19200
9	4700	4	18800
10	4600	4	18400
11	5000	4	20000
12	5000	5	25000
13	5000	6	30000
14	5000	7	35000
15	5000	8	40000
16	5000	4	20000
17	5000	3	15000
18	5000	2	10000
19	5000	1	5000
20	5000	4	20000
21	5000	4	20000
22	5500	5	27500
23	6000	6	36000
24	6500	7	45500
25	7000	8	56000

CH08PR06

Chapter 8 Problem 6

PRACTICE PROBLEMS

PRACTICE PROBLEMS

PRACTICE PRACTICE PRACTICE PRACTICE PRACTICE PRACTICE

Given
- Budgeted DL Hours
- Variable OH Rate
- Fixed OH

Compute
- Variable Overhead
- Fixed Overhead
- Total

Please work these problems.
Compare your results with the solution.

Item No.	Budget DL Hours	Variable OH Rate	Fixed OH	Total
1	5250	2	15000	25500
2	7750	2	15000	30500
3	9750	2	15000	34500
4	9750	2	15000	34500
5	9750	2	15000	34500
6	9750	2	15000	34500
7	9750	3	15000	44250
8	9750	4	15000	54000
9	9750	5	15000	63750
10	9750	6	15000	73500
11	5250	2	15000	25500
12	5050	2	15000	25100
13	4850	2	15000	24700
14	4650	2	15000	24300
15	4450	2	15000	23900
16	9750	2	17000	36500
17	9750	2	19000	38500
18	9750	2	21000	40500
19	9750	2	23000	42500
20	9750	2	25000	44500
21	5750	4	15000	38000
22	6750	6	15000	55500
23	7750	8	15000	77000
24	8750	10	15000	102500
25	9750	12	15000	132000

Chapter 8 Problem 7

PRACTICE PROBLEMS

PRACTICE PROBLEMS

Given
- Annual quantity used in units
- Cost of placing one order
- annual cost of carrying one unit

Compute
- Economic order quantity

Please work these problems.
Compare your results with the solution.

Item No.	Annual Qty Used	Cost 1 order	Annual Cost 1	EOQ
1	3000	10	.8	274
2	4000	10	.8	316
3	5000	10	.8	354
4	6000	10	.8	387
5	7000	10	.8	418
6	3000	10	.8	274
7	2500	10	.8	250
8	2000	10	.8	224
9	1500	10	.8	194
10	1000	10	.8	158
11	3000	10	.8	274
12	3000	11	.8	287
13	3000	12	.8	300
14	3000	13	.8	312
15	3000	14	.8	324
16	3000	10	.8	274
17	3000	9	.8	260
18	3000	8	.8	245
19	3000	7	.8	229
20	3000	6	.8	212
21	3000	10	1	245
22	4000	12	1	310
23	5000	14	1	374
24	6000	16	1	438
25	7000	18	1	502

CH08PR08

Chapter 8 Problem 8

PRACTICE PROBLEMS

PRACTICE PROBLEMS

Given
- units produced each year
- setup costs to change production
- annual cost of carrying one unit

Compute
- Economic production run

Please work these problems.
Compare your results with the solution.

Item No.	Units Produced	Setup Costs	Annual Cost	Econ Prod Run
1	15000	150	2	1500
2	16000	150	2	1549
3	17000	150	2	1597
4	18000	150	2	1643
5	19000	150	2	1688
6	15000	150	2	1500
7	14000	150	2	1449
8	13000	150	2	1396
9	12000	150	2	1342
10	11000	150	2	1285
11	15000	160	2	1549
12	15000	170	2	1597
13	15000	180	2	1643
14	15000	190	2	1688
15	15000	200	2	1732
16	15000	150	2	1500
17	15000	140	2	1449
18	15000	130	2	1396
19	15000	120	2	1342
20	15000	110	2	1285
21	15000	150	3	1225
22	15000	150	4	1061
23	15000	150	5	949
24	15000	150	6	866
25	15000	150	7	802

PRACTICE PRACTICE PRACTICE PRACTICE PRACTICE PRACTICE

Given
- Maximum expected usage per week
- Average usage per week
- Lead time (weeks)

Compute
- Maximum expected usage per week
- Average usage per week
- Excess
- Lead time (weeks)
- Safety Stock

Please work these problems.
Compare your results with the solution.

Item No.	Maximum Usage	Average Usage	Lead Time weeks	Safety Stock
1	65	50	3	45
2	70	50	3	60
3	75	50	3	75
4	80	50	3	90
5	85	50	3	105
6	65	50	3	45
7	55	50	3	15
8	45	50	3	-15
9	35	50	3	-45
10	25	50	3	-75
11	65	50	3	45
12	65	53	3	36
13	65	56	3	27
14	65	59	3	18
15	65	62	3	9
16	65	50	3	45
17	65	50	4	60
18	65	50	5	75
19	65	50	6	90
20	65	50	7	105
21	65	50	3	45
22	70	48	4	88
23	75	46	5	145
24	80	44	6	216
25	85	42	7	301

9 Variance Analysis

Condensed List of Items

Item No.	Variances	*Problems*
CH09PR01	Material—Price	5
CH09PR02	Material—Quantity	5
CH09PR03	Material—Price and Quantity	5
CH09PR04	Labor—Rate	5
CH09PR05	Labor—Efficiency	5
CH09PR06	Labor—Rate and Efficiency	5
CH09PR07	Overhead—Rate	5
CH09PR08	Overhead—Efficiency	5
CH09PR09	Overhead—Rate and efficiency	5
CH09PR10	Overhead—Rate and efficiency	25
CH09PR11	Overhead—Spending and efficiency	
CH09PR12	Overhead—Budget and Volume	
CH09PR13	Overhead—Three Way	
CH09PR14	Overhead—Four Way	
CH09PR15	Overhead—Garrison	25
CH09PR16	Overhead—Three Way and Four Way	
CH09PR17	Overhead—One, Two and Three Way	25
	Total	120

PRICE VARIANCE

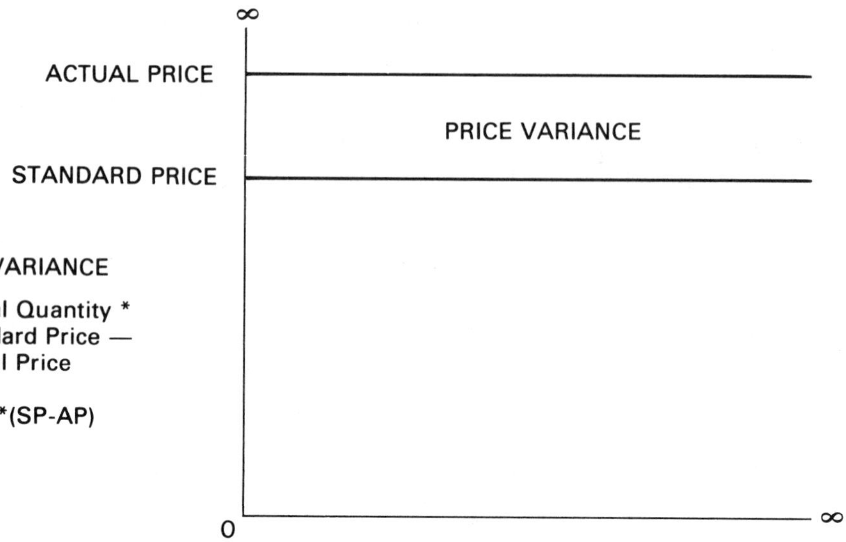

PRICE VARIANCE

Actual Quantity *
Standard Price —
Actual Price

AQ*(SP-AP)

QUANTITY VARIANCE

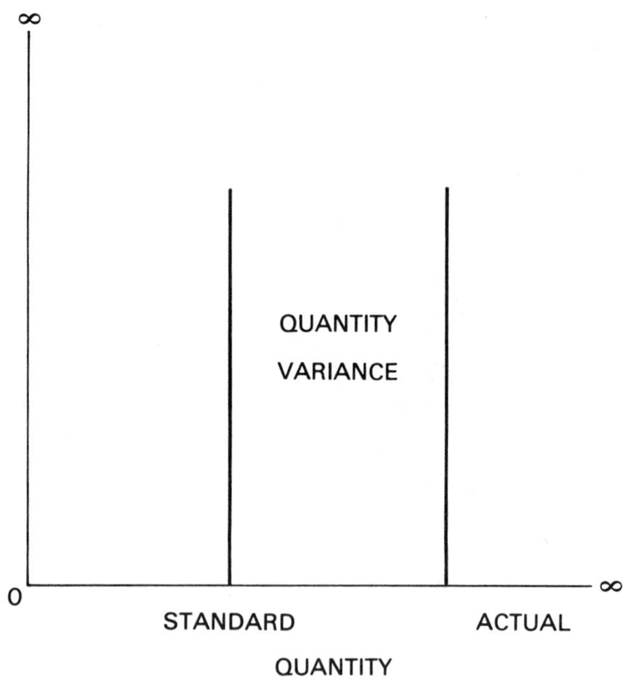

QUANTITY VARIANCE

Actual Price *
Standard Quantity —
Actual Quantity

AP*(SQ-AQ)

CH09PR01

Chapter 9 Problem 1

Given

```
   Actual               Quantity    Price
   Standard             Quantity    Price
Compute
   Price Variance
   Quantity Variance
   Total Variance
```

SCREEN DISPLAY

```
FACTS                  FACTS
Direct Materials
                        Quantity     Price
Actual                    124000      7.96    987040
Standard                  124000      8.00    992000
                                                4960
SOLUTION               SOLUTION
Price Variance                        4960
Quantity Variance                        0
Total Variance                                  4960
```

CELL CONTENT

	A	B	C	D	E
1	FACTS		FACTS		
2	Direct Ma	terials			
3			Quantity	Price	
4	Actual		124000	7.96	+C4*D4
5	Standard		124000	8	+C5*D5
6					+E5-E4
7	SOLUTION		SOLUTION		
8	Price Var	iance		+C4*(D5-D4	
9	Quantity	Variance		+D5*(C5-C4	
10	Total Var	iance			+D8+D9

Chapter 9 Problem 2

CH09PR02

```
Given
   Actual              Quantity    Price
   Standard            Quantity    Price
Compute
   Price Variance
   Quantity Variance
   Total Variance
```

SCREEN DISPLAY

```
FACTS                  FACTS
Direct Materials
                        Quantity     Price
Actual                    124000      8.00     992000
Standard                  120000      8.00     960000
                                               -32000
SOLUTION               SOLUTION
Price Variance                           0
Quantity Variance                   -32000
Total Variance                                 -32000
```

CELL CONTENT

	A	B	C	D	E
1	FACTS		FACTS		
2	Direct Ma	terials			
3			Quantity	Price	
4	Actual		124000	8	+C4*D4
5	Standard		120000	8	+C5*D5
6					+E5-E4
7	SOLUTION		SOLUTION		
8	Price Var	iance		+C4*(D5-D4	
9	Quantity	Variance		+D5*(C5-C4	
10	Total Var	iance			+D8+D9

CH09PR03

Chapter 9 Problem 3

```
Given
   Actual              Quantity    Price
   Standard            Quantity    Price
Compute
   Price Variance
   Quantity Variance
   Total Variance
```

SCREEN DISPLAY

```
FACTS                FACTS
Direct Materials
                      Quantity    Price
Actual                  124000     7.96
Standard                120000     8.00

SOLUTION             SOLUTION
Price Variance                     4960
Quantity Variance                -32000
Total Variance                              -27040
```

CELL CONTENT

	A	B	C	D	E
1	FACTS		FACTS		
2	Direct Ma	terials			
3			Quantity	Price	
4	Actual		124000	7.96	
5	Standard		120000	8	
6					
7	SOLUTION		SOLUTION		
8	Price Var	iance		+C4*(D5-D4	
9	Quantity	Variance		+D5*(C5-C4	
10	Total Var	iance			+D8+D9

CH09PR04 Chapter 9 Problem 4

```
Given
   Actual      Hours    Rate
   Standard    Hours    Rate
Compute
   Actual Cost
   Rate Variance
   Efficiency Variance
       Total Variance
   Standard Cost
```

SCREEN DISPLAY

```
FACTS              FACTS
Direct Labor
            Hours    Rate
Actual       20000    14.84
Standard     20000    14.00
SOLUTION           SOLUTION
Actual Cost                                  296800
Rate Variance                       -16800
Efficiency Variance                      0
    Total Variance                           -16800
Standard Cost                                280000
```

CELL CONTENT

	A	B	C	D	E
1	FACTS		FACTS		
2	Direct La	bor			
3		Hours	Rate		
4	Actual	20000	14.84		
5	Standard	20000	14		
6	SOLUTION		SOLUTION		
7	Actual Co	st			+B4*C4
8	Rate Vari	ance		+B4*(C5-C4	
9	Efficienc	y Varianc	e	+C5*(B5-B4	
10	Total	Variance			+D8+D9
11	Standard	Cost			+B5*C5

CH09PR05

Chapter 9 Problem 5

Given
- Actual Hours Rate
- Standard Hours Rate

Compute
- Actual Cost
- Rate Variance
- Efficiency Variance
  - Total Variance
- Standard Cost

SCREEN DISPLAY

```
FACTS               FACTS
Direct Labor
            Hours    Rate
Actual       19200    14.00
Standard     20000    14.00
SOLUTION            SOLUTION
Actual Cost                                  268800
Rate Variance                          0
Efficiency Variance                11200
    Total Variance                            11200
Standard Cost                                280000
```

CELL CONTENT

	A	B	C	D	E
1	FACTS		FACTS		
2	Direct La	bor			
3		Hours	Rate		
4	Actual	19200	14		
5	Standard	20000	14		
6	SOLUTION		SOLUTION		
7	Actual Co	st			+B4*C4
8	Rate Vari	ance		+B4*(C5-C4	
9	Efficienc	y Varianc	e	+C5*(B5-B4	
10	Total	Variance			+D8+D9
11	Standard	Cost			+B5*C5

CH09PR06

Chapter 9 Problem 6

```
Given
   Actual      Hours    Rate
   Standard    Hours    Rate
Compute
   Actual Cost
   Rate Variance
   Efficiency Variance
       Total Variance
   Standard Cost
```

SCREEN DISPLAY

```
FACTS              FACTS
Direct Labor
            Hours    Rate
Actual       19200    14.84
Standard     20000    14.00
SOLUTION           SOLUTION
Actual Cost                                    284928
Rate Variance                       -16128
Efficiency Variance                  11200
    Total Variance                              -4928
Standard Cost                                  280000
```

CELL CONTENT

	A	B	C	D	E
1	FACTS		FACTS		
2	Direct La	bor			
3		Hours	Rate		
4	Actual	19200	14.84		
5	Standard	20000	14		
6	SOLUTION		SOLUTION		
7	Actual Co	st			+B4*C4
8	Rate Vari	ance		+B4*(C5-C4	
9	Efficienc	y Varianc	e	+C5*(B5-B4	
10	Total	Variance			+D8+D9
11	Standard	Cost			+B5*C5

CH09PR07

Chapter 9 Problem 7

```
Given
   Actual    Quantity    Price
   Standard  Quantity    Price
Compute
   Actual Cost
   Rate Variance
   Efficiency Variance
       Total Variance
   Standard Cost
```

SCREEN DISPLAY

```
FACTS               FACTS
Variable Overhead
          Quantity    Price
Actual        1440     5.50
Standard      1440     5.00
SOLUTION            SOLUTION
Actual Cost                                      7920
Rate Variance                          -720
Efficiency Variance                       0
    Total Variance                               -720
Standard Cost                                    7200
```

CELL CONTENT

	A	B	C	D	E
1	FACTS		FACTS		
2	Variable	Overhead			
3		Quantity	Price		
4	Actual	1440	5.5		
5	Standard	1440	5		
6	SOLUTION		SOLUTION		
7	Actual Co	st			+B4*C4
8	Rate Vari	ance		+B4*(C5-C4	
9	Efficienc	y Varianc	e	+C5*(B5-B4	
10	Total	Variance			+D8+D9
11	Standard	Cost			+B5*C5

CH09PR08 Chapter 9 Problem 8

```
Given
   Actual    Quantity    Price
   Standard  Quantity    Price
Compute
   Actual Cost
   Rate Variance
   Efficiency Variance
       Total Variance
   Standard Cost
```

SCREEN DISPLAY

```
FACTS                 FACTS
Variable Overhead
           Quantity     Price
Actual         1360      5.00
Standard       1440      5.00
SOLUTION              SOLUTION
Actual Cost                                  6800
Rate Variance                         0
Efficiency Variance                 400
    Total Variance                            400
Standard Cost                                7200
```

CELL CONTENT

	A	B	C	D	E
1	FACTS		FACTS		
2	Variable	Overhead			
3		Quantity	Price		
4	Actual	1360	5		
5	Standard	1440	5		
6	SOLUTION		SOLUTION		
7	Actual Co	st			+B4*C4
8	Rate Vari	ance		+B4*(C5-C4	
9	Efficienc	y Varianc	e	+C5*(B5-B4	
10	Total	Variance			+D8+D9
11	Standard	Cost			+B5*C5

CH09PR09 Chapter 9 Problem 9

```
Given
   Actual    Quantity    Price
   Standard  Quantity    Price
Compute
   Actual Cost
   Rate Variance
   Efficiency Variance
       Total Variance
   Standard Cost
```

SCREEN DISPLAY

```
FACTS              FACTS
Overhead
          Quantity     Price
Actual        1360      5.50
Standard      1440      5.00
SOLUTION           SOLUTION
Actual Cost                                        7480
Rate Variance                             -680
Efficiency Variance                        400
    Total Variance                                 -280
Standard Cost                                      7200
```

CELL CONTENT

	A	B	C	D	E
1	FACTS		FACTS		
2	Overhead				
3		Quantity	Price		
4	Actual	1360	5.5		
5	Standard	1440	5		
6	SOLUTION		SOLUTION		
7	Actual Co	st			+B4*C4
8	Rate Vari	ance		+B4*(C5-C4	
9	Efficienc	y Varianc	e	+C5*(B5-B4	
10	Total	Variance			+D8+D9
11	Standard	Cost			+B5*C5

Chapter 9 Problem 10

CH09PR10

```
Given        Quantity    Price
   Actual    Quantity    Price
   Standard  Quantity    Price
Compute
   Actual Cost
   Rate Variance
   Efficiency Variance
       Total Variance
   Standard Cost
```

SCREEN DISPLAY

```
FACTS              FACTS
Overhead
          Quantity    Price
Actual         890      2.3
Standard       800        2
SOLUTION           SOLUTION
Actual Cost                               2047
Rate Variance                     -267
Efficiency Variance               -180
    Total Variance                        -447
Standard Cost                             1600
```

CELL CONTENT

	A	B	C	D	E
1	FACTS		FACTS		
2	Overhead				
3		Quantity	Price		
4	Actual	890	2.3		
5	Standard	800	2		
6	SOLUTION		SOLUTION		
7	Actual Co	st			+B4*C4
8	Rate Vari	ance		+B4*(C5-C4	
9	Efficienc	y Varianc	e	+C5*(B5-B4	
10	Total	Variance			+D8+D9
11	Standard	Cost			+B5*C5

Chapter 9 Problem 11

CH09PR11

Given
- Standard Hours Cost
- Actual Hours Cost

Compute
- Actual
- Spending variance
- Efficiency var.
- Total variance
- Standard

SCREEN DISPLAY

FACTS	FACTS		
Overhead			
	Hours	Cost	
Standard	6500	.5	
Actual	6800	.6	
SOLUTION	SOLUTION		
Actual			4080
Spending variance		-680	
Efficiency var.		-150	
Total variance			-830
Standard			3250

CELL CONTENT

	A	B	C	D
1	FACTS		FACTS	
2	Overhead			
3		Hours	Cost	
4	Standard	6500	.5	
5	Actual	6800	.6	
6				
7	SOLUTION		SOLUTION	
8	Actual			+B5*C5
9	Spending	variance	+B5*(C4-C5)	
10	Efficienc	y var.	+C4*(B4-B5)	
11	Total var	iance		+C9+C10
12	Standard			+B4*C4

Chapter 9 Problem 12

CH09PR12

```
Given
   Denominator          Hours     Cost
   Standard             Hours
   Actual               Hours     Cost
Compute
   Actual
   Budget variance
   Budget
   Volume variance
   Applied fixed
```

SCREEN DISPLAY

```
FACTS                 FACTS
Fixed overhead variances
                        Hours      Cost
Denominator               6000      9000
Standard                  6500
Actual                    6800      9450
SOLUTION              SOLUTION
Actual                              9450
Budget variance                     -450
Budget                              9000
Volume variance                      750
Applied fixed                       9750
```

CELL CONTENT

	A	B	C	D
1	FACTS		FACTS	
2	Fixed ove	rhead var	iances	
3			Hours	Cost
4	Denominat	or	6000	9000
5	Standard		6500	
6	Actual		6800	9450
7	SOLUTION		SOLUTION	
8	Actual			+D6
9	Budget va	riance		+D4-D6
10	Budget			+D4
11	Volume va	riance		(D4/C4)*(C 5-C4)
12	Applied f	ixed		+C5*(D4/C4)

CH09PR13

SCREEN DISPLAY

```
    INDEX     INDEX     INDEX



FACTS     Overhead Overhead
Hours     Per Hour
     3475 2.124892 Actual-total
     3400      1.2 Std. variable
                .8 Std. fixed
     4000          Normal capacity
              3200 Budget - fixed
```

SCREEN DISPLAY

```
SOLUTION                         THREE WAY
ACTUAL OVERHEAD                     7384
Spending variance                    -14
BUDGET-ACT. HOURS                   7370
Idle Capacity                       -420
Efficiency-Total                    -150
OH APPLIED                          6800
```

CELL CONTENT

	A	B	C	D	E
1	INDEX	INDEX	INDEX		
2					
3					
4					
5					
6	FACTS	Overhead	Overhead		
7	Hours	Per Hour			
8	3475	7384/3475	Actual-t	otal	
9	3400	1.2	Std. var	iable	
10		.8	Std. fix	ed	
11	4000		Normal c	apacity	
12		3200	Budget -	fixed	
13	SOLUTION			THREE W	AY
14	ACTUAL OV	ERHEAD		+A8*B8	
15	Spending	variance		((+A8*B9)+B12)-D14	
16	BUDGET-AC	T. HOURS		(+A8*B9)+B12	
17	Idle Capa	city		(A8*(B9+B10)-D16	
18	Efficienc	y-Total		(A9-A8)*(B9+B10)	
19	OH APPLIE	D		+A9*(B9+B10)	

CH09PR14

SCREEN DISPLAY

```
            INDEX      INDEX      INDEX




          FACTS     Overhead Overhead
          Hours     Per Hour
               3475 2.124892 Actual-total
               3400      1.2 Std. variable
                          .8 Std. fixed
               4000          Normal capacity
                        3200 Budget - fixed
```

SCREEN DISPLAY

```
SOLUTION                                       FOUR WAY
ACTUAL OVERHEAD                                  7384
Controllable
Spending variance                                 -14
BUDGET-STD. HOURS
BUDGET-ACT. HOURS                                7370
Volume
Idle Capacity                                    -420
Efficiency-Total
Efficiency-Variable                             -7370
Efficiency-Fixed                                  -60
OH APPLIED                                       6800
```

CELL CONTENT

	A	B	C	D	E
1		INDEX	INDEX		
2					
3					
4					
5					
6	FACTS	"Overhead	Overhead		
7	Hours	"Per Hour			
8	3475	7384/3475	Actual-t	otal	
9	3400	1.2	Std. var	iable	
10		.8	Std. fix	ed	
11	4000		Normal c	apacity	
12		3200	Budget -	fixed	
13	SOLUTION				FOUR WA
14	ACTUAL OV	ERHEAD			+A8*B8
15	Controlla	ble			
16	Spending	variance			((+A8*B9)+B12)-E14
17	BUDGET-ST	D. HOURS			
18	BUDGET-AC	T. HOURS			(+A8*B9)+B12
19	Volume				
20	Idle Capa	city			(A8*(B9+B10)-E18
21	Efficienc	y-Total			
22	Efficienc	y-Variable			+C17-E18
23	Efficienc	y-Fixed			(A9-A8)*B10
24	OH APPLIE	D			+A9*(B9+B10)

Chapter 9 Problem 15

CH09PR15

```
    Given    VE costs  Actual   Budget
             FE costs  Actual   Budget
             Hours     Actual   Budget  Standard
             V.E.                 V.E.              F.E.
   Compute                      Variable
             Actual                        Actual
             Spending                      Budget
             Efficiency                    Volume
             Applied                       Applied
```

SCREEN DISPLAY

```
FACTS
           Actual    Budget  Standard
VE costs      4080      3000
FE costs      9450      9000
Hours         6800      6000      6500
SOLUTION         SOLUTION                     SOLUTION
V.E.          0.60   V.E.         0.50  F.E.      1.50
                   Variable                      Fixed
Actual                  4080  Actual              9450
Spending                -680  Budget              -450
Efficiency              -150  Volume               750
Applied                 3250  Applied             9000
```

CELL CONTENT

	A	B	C	D	E	F
1	FACTS					
2		Actual	Budget	Standard		
3	VE costs	4080	3000			
4	FE costs	9450	9000			
5	Hours	6800	6000	6500		
6	SOLUTION		SOLUTION			SOLUTION
7	V.E.	+B3/B5	V.E.	+C3/C5	F.E.	+C4/C5
8			Variable			Fixed
9	Actual		+B3	Actual		+B4
10	Spending		+B5*(D7-B7	Budget		+C4-B4
11	Efficienc	y	+D7*(D5-B5	Volume		+F7*(D5 -C5)
12	Applied		+D5*(C3/C5	Applied		+C5*F7

SCREEN DISPLAY

CH09PR16

```
FACTS                                   Dollars
               Hours    Total    Variable    Fixed
Budget          4000     8000       4800       3200
Actual          3475     7384
Standard        3400
SOLUTION              Overall    Two Way
Actual                   7384       7384
Overall    ---> 1        -584
Contrlble                           -104   1 <---
Budget                              7280
Volume                              -480   2 <---
Applied                  6800       6800
```

SCREEN DISPLAY

```
                     Three Way Four Way
Actual                    7384
Spending    ---> 1         -14              1 <---
                          7370      7370
Idle Cap.   ---> 2        -420      -420    2 <---
                          6950      6950
Effic       ---> 3        -150
Eff-Var                              -90    3 <---
Eff-Fixed                            -60    4 <---
Applied                   6800      6800
```

CELL CONTENT

	A	B	C	D	E
1	FACTS			Dollars	
2		Hours	Total	Variable	Fixed
3	Budget	4000	8000	4800	3200
4	Actual	3475	7384		
5	Standard	3400			
6	SOLUTION		Overall	Two Way	
7	Actual		+C4	+C4	
8	Overall	---> 1	(+B5*(C3/B3))-C4		
9	Contrlble			(+E3+(B5*(D3/B3))-C4	1 <---
10	Budget			+E3+(B5*(D3/B3)	
11	Volume			(+B5*(C3/B3))-D10	2 <---
12	Applied		+B5*(C3/B3)	+B5*(C3/B3)	
13					
14			Three Way	Four Way	
15	Actual		+C4		
16	Spending	---> 1	(+E3+(B4*(D3/B3))-C15		1 <---
17			+E3+(B4*(D3/B3)	+E3+(B4*(D3/B3)	
18	Idle Cap.	---> 2	+B4*(C3/B3)-(E3+(B4*(D3/B3)	+B4*(C3/B3)-(E3+(B4*(D3/B3)	2 <---
19			+B4*(C3/B3)	+B4*(C3/B3)	
20	Effic	---> 3	+B5*(C3/B3)-(B4*(C3/B3)		
21	Eff-Var			(+E3+(B5*(D3/B3))-D17	3 <---
22	Eff-Fixed			(B5-B4)*(E3/B3)	4 <---
23	Applied		+B5*(C3/B3)	+B5*(C3/B3)	

CH09PR17

Chapter 9 Problem 17

Given

	Units	Variable	Fixed
Budget			
Actual			
Standard			

Compute

	1 Way	2 Way	3 Way
Incurred			
Combined			
Volume			
Budget			
Spending			
Effic.			
Applied			

SCREEN DISPLAY

FACTS		Units	Variable	Fixed
Budget		10000	17000	10000
Actual		7900	14250	10200
Standard		8000		
SOLUTION		1 Way	2 Way	3 Way
	Incurred	24450	24450	24450
	Combined	-2850		
	Volume		-2000	-2000
	Budget		-850	
	Spending			-1020
	Effic.			170
	Applied	21600	21600	21600

CELL CONTENT

	A	B	C	D	E
1	FACTS	Units	Variable	Fixed	
2	Budget	10000	17000	10000	
3	Actual	7900	14250	10200	
4	Standard	8000			
5	SOLUTION		1 Way	2 Way	3 Way
6		Incurred	+C3+D3	+C3+D3	+C3+D3
7		Combined	(+B4*(B2+C 2/D2))-(C3 +D3)		
8		Volume		((B4*(B2+C 2/D2)-(B4* (C2/D2)+D2	((B4*(B2+C 2/D2)-(B4* (C2/D2)+D2
9		Budget		((B4*(C2/D 2)+D2)-(C3 +D3)	
10		Spending			((+B3*(C2/ D2))+D2)-E 6
11		Effic.			(B4*(C2/D2)+D2)-((+B 3*(C2/D2)) +D2)
12		Applied	+B4*(B2+C2 /D2)	+B4*(B2+C2 /D2)	+B4*(B2+C2 /D2)

PRACTICE PROBLEMS

Chapter 9

Please work these problems.

Problem 1

Given

Actual	Quantity	Price
Standard	Quantity	Price

Compute
- Price Variance
- Quantity Variance
- Total Variance

Item No.	Quantity		Price		Variance	
	Actual	Standard	Actual	Standard	Price	Quantity
1	120000	120000	7.96	8.00	4800	0
2	120000	120000	7.96	8.00	4800	0
3	120000	120000	7.96	8.00	4800	0
4	120000	120000	7.96	8.00	4800	0
5	120000	120000	7.96	8.00	4800	0

Problem 2 PRACTICE PRACTICE PRACTICE PRACTICE PRACTICE PRACTICE

Given

Actual	Quantity	Price
Standard	Quantity	Price

Compute
- Price Variance
- Quantity Variance
- Total Variance

Item No.	Quantity		Price		Variance	
	Actual	Standard	Actual	Standard	Price	Quantity
1	124000	120000	8.00	8.00	0	-32000
2	124100	120000	8.00	8.00	0	-32800
3	124200	120000	8.00	8.00	0	-33600
4	124300	120000	8.00	8.00	0	-34400
5	124400	120000	8.00	8.00	0	-35200

Problem 3 PRACTICE PRACTICE PRACTICE PRACTICE PRACTICE PRACTICE

Given

Actual	Quantity	Price
Standard	Quantity	Price

Compute
- Price Variance
- Quantity Variance
- Total Variance

Item No.	Quantity		Price		Variance	
	Actual	Standard	Actual	Standard	Price	Quantity
1	124000	120000	7.96	8.00	4960	-32000
2	124100	120000	7.96	8.00	4964	-32800
3	124200	120000	7.96	8.00	4968	-33600
4	124300	120000	7.96	8.00	4972	-34400
5	124400	120000	7.96	8.00	4976	-35200

Problem 4

Given
- Actual Hours Rate
- Standard Hours Rate

Compute
- Actual Cost
- Rate Variance
- Efficiency Variance
- Total Variance
- Standard Cost

Item No.	Quantity Actual	Quantity Standard	Price Actual	Price Standard	Variance Rate	Variance Efficiency
1	20000	20000	14.84	14.00	-16800	0
2	20000	20000	14.94	14.00	-18800	0
3	20000	20000	15.04	14.00	-20800	0
4	20000	20000	15.14	14.00	-22800	0
5	20000	20000	15.24	14.00	-24800	0

Problem 5 PRACTICE PRACTICE PRACTICE PRACTICE PRACTICE PRACTICE

Given
- Actual Hours Rate
- Standard Hours Rate

Compute
- Actual Cost
- Rate Variance
- Efficiency Variance
- Total Variance
- Standard Cost

Item No.	Quantity Actual	Quantity Standard	Price Actual	Price Standard	Variance Rate	Variance Efficiency
1	19200	20000	14.00	14.00	0	11200
2	19300	20000	14.00	14.00	0	9800
3	19400	20000	14.00	14.00	0	8400
4	19500	20000	14.00	14.00	0	7000
5	19600	20000	14.00	14.00	0	5600

Problem 6 PRACTICE PRACTICE PRACTICE PRACTICE PRACTICE PRACTICE

Given
- Actual Hours Rate
- Standard Hours Rate

Compute
- Actual Cost
- Rate Variance
- Efficiency Variance
- Total Variance
- Standard Cost

Item No.	Quantity Actual	Quantity Standard	Price Actual	Price Standard	Variance Rate	Variance Efficiency
1	19200	20000	14.84	14.00	-16128	11200
2	19300	20000	14.84	14.00	-16212	9800
3	19400	20000	14.84	14.00	-16296	8400
4	19500	20000	14.84	14.00	-16380	7000
5	19600	20000	14.84	14.00	-16464	5600

Please work these problems.

Problem 7

Given
 Actual Quantity Price
 Standard Quantity Price
Compute
 Actual Cost
 Rate Variance
 Efficiency Variance
 Total Variance
 Standard Cost

	Quantity		Price		Variance	
Item No.	Actual	Standard	Actual	Standard	Rate	Efficiency
1	1440	1440	5.50	5.00	-720	0
2	1440	1440	5.50	5.00	-720	0
3	1440	1440	5.50	5.00	-720	0
4	1440	1440	5.50	5.00	-720	0
5	1440	1440	5.50	5.00	-720	0

Problem 8 PRACTICE PRACTICE PRACTICE PRACTICE PRACTICE PRACTICE

Given
 Actual Quantity Price
 Standard Quantity Price
Compute
 Actual Cost
 Rate Variance
 Efficiency Variance
 Total Variance
 Standard Cost

	Quantity		Price		Variance	
Item No.	Actual	Standard	Actual	Standard	Rate	Efficiency
1	1360	1440	5.00	5.00	0	400
2	1460	1440	5.00	5.00	0	-100
3	1560	1440	5.00	5.00	0	-600
4	1660	1440	5.00	5.00	0	-1100
5	1760	1440	5.00	5.00	0	-1600

Problem 9

Given
 Actual Quantity Price
 Standard Quantity Price
Compute
 Actual Cost
 Rate Variance
 Efficiency Variance
 Total Variance
 Standard Cost

	Quantity		Price		Variance	
Item No.	Actual	Standard	Actual	Standard	Rate	Efficiency
1	1360	1440	5.50	5.00	-680	400
2	1460	1440	5.50	5.00	-730	-100
3	1560	1440	5.50	5.00	-780	-600
4	1660	1440	5.50	5.00	-830	-1100
5	1760	1440	5.50	5.00	-880	-1600

CH09PR10

Chapter 9 Problem 10

PRACTICE PROBLEMS PRACTICE PROBLEMS

PRACTICE PRACTICE PRACTICE PRACTICE PRACTICE PRACTICE

Given Quantity Price
 Actual Quantity Price
 Standard Quantity Price
Compute
 Actual Cost
 Rate Variance
 Efficiency Variance
 Total Variance
 Standard Cost

Please work these problems.
Compare your results with the solution.

Standard
800 Quantity
2.00 Price

	Actual		Variance		
	Quantity	Price	Rate	Efficiency	Total
Item No.					
1	890	2.30	-267	-180	-447
2	900	2.30	-270	-200	-470
3	910	2.30	-273	-220	-493
4	920	2.30	-276	-240	-516
5	930	2.30	-279	-260	-539
6	900	2.40	-270	-200	-470
7	890	2.50	-267	-180	-447
8	880	2.60	-264	-160	-424
9	870	2.70	-261	-140	-401
10	860	2.80	-258	-120	-378
11	850	2.30	-255	-100	-355
12	840	2.30	-252	-80	-332
13	830	2.30	-249	-60	-309
14	820	2.30	-246	-40	-286
15	810	2.30	-243	-20	-263
16	900	2.30	-270	-200	-470
17	910	2.20	-273	-220	-493
18	920	2.10	-276	-240	-516
19	930	2.00	-279	-260	-539
20	940	1.90	-282	-280	-562
21	930	2.40	-279	-260	-539
22	920	2.30	-276	-240	-516
23	910	2.20	-273	-220	-493
24	900	2.10	-270	-200	-470
25	890	2.00	-267	-180	-447

CH09PR15

Given	VE costs	Actual	Budget		
	FE costs	Actual	Budget		
	Hours	Actual	Budget	Standard	
	V.E.		V.E.		F.E.
			Variable		
Compute	Actual			Actual	
	Spending			Budget	
	Efficiency			Volume	
	Applied			Applied	

Please work these problems.
Compare your results with the solution.

	Actual	Budget	Standard
VE costs	4080	3000	
FE costs	9450	9000	
Hours	6800		
Act Rate	0.60	Variable	

Item No.	Budget Hours	Standard Hours	Variances Spending	Effic.	Budget	Volume
1	6000	6500	-680	-150	-450	750
2	6100	6500	-736	-148	-450	590
3	6200	6500	-790	-145	-450	435
4	6300	6500	-842	-143	-450	286
5	6400	6500	-893	-141	-450	141
6	6000	6500	-680	-150	-450	750
7	5900	6500	-622	-153	-450	915
8	5800	6500	-563	-155	-450	1086
9	5700	6500	-501	-158	-450	1263
10	5600	6500	-437	-161	-450	1446
11	6000	6500	-680	-150	-450	750
12	6000	6600	-680	-100	-450	900
13	6000	6700	-680	-50	-450	1050
14	6000	6800	-680	0	-450	1200
15	6000	6900	-680	50	-450	1350
16	6000	6500	-680	-150	-450	750
17	6000	6400	-680	-200	-450	600
18	6000	6300	-680	-250	-450	450
19	6000	6200	-680	-300	-450	300
20	6000	6100	-680	-350	-450	150
21	6000	6500	-680	-150	-450	750
22	5900	6600	-622	-102	-450	1068
23	5800	6700	-563	-52	-450	1397
24	5700	6800	-501	0	-450	1737
25	5600	6900	-437	54	-450	2089

CH09PR17

		Units	Variable	Fixed	
Given	Budget				
	Actual				
	Standard				
Compute			1 Way	2 Way	3 Way
	Incurred				
	Combined				
	Volume				
	Budget				
	Spending				
	Effic.				
	Applied				

Please work these problems.
Compare your results with the solution.

	Units	Variable	Fixed
Budget	10000	17000	10000
Actual			10200
Standard	8000		

Item No.	Units Actual	Standard	Volume	Spending	Effic.
1	7900	8000	-2000	-1020	170
2	8000	8000	-2000	-850	0
3	8100	8000	-2000	-680	-170
4	8200	8000	-2000	-510	-340
5	8300	8000	-2000	-340	-510
6	7900	8000	-2000	-1020	170
7	7800	8000	-2000	-1190	340
8	7700	8000	-2000	-1360	510
9	7600	8000	-2000	-1530	680
10	7500	8000	-2000	-1700	850
11	7900	8100	-2000	-1020	170
12	7900	8300	-2000	-1020	170
13	7900	8400	-2000	-1020	170
14	7900	8500	-2000	-1020	170
15	7900	8600	-2000	-1020	170
16	7900	7900	-2000	-1020	170
17	7900	7800	-2000	-1020	170
18	7900	7700	-2000	-1020	170
19	7900	7600	-2000	-1020	170
20	7900	7500	-2000	-1020	170
21	7900	8000	-2000	-1020	170
22	7900	8000	-2000	-1020	170
23	8000	8000	-2000	-850	0
24	8100	7900	-2000	-680	-170
25	8200	7800	-2000	-510	-340

10 Capital Budgeting

Condensed List of Items

Item No.		*Problems*
CH10PR01	Compound amount	25
CH10PR02	Present value	25
CH10PR03	Future value annuity in arrears	25
CH10PR04	Present value annuity in arrears	25
CH10PR05	Payback period	25
CH10PR06	Payback period	25
CH10PR07	Simple rate of return	25
CH10PR08	Profitability index	25
CH10PR09	Simple rate of return	25
CH10PR10	Net present value	25
CH10PR11	After Tax—Proposed expenses	25
CH10PR12	Cash inflow	25
	Total	300

COMPOUND AMOUNT

Interest is the reward for keeping a deposit in a savings account. The amount of money on deposit may be identified as PRINCIPAL. The amount of interest depends on the length of TIME the money is deposited as well as the RATE of interest and the PRINCIPAL. The principal deposited at the PRESENT time will be increased by interest and that is the amount the depositor will receive in the FUTURE. In this situation, the lump sum at the PRESENT time is known and the FUTURE lump sum is computed.

	PRESENT	FUTURE
(1+i)^n	KNOWN	UNKNOWN

PRESENT VALUE

A company may want to know how much to deposit in a savings account at the PRESENT time in order to receive a known amount at some time in the future. It is necessary to know the desired FUTURE amount as well as the number of periods and the rate of interest. In this case, the FUTURE lump sum is known and the lump sum at the PRESENT time will be computed. Please recognize the compound amount formula included in this formula.

	PRESENT	FUTURE
1/(1+i)^n	UNKNOWN	KNOWN

FUTURE VALUE OF ANNUITY

An annuity involves a series of payments. These may be called rents or installments. The periodic payments during the period of the contract are known. It is desired to know the lump sum at a FUTURE time. This problem will be solved with the formula for the future value of an annuity. It will also be necessary to know the length of time and the rate of interest, in addition to the known periodic payments. Note that the formula includes the compound amount formula.

	PRESENT	FUTURE
$\frac{(1+i)^n - 1}{i}$	$ $ $ $	UNKNOWN

PRESENT VALUE OF ANNUITY

How much does a company deposit at the PRESENT time in order to receive specified installments in the FUTURE? The answer to this query rests with the formula for the present value of an annuity. The present value of an annuity involves known installments in the FUTURE and the PRESENT value is computed. It is also necessary to know the rate of interest and the length of time. Observe the present value formula included in this computation.

	PRESENT	FUTURE
$\left\{1 - \frac{1}{(1+i)^n}\right\} * \frac{1}{i}$	UNKNOWN	$ $ $ $

CH10PR01 Chapter 10 Problem 1

```
Given
   Principal
   Interest rate
   Periods
Compute
   Compound Amount
```

SCREEN DISPLAY

```
Compound Interest
FACTS                FACTS
     1000  Principal
      .12  Interest rate
        5  Periods

SOLUTION             SOLUTION
          Compound  Amount      1762.34
```

CELL CONTENT

	A	B	C	D
1	Compound	Interest		
2	FACTS		FACTS	
3	1000	Princip	al	
4	.12	Interes	t rate	
5	5	Periods		
6				
7	SOLUTION		SOLUTION	
8		Compound	Amount	+A3*((1 +A4)^A5)
9				

Chapter 10 Problem 2

CH10PR02

```
Given
   Principal
   Interest rate
   Periods
Compute
   Present Value
```

SCREEN DISPLAY

```
Present Value
FACTS                FACTS
      200  Principal
      .12  Interest rate
        2  Periods

SOLUTION             SOLUTION
          Present    Value          159.44
```

CELL CONTENT

	A	B	C	D
1	Present V	alue		
2	FACTS		FACTS	
3	200	Princip	al	
4	.12	Interes	t rate	
5	2	Periods		
6				
7	SOLUTION		SOLUTION	
8		Present	Value	+A3/((1+A4)^A5)

CH10PR03

Chapter 10 Problem 3

```
Given
   Principal
   Interest rate
   Periods
Compute
   Future value annuity in arrears
```

SCREEN DISPLAY

```
 Future value of a annuity in arrears
FACTS              FACTS
   100.00  Principal
     0.12  Interest rate
     5.00  Periods

SOLUTION           SOLUTION
 FV annuity in arrears         635.28
```

CELL CONTENT

	A	B	C	D
1	Future va	lue of an	nuity in	arrears
2	FACTS		FACTS	
3	100	Princip	al	
4	.12	Interes	t rate	
5	5	Periods		
6				
7	SOLUTION		SOLUTION	
8	FV annui	ty in arr	ears	+A3*((((1+ A4)^A5)-1) /A4)

CH10PR04

Chapter 10 Problem 4

```
Given
   Principal
   Interest rate
   Periods
Compute
   Present value annuity in arrears
```

SCREEN DISPLAY

```
Present value of a annuity in arrears
FACTS                FACTS
   100.00  Principal
     0.12  Interest rate
     5.00  Periods

SOLUTION             SOLUTION
 PV annuity in arrears          360.48
```

CELL CONTENT

	A	B	C	D	
1	Present v	alue of a	annuity	in arrear	s
2	FACTS		FACTS		
3	100	Princip	al		
4	.12	Interes	t rate		
5	5	Periods			
6					
7	SOLUTION		SOLUTION		
8	PV annui	ty in arr	ears	+A3*((1/A4)*(1-(1/(1 +A4)^A5)))	

CH10PR05 Chapter 10 Problem 5

Given
   Investment required- Option A
   Investment required- Option B
   Net cash inflows-Option A
   Net cash inflows-Option B
Compute
   Payback period-Option A
   Payback period-Option B

SCREEN DISPLAY

```
Payback method
FACTS              FACTS
    15000 Investment required
     5000 Net cash inflows

  Payback Period          3 Years
```

CELL CONTENT

	A	B	C	D
1	Payback m	ethod		
2	FACTS		FACTS	
3	15000	Investme	nt requir	ed
4	5000	Net cash	inflows	
5				
6	Payback	Period	+A3/A4	Years

CH10PR06

Chapter 10 Problem 6

Given
- Investment required- Option A
- Investment required- Option B
- Net cash inflows-Option A
- Net cash inflows-Option B

Compute
- Payback period-Option A
- Payback period-Option B

SCREEN DISPLAY

```
Payback method
FACTS                FACTS
Option A .Option B
    15000     12000 Investment required
     5000      5000 Net cash inflows

        3       2.4 Years Payback
```

CELL CONTENT

	A	B	C	D	E
1	Payback m	ethod			
2	FACTS		FACTS		
3	Option A	Option B			
4	15000	12000	Investme	nt requir	ed
5	5000	5000	Net cash	inflows	
6					
7	+A4/A5	+B4/B5	Years Pa	yback	

CH10PR07

Chapter 10 Problem 7

```
Given
   Incremental revenues
   Cash operating revenues
   Depreciation
   Initial investment
Compute
   Simple rate of return
```

SCREEN DISPLAY

```
Simple rate of return
FACTS                  FACTS
    10000 Incremental revenues
     4000 Cash operating revenues
     2000 Depreciation
    24000 Initial Investment

Solution
  Simple rate of return        16.67
```

CELL CONTENT

	A	B	C	D
1	Simple ra	te of ret	urn	
2	FACTS		FACTS	
3	10000	Incremen	tal reven	ues
4	4000	Cash ope	rating re	venues
5	2000	Deprecia	tion	
6	24000	Initial	Investmen	t
7				
8	Solution			
9	Simple	rate of r	eturn	((+A3-(A4+A5))/A6)*100

CH10PR08 Chapter 10 Problem 8

```
Given
   Option A
     Present value-cash inflows
     Investment required
   Option B
     Present value-cash inflows
     Investment required
Compute
   Profitability index-option A
   Profitability index-option B
```

SCREEN DISPLAY

```
Profitability index
FACTS                FACTS
Option A Option B
    51000     6000 Present value - cash inflows
    50000     5000 Investment required


Solution
Option A Option B
     1.02      1.2 Profitability index
```

CELL CONTENT

	A	B	C	D	E	F
1	Profitabi	lity inde	x			
2	FACTS		FACTS			
3	Option A	Option B				
4	51000	6000	Present	value - c	ash inflo	ws
5	50000	5000	Investme	nt requir	ed	
6						
7						
8	Solution					
9	Option A	Option B				
10	+A4/A5	+B4/B5	Profitab	ility ind	ex	

CH10PR09 Chapter 10 Problem 9

Given
- Reduction in costs-Options A and B
- Depreciation and taxes-Options A and B
- Investment required-Options A and B

Compute
- Simple rate of return-Options A and B

SCREEN DISPLAY

```
Simple Rate of Return - Reduction in Costs
FACTS              FACTS
Option A Option B
    12000     6000  Reduction in costs
     3500     2000  Depreciation and taxes
   100000    50000  Investment required


Solution
Option A Option B
     .085      .08 Simple rate of return
```

CELL CONTENT

	A	B	C	D	E
1	Simple Ra	te of Ret	urn - Red	uction in	Costs
2	FACTS		FACTS		
3	Option A	Option B			
4	12000	6000	Reducti	on in cos	ts
5	3500	2000	Depreci	ation and	taxes
6	100000	50000	Investm	ent requi	red
			e		
7					
8					
9	Solution				
10	Option A	Option B			
11	+A4-A5/A6	+B4-B5/B6	Simple r	ate of re	turn

CH10PR10

Chapter 10 Problem 10

Given
- Initial cost
- Life of the project (years)
- Annual net cash inflow
- Desired rate of return

Compute
- Annual net cash inflow
- Initial investment

SCREEN DISPLAY

```
Net Present value method
                  FACTS
     3170 Initial Cost
        4 Life of the project(years)
     1000 Annual net cash inflow
     0.10 Desired rate of return
SOLUTION          SOLUTION          SOLUTION

Annual Net cash inflow        3169.87
Initial investment            3170.00

Net present value               -0.13
```

CELL CONTENT

	A	B	C	D	E
1	Net Prese	nt value	method		
2			FACTS		
3	3170	Initial	Cost		
4	4	Life of	the proje	ct(years)	
5	1000	Annual n	et cash i	nflow	
6	.1	Desired	rate of r	eturn	
7	SOLUTION		SOLUTION		SOLUTION
8					
9	Annual Ne	t cash in	flow	+A5*((1 /A6)*(1-(1 /(1+A6)^A4	
10	Initial i	nvestment		+A3	
11					
12	Net prese	nt value		+D9-D10	

CH10PR11 Chapter 10 Problem 11

```
Given
   Sales
   Expenses-present
   Expenses-proposed increase
   Income tax rate %
Compute
   Net income after tax
   After tax-proposed expenses
```

SCREEN DISPLAY

```
Computation of after-tax cost
FACTS              FACTS
  Co. A     Co. B
    15000     15000 Sales
     5000      5000 Expenses - present
     2000           Expenses - proposed increase
     0.40      0.40 Income tax
SOLUTION           SOLUTION
     4800      6000 Net Income after tax
     2000           Expenses - proposed increase
               1200 After tax - proposed expenses
```

CELL CONTENT

	A	B	C	D	E	F
1	Computati	on of aft	er-tax co	st		
2	FACTS		FACTS			
3	Co. A	Co. B				
4	15000	15000	Sales			
5	5000	5000	Expenses	- presen	t	
6	2000		Expenses	- propos	ed increa	se
7	.4	.4	Income t	ax		
8	SOLUTION		SOLUTION			
9	(+A4-(A5+A 6))*(1-A7	(+B4-(B5+B 6))*(1-B7	Net Inco	me after	tax	
10	+E6		Expenses	- propos	ed increa	se
11		+B9-A9	After ta	x - propo	sed expen	ses

CH10PR12

Chapter 10 Problem 12

Given		
Sales	Co. A	Co. B
Expenses-cash	Co. A	Co. B
Depreciation	Co. A	Co. B
Income tax rate %	Co. A	Co. B
Compute		
Net income after tax	Co. A	Co. B
Non-cash depreciation	Co. A	
Cash inflow	Co. A	Co. B

SCREEN DISPLAY

```
Comparison of cash costs
FACTS              FACTS
  Co. A     Co. B
    20000     20000 Sales
    10000     10000 Expenses - cash
     2500           Depreciation
     0.40      0.40 Income tax
SOLUTION           SOLUTION
     4500      6000 Net Income after tax
     2500           Non-cash depreciation
     7000      6000 Cash inflow
```

CELL CONTENT

	A	B	C	D	E
1	Compariso	n of cash	costs		
2	FACTS		FACTS		
3	Co. A	Co. B			
4	20000	20000	Sales		
5	10000	10000	Expenses	- cash	
6	2500		Deprecia	tion	
7	.4	.4	Income t	ax	
8	SOLUTION		SOLUTION		
9	(+A4-A5-A6)*(1-A7	(+B4-B5-B6)*(1-B7	Net Inco	me after	tax
10	+A6		Non-cash	deprecia	tion
11	+A9+A10	+B9+B10	Cash inf	low	

CH10PR01

Chapter 10 Problem 1

PRACTICE PROBLEMS

PRACTICE PROBLEMS

PRACTICE PRACTICE PRACTICE PRACTICE PRACTICE PRACTICE

Given
- Principal
- Interest rate
- Periods

Compute
- Compound Amount

Please work these problems.
Compare your results with the solution.

Item No.	Princ.	Rate	Periods	Compound Amount
1	1000	.12	5	1762.34
2	2000	.12	5	3524.68
3	3000	.12	5	5287.03
4	4000	.12	5	7049.37
5	5000	.12	5	8811.71
6	1000	.13	5	1842.44
7	1000	.14	5	1925.41
8	1000	.15	5	2011.36
9	1000	.16	5	2100.34
10	1000	.17	5	2192.45
11	1000	.12	6	1973.82
12	1000	.12	7	2210.68
13	1000	.12	8	2475.96
14	1000	.12	9	2773.08
15	1000	.12	10	3105.85
16	2000	.12	11	6957.10
17	3000	.12	12	11687.93
18	4000	.12	13	17453.97
19	5000	.12	14	24435.56
20	6000	.12	15	32841.39
21	5000	.11	14	21552.20
22	4000	.10	13	13809.08
23	3000	.09	12	8437.99
24	2000	.08	11	4663.28
25	1000	.07	10	1967.15

CH10PR02

Chapter 10 Problem 2

PRACTICE PROBLEMS PRACTICE PROBLEMS

PRACTICE PRACTICE PRACTICE PRACTICE PRACTICE PRACTICE

Given
- Principal
- Interest rate
- Periods

Compute
- Present Value

Please work these problems.
Compare your results with the solution.

Item No.	Princ.	Rate	Periods	Compound Amount
1	200	.12	2	159.44
2	200	.13	2	156.63
3	200	.14	2	153.89
4	200	.15	2	151.23
5	200	.16	2	148.63
6	300	.12	5	170.23
7	400	.12	5	226.97
8	500	.12	5	283.71
9	600	.12	5	340.46
10	700	.12	5	397.20
11	200	.12	6	101.33
12	300	.12	7	135.70
13	400	.12	8	161.55
14	500	.12	9	180.31
15	600	.12	10	193.18
16	200	.12	11	57.50
17	200	.12	12	51.34
18	200	.12	13	45.83
19	200	.12	14	40.92
20	200	.12	15	36.54
21	300	.11	14	69.60
22	400	.10	13	115.87
23	500	.09	12	177.77
24	600	.08	11	257.33
25	700	.07	10	355.84

CH10PR03

Chapter 10 Problem 3

PRACTICE PROBLEMS

PRACTICE PROBLEMS

PRACTICE PRACTICE PRACTICE PRACTICE PRACTICE PRACTICE

Given
- Principal
- Interest rate
- Periods

Compute
- Future value annuity in arrears

Please work these problems.
Compare your results with the solution.

Item No.	Princ.	Rate	Periods	Compound Amount
1	100	0.12	5.00	635.28
2	200	0.12	5.00	1270.57
3	300	0.12	5.00	1905.85
4	400	0.12	5.00	2541.14
5	500	0.12	5.00	3176.42
6	600	0.13	5.00	3888.16
7	700	0.14	5.00	4627.07
8	800	0.15	5.00	5393.91
9	900	0.16	5.00	6189.42
10	1000	0.17	5.00	7014.40
11	1100	0.12	6.00	8926.71
12	1200	0.12	7.00	12106.81
13	1300	0.12	8.00	15989.60
14	1400	0.12	9.00	20685.92
15	1500	0.12	10.00	26323.10
16	1600	0.12	11.00	33047.33
17	1700	0.12	12.00	41026.33
18	1800	0.12	13.00	50452.40
19	1900	0.12	14.00	61545.94
20	2000	0.12	14.50	69533.89
21	2100	0.11	13.50	59015.53
22	2200	0.10	12.50	50415.45
23	2300	0.09	11.50	43292.24
24	2400	0.08	10.50	37308.62
25	2500	0.07	9.50	32204.18

CH10PR04

Chapter 10 Problem 4

PRACTICE PROBLEMS

PRACTICE PROBLEMS

Given
   Principal
   Interest rate
   Periods
Compute
   Present value annuity in arrears

   PV annuity in arrears
      annuity in arrears
      annuity in arrears

Please work these problems.
Compare your results with the solution.

Item No.	Princ.	Rate	Periods	Compound Amount
1	100	0.12	5.00	360.48
2	200	0.12	5.00	720.96
3	300	0.12	5.00	1081.43
4	400	0.12	5.00	1441.91
5	500	0.12	5.00	1802.39
6	600	0.13	5.00	2110.34
7	700	0.14	5.00	2403.16
8	800	0.15	5.00	2681.72
9	900	0.16	5.00	2946.86
10	1000	0.17	5.00	3199.35
11	1100	0.12	6.00	4522.55
12	1200	0.12	7.00	5476.51
13	1300	0.12	8.00	6457.93
14	1400	0.12	9.00	7459.55
15	1500	0.12	10.00	8475.33
16	1600	0.12	11.00	9500.32
17	1700	0.12	12.00	10530.44
18	1800	0.12	13.00	11562.39
19	1900	0.12	14.00	12593.52
20	2000	0.12	14.50	13444.21
21	2100	0.11	13.50	14424.68
22	2200	0.10	12.50	15316.34
23	2300	0.09	11.50	16069.61
24	2400	0.08	10.50	16628.76
25	2500	0.07	9.50	16934.26

CH10PR05

Chapter 10 Problem 5

PRACTICE PROBLEMS

Given
   Investment required- Option A
   Investment required- Option B
   Net cash inflows-Option A
   Net cash inflows-Option B
Compute
   Payback period-Option A
   Payback period-Option B

Please work these problems.
Compare your results with the solution.

Item No.	Invest. Required	Net cash inflows	Payback Period
1	15000	5000	3.00
2	17000	5000	3.40
3	19000	5000	3.80
4	21000	5000	4.20
5	23000	5000	4.60
6	15000	5000	3.00
7	15000	6000	2.50
8	15000	7000	2.14
9	15000	8000	1.88
10	15000	9000	1.67
11	15000	5000	3.00
12	14000	5000	2.80
13	13000	5000	2.60
14	12000	5000	2.40
15	11000	5000	2.20
16	15000	4500	3.33
17	15000	4000	3.75
18	15000	3500	4.29
19	15000	3000	5.00
20	15000	2500	6.00
21	14500	4500	3.22
22	14000	4000	3.50
23	13500	3500	3.86
24	13000	3000	4.33
25	12500	2500	5.00

CH10PR06

Chapter 10 Problem 6

PRACTICE PROBLEMS

PRACTICE PROBLEMS

PRACTICE PRACTICE PRACTICE PRACTICE PRACTICE PRACTICE

Given
- Investment required- Option A
- Investment required- Option B
- Net cash inflows-Option A
- Net cash inflows-Option B

Compute
- Payback period-Option A
- Payback period-Option B

Please work these problems.
Compare your results with the solution.

	<------ Option A		------>	<------ Option B		------>
Item No.	Invest. Required	Cash Inflows	Payback Years	Invest. Required	Cash Inflows	Payback Years
1	15000	5000	3.00	14000	5000	2.80
2	15000	6000	2.50	13000	5000	2.60
3	15000	7000	2.14	12000	5000	2.40
4	15000	8000	1.88	11000	5000	2.20
5	15000	9000	1.67	10000	5000	2.00
6	16000	5000	3.20	15000	6000	2.50
7	17000	5000	3.40	15000	7000	2.14
8	18000	5000	3.60	15000	8000	1.88
9	19000	5000	3.80	15000	9000	1.67
10	20000	5000	4.00	15000	10000	1.50
11	20500	4500	4.56	14800	3000	4.93
12	21000	4000	5.25	14600	2500	5.84
13	21500	3500	6.14	14400	2000	7.20
14	22000	3000	7.33	14200	1500	9.47
15	22500	2500	9.00	14000	1000	14.00
16	2000	500	4.00	15000	5000	3.00
17	2200	600	3.67	14700	5500	2.67
18	2400	700	3.43	14400	6000	2.40
19	2600	800	3.25	14100	6500	2.17
20	2800	900	3.11	13800	7000	1.97
21	15000	5000	3.00	12500	4000	3.13
22	16000	5000	3.20	12000	3000	4.00
23	17000	3500	4.86	11500	3500	3.29
24	18000	5000	3.60	11000	4000	2.75
25	19000	5000	3.80	10500	4500	2.33

CH10PR07

Chapter 10 Problem 7

PRACTICE PROBLEMS PRACTICE PROBLEMS

PRACTICE PRACTICE PRACTICE PRACTICE PRACTICE PRACTICE

Given
- Incremental revenues
- Cash operating revenues
- Depreciation
- Initial investment

Compute
- Simple rate of return

Please work these problems.
Compare your results with the solution.

Item No.	Increment Revenue	Cash Revenues	Deprec.	Initial Invest.	Simple ROR
1	10000	4000	2000	24000	16.67
2	12000	4000	2000	24000	25.00
3	14000	4000	2000	24000	33.33
4	16000	4000	2000	24000	41.67
5	18000	4000	2000	24000	50.00
6	10000	5000	2000	24000	12.50
7	10000	6000	2000	24000	8.33
8	10000	7000	2000	24000	4.17
9	20000	8000	2000	24000	41.67
10	20000	9000	2000	24000	37.50
11	20000	4000	3000	24000	54.17
12	20000	4000	4000	24000	50.00
13	20000	4000	5000	24000	45.83
14	20000	4000	6000	24000	41.67
15	20000	4000	7000	24000	37.50
16	10000	4000	2000	26000	15.38
17	10000	4000	2000	28000	14.29
18	10000	4000	2000	30000	13.33
19	10000	4000	2000	32000	12.50
20	10000	4000	2000	34000	11.76
21	12000	5000	4000	36000	8.33
22	14000	6000	6000	38000	5.26
23	16000	7000	8000	40000	2.50
24	28000	8000	10000	42000	23.81
25	30000	12000	12000	44000	13.64

CH10PR08

Chapter 10 Problem 8

Given
- Option A
  - Present value-cash inflows
  - Investment required
- Option B
  - Present value-cash inflows
  - Investment required

Compute
- Profitability index-option A
- Profitability index-option B

	<----- Option A	---->		<----- Option B	---->	
Item No.	PV- Cash Inflows	Invest. Required	Prof Index	PV- Cash Inflows	Invest. Required	Prof Index
1	51000	50000	1.02	6000	5000	1.20
2	56000	50000	1.12	8000	5000	1.60
3	61000	50000	1.22	10000	5000	2.00
4	66000	50000	1.32	12000	5000	2.40
5	71000	50000	1.42	14000	5000	2.80
6	51000	55000	0.93	6000	5500	1.09
7	51000	60000	0.85	6000	6000	1.00
8	51000	65000	0.78	6000	6500	0.92
9	51000	70000	0.73	6000	7000	0.86
10	51000	75000	0.68	6000	7500	0.80
11	45000	42000	1.07	5600	4800	1.17
12	40000	40000	1.00	5200	4600	1.13
13	35000	38000	0.92	4800	4400	1.09
14	30000	36000	0.83	4400	4200	1.05
15	25000	34000	0.74	4000	4000	1.00
16	50000	48000	1.04	5000	5000	1.00
17	49000	46000	1.07	5200	5000	1.04
18	48000	44000	1.09	5400	5000	1.08
19	47000	42000	1.12	5600	5000	1.12
20	46000	40000	1.15	5800	5000	1.16
21	51000	40000	1.28	6000	5000	1.20
22	51000	38000	1.34	6000	4500	1.33
23	51000	36000	1.42	6000	4000	1.50
24	51000	34000	1.50	6000	3500	1.71
25	51000	32000	1.59	6000	3000	2.00

CH10PR09

Chapter 10 Problem 9

PRACTICE PROBLEMS

PRACTICE PROBLEMS

PRACTICE PRACTICE PRACTICE PRACTICE PRACTICE PRACTICE

Given
Reduction in costs-Options A and B
Depreciation and taxes-Options A and B
Investment required-Options A and B
Compute
Simple rate of return-Options A and B

Please work these problems.
Compare your results with the solution.

Item No.	Reduction in costs	Deprec & Taxes	Invest. Required	Simple ROR
1	12000	3500	100000	8.50
2	14000	3500	100000	10.50
3	16000	3500	100000	12.50
4	18000	3500	100000	14.50
5	20000	3500	100000	16.50
6	12000	4000	110000	7.27
7	12000	4500	120000	6.25
8	12000	5000	130000	5.38
9	12000	5500	140000	4.64
10	12000	6000	150000	4.00
11	11000	3500	100000	7.50
12	10000	3500	100000	6.50
13	9000	3500	100000	5.50
14	8000	3500	100000	4.50
15	7000	3500	100000	3.50
16	12000	3500	100000	8.50
17	12000	3000	100000	9.00
18	12000	2500	100000	9.50
19	12000	2000	100000	10.00
20	12000	1500	100000	10.50
21	12000	3500	90000	9.44
22	12000	3500	80000	10.63
23	12000	3500	70000	12.14
24	12000	3500	60000	14.17
25	12000	3500	50000	17.00

CH10PR10

Chapter 10 Problem 10

PRACTICE PROBLEMS

PRACTICE PRACTICE PRACTICE PRACTICE PRACTICE PRACTICE

Given
- Initial cost
- Life of the project (years)
- Annual net cash inflow
- Desired rate of return

Compute
- Annual net cash inflow
- Initial investment

Please work these problems.
Compare your results with the solution.

Item No.	Initial Cost	Life of Project	Annual Cash in	Desired ROR	Annual cash in	Net PV
1	3170	4	1000	0.10	3169.87	0.13
2	3300	4	1000	0.10	3169.87	130.13
3	3400	4	1000	0.10	3169.87	230.13
4	3500	4	1000	0.10	3169.87	330.13
5	3600	4	1000	0.10	3169.87	430.13
6	3170	4	1100	0.10	3486.85	-316.85
7	3170	4	1200	0.10	3803.84	-633.84
8	3170	4	1300	0.10	4120.83	-950.83
9	3170	4	1400	0.10	4437.81	-1267.81
10	3170	4	1500	0.10	4754.80	-1584.80
11	3270	4	1100	0.10	3486.85	-216.85
12	3370	4	1200	0.10	3803.84	-433.84
13	3470	4	1300	0.10	4120.83	-650.83
14	3570	4	1400	0.10	4437.81	-867.81
15	3670	4	1500	0.10	4754.80	-1084.80
16	3170	5	1000	0.10	3790.79	-620.79
17	3170	6	1000	0.10	4355.26	-1185.26
18	3170	7	1000	0.10	4868.42	-1698.42
19	3170	8	1000	0.10	5334.93	-2164.93
20	3170	9	1000	0.10	5759.02	-2589.02
21	3170	4	1000	0.12	3037.35	132.65
22	3170	4	1000	0.14	2913.71	256.29
23	3170	4	1000	0.16	2798.18	371.82
24	3170	4	1000	0.18	2690.06	479.94
25	3170	4	1000	0.20	2588.73	581 27

PRACTICE PROBLEMS PRACTICE PROBLEMS

PRACTICE PRACTICE PRACTICE PRACTICE PRACTICE PRACTICE

Given
- Sales
- Expenses-present
- Expenses-proposed increase
- Income tax rate %

Compute
- Net income after tax
- After tax-proposed expenses

Please work these problems.
Compare your results with the solution.

Item No.	Tax rate	Change in Expenses Amount	After Tax
1	0.40	2000	1200
2	0.35	3000	1950
3	0.30	4000	2800
4	0.25	5000	3750
5	0.20	6000	4800
6	0.40	2000	1200
7	0.40	1800	1080
8	0.40	1600	960
9	0.40	1400	840
10	0.40	1200	720
11	0.35	3000	1950
12	0.30	4000	2800
13	0.25	5000	3750
14	0.20	6000	4800
15	0.15	7000	5950
16	0.40	10000	6000
17	0.41	15000	8850
18	0.42	20000	11600
19	0.43	25000	14250
20	0.44	30000	16800
21	0.40	8000	4800
22	0.39	9000	5490
23	0.38	10000	6200
24	0.37	11000	6930
25	0.36	12000	7680

Chapter 10 Problem 12

CH10PR12

PRACTICE PROBLEMS

PRACTICE PROBLEMS

PRACTICE PRACTICE PRACTICE PRACTICE PRACTICE PRACTICE

Given		
Sales	Co. A	Co. B
Expenses-cash	Co. A	Co. B
Depreciation	Co. A	Co. B
Income tax rate %	Co. A	Co. B
Compute		
Net income after tax	Co. A	Co. B
Non-cash depreciation	Co. A	
Cash inflow	Co. A	Co. B

Please work these problems.
Compare your results with the solution.

Item No.	Income Before Tax	Tax Rate	Income After Tax	Deprec.	Cash Inflow
1	7500	0.40	4500	2500	7000
2	8500	0.40	5100	2500	7600
3	9500	0.40	5700	2500	8200
4	10500	0.40	6300	2500	8800
5	11500	0.40	6900	2500	9400
6	7500	0.41	4425	2500	6925
7	7500	0.42	4350	2500	6850
8	7500	0.43	4275	2500	6775
9	7500	0.44	4200	2500	6700
10	7500	0.45	4125	2500	6625
11	7500	0.40	4500	3000	7500
12	7500	0.40	4500	3500	8000
13	7500	0.40	4500	4000	8500
14	7500	0.40	4500	4500	9000
15	7500	0.40	4500	5000	9500
16	8500	0.39	5185	2500	7685
17	9500	0.38	5890	3000	8890
18	10500	0.37	6615	3500	10115
19	11500	0.36	7360	4000	11360
20	12500	0.35	8125	4500	12625
21	13500	0.34	8910	5000	13910
22	14500	0.33	9715	5500	15215
23	15500	0.32	10540	6000	16540
24	16500	0.31	11385	6500	17885
25	17500	0.30	12250	7000	19250

11 Service Department Allocation Percent Basics

Condensed List of Items

Item No.		*Problems*
CH11PR01	Allocated service department costs	25
CH11PR02	Allocated service department costs-step	6
CH11PR03	Allocated service department costs-step	6
CH11PR04	Allocated service department costs-step	3
CH11PR05	Allocated service department costs-direct	3
CH11PR06	Rate per machine hour	3
CH11PR07	Allocate cost by department	25
CH11PR08	Determine percentage	25
CH11PR09	Determine percent	25
CH11PR10	Determine base	25
	Total	146

DIRECT METHOD

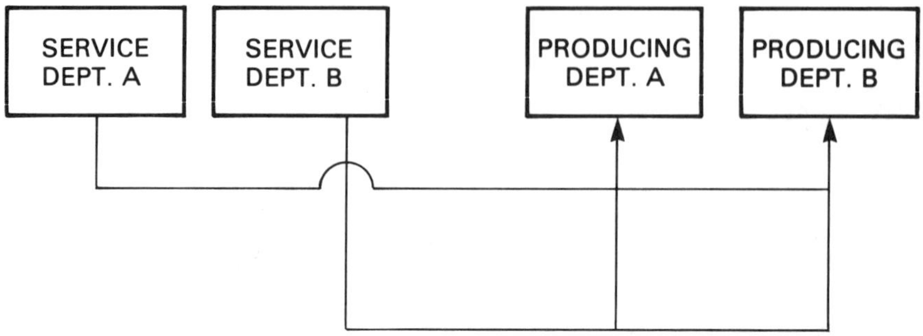

STEP METHOD

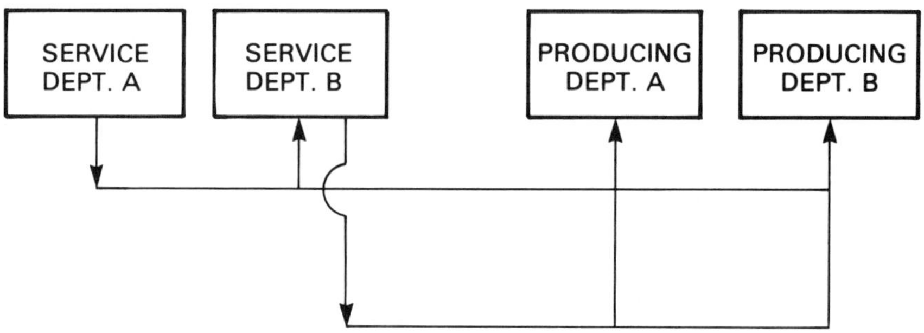

Chapter 11 Problem 1

CH11PR01

```
Allocated service department costs
FACTS    FACTS    FACTS
     5000 Budgeted direct labor-hours
                  Cost per
Variable overhead labor hr.
Indirect labor         0.20
Indirect materials     0.10
Utilities               .05
Service department     0.15
Total                  0.50
Fixed overhead         8500
```

SCREEN DISPLAY

```
SOLUTION

Direct Labor Hours      4000     5000     6000
Variable rate           0.50     0.50     0.50
Variable costs          2000     2500     3000
Fixed costs             8500     8500     8500
Total                  10500    11000    11500

Predetermined rate               2.20
```

CELL CONTENT

	A	B	C	D	E
1	Allocated	service	departmen	t costs	
2	FACTS	FACTS	FACTS		
3	5000	Budgeted	direct l	abor-hour	s
4			Cost per		
5	Variable	overhead	labor hr.		
6	Indirect	labor	.2		
7	Indirect	materials	.1		
8	Utilities		.05		
9	Service d	epartment	.15		
10	Total		@SUM(C6 ...C9		
11	Fixed ove	rhead	8500		
12					
13	SOLUTION				
14					
15	Direct La	bor Hours	+A3-1000	+A3	+D15+1000
16	Variable	rate	+C10	+C10	+C10
17	Variable	costs	+C15*C10	+D15*C10	+E15*C10
18	Fixed cos	ts	+C11	+C11	+C11
19	Total		+C17+C18	+D17+D18	+E17+E18
20					
21	Predeterm	ined rate		+D19/Dl 5	

CH11PR02

Chapter 11 Problem 2

Given
  By department
    Labor hours
    Overhead
Required
  Allocate the cost of a service department
  using the step method.

SCREEN DISPLAY

```
Allocation service department
Step method
FACTS     FACTS     FACTS
                        D E P A R T M E N T S
                      Service       Producing
             A          B          1          2        Total
Labor Hrs    ---        5000      10000      25000      40000
Overhead    200000     45000     200000     300000     745000
SOLUTION
Alloc.  A   200000     25000      50000     125000     200000
Total            0     70000     250000     425000     745000
```

CELL CONTENT

	A	B	C	D	E	F
1	Allocatio	n service	departme	nt		
2	Step meth	od	Chapter 1	1 Problem	2	
3	FACTS	FACTS	FACTS			
4			D E P	A R T M	E N T S	
5			Service	Pro	ducing	
6		A	B	1	2	Total
7	Labor Hrs	---	5000	10000	25000	@SUM(B7...E7
8	Overhead	200000	45000	200000	300000	@SUM(B8... E8
9	SOLUTION					
10	Alloc. A	+B8	+C7/F7*B10	+D7/F7*B10	+E7/F7*B10	+F7/F7*B10
11	Total	+B8-B10	+C8+C10	+D8+D10	+E8+E10	+F8
12						

CH11PR03 Chapter 11 Problem 3

Given
  By department
    Space - feet
    Overhead
Required
  Allocate the cost of a service department
  using the step method.

SCREEN DISPLAY

```
Allocation service department-Step method
FACTS     FACTS     FACTS
                    Service depts.    Producing
          A         B          1          2        Total
Space-ft.                  50000      40000        90000

SOLUTION  A         B          1          2        Total
Overhead               70000  200000     300000   570000
Alloc B                70000   38889      31111    70000
Total                      0  238889     331111   570000
```

CELL CONTENT

	A	B	C	D	E	F
1			Chapter	11 Proble	m 3	
2	Allocatio	n service	departme	nt-Step m	ethod	
3	FACTS	FACTS	FACTS			
4			Service d	epts.	Producing	
5		A	B	1	2	Total
6	Space-ft.			50000	40000	@SUM(B6... E6
7						
8	SOLUTION	A	B	1	2	Total
9	Overhead		70000	200000	300000	@SUM(B9... E9
10	Alloc B		+C9	+D6/F6* C10	+E6/F6* C10	+F6/F6* C10
11	Total		+C9-C10	+D9+D10	+E9+E10	+F9

Given
  By department
    Labor hours
    Space - feet
    Overhead
Required
  Allocate service department costs
  using the step method.

SCREEN DISPLAY

Allocation service department

FACTS		Service depts.	Producing		
	A	B	1	2	Total
Labor Hrs		5000	10000	25000	40000
Space-ft.			50000	40000	90000
Overhead	200000	45000	200000	300000	745000
SOLUTION					
Alloc A	200000	25000	50000	125000	200000
Alloc B			38889	31111	70000
Total	0	0	238889	456111	745000

CELL CONTENT

	A	B	C	D	E	F
1						
2		Allocatio	n service	departme	nt	
3	FACTS		Service d	epts.	Producing	
4		A	B	1	2	Total
5	Labor Hrs		5000	10000	25000	@SUM(B5... E5
6	Space-ft.			50000	40000	@SUM(B6... E6
7	Overhead	200000	45000	200000	300000	@SUM(B7... E7
8	SOLUTION					
9	Alloc A	200000	+B9*(C5/F5	+B9*(D5/F5	+B9*(E5/F5	+B9*(F5/F5
10	Alloc B			(C7+C9) *D6/F6	(C7+C9) *E6/F6	(C7+C9) *F6/F6
11	Total	+B7-B9	+C7+C9-C7-C9	+D7+D10	@SUM(E7 ...E10	+F7

CH11PR05

Chapter 11 Problem 5

Given
- By department
  - Labor hours
  - Space - feet
  - Overhead

Required
- Allocate service department costs using the direct method.

SCREEN DISPLAY

Allocation service department-Direct method

FACTS	FACTS D E P A R T M E N T S				
	Service		Producing		
	A	B	1	2	Total
Labor Hrs		5000	10000	25000	40000
Space-ft.			50000	40000	90000
Overhead	200000	45000	200000	300000	745000
SOLUTION					
Alloc. A	200000		57143	142857	
Alloc. B		45000	25000	20000	
Total	0	0	282143	462857	745000

CELL CONTENT

	A	B	C	D	E	F
1			Chapter 1	1 Problem	5	
2	Allocatio	n service	departme	nt-Direct	method	
3	FACTS	FACTS	D E P A R	T M E N	T S	
4		Servi	ce	Produ	cing	
5		A	B	1	2	Total
6	Labor Hrs		5000	10000	25000	@SUM(B6...E6
7	Space-ft.			50000	40000	@SUM(B7...E7
8	Overhead	200000	45000	200000	300000	@SUM(B8...E8
9	SOLUTION					
10	Alloc. A	+B8		+B10*(D6/(D6+E6)	+B10*(E6/(D6+E6)	
11	Alloc. B		+C8	/FI+C11*(D7/F7)	+C11*(E7/F7)	
12	Total	+B8-B10	+C8-C11	+D8+D10+D11	+E8+E10+E11	@SUM(B12...E12

CH11PR06

Chapter 11 Problem 6

Given
  Comparative by departments
    Service department - fixed costs
    Machine - hours
  Required
    Compute rate per machine hour.

SCREEN DISPLAY

```
Allocation service department-Fixed Cost
FACTS     FACTS     FACTS     Year 1    Year 2
Service dept. fixed               30000     30000
Machine hours
  Dept. A                         15000     15000
  Dept. B                         15000      5000

SOLUTION            SOLUTION
Total Hours                       30000     20000
Rate per machine hour              1.00      1.50
```

CELL CONTENT

	A	B	C	D	E
1					
2	Allocatio	n service	departme	nt-Fixed	Cost
3	FACTS	FACTS	FACTS	Year 1	Year 2
4	Service d	ept. fixe	d	30000	30000
5	Machine h	ours			
6	Dept. A			15000	15000
7	Dept. B			15000	5000
8					
9	SOLUTION		SOLUTION		
10	Total Hou	rs		+D6+D7	+E6+E7
11	Rate per	machine h	our	+D4/(D10	+E4/(E10

Given
  Variable - rate per hour
  Fixed cost
  Budget and Peak Period - by department
    Hours

  Required
    Allocate cost by department.

SCREEN DISPLAY

```
Allocation service department
FACTS    FACTS    FACTS    Budgeted Peak Period
Producing Dept. A hours        12000     18000
Producing Dept. B hours        10000     12000
Variable rate          0.10
Fixed Cost            10000
SOLUTION          SOLUTION
                            Dept. A  Dept. B
Variable                       1200     1000
Fixed                          6000     4000
Allocated cost                 7200     5000
```

CELL CONTENT

	A	B	C	D	E	F
1	Allocatio	n service	departme	nt		
2	FACTS	FACTS	FACTS	Budgeted	Peak Peri	od
3	Producing	Dept. A	hours	12000	18000	
4	Producing	Dept. B	hours	10000	12000	
5	Variable	rate	.1			
6	Fixed Cos	t	10000			
7	SOLUTION		SOLUTION			
8				Dept. A	Dept. B	
9	Variable			+D3*C5	+D4*C5	
10	Fixed			+C6*E3/(E3 +E4)	+C6*E4/(E3 +E4)	
11	Allocated	cost		+D9+D10	+E9+E10	

CH11PR08 Chapter 11 Problem 8

Given
Base
Percent

Required

Percentage

SCREEN DISPLAY

```
Compute Percentage
FACTS                FACTS                FACTS
      100  Base
       25  Percent

SOLUTION             SOLUTION

         Percentage                  25
```

CELL CONTENT

	A	B	C	D	E
1			Chapter 1	1 Problem	8
2	Compute P	ercentage			
3	FACTS		FACTS		FACTS
4	100	Base			
5	25	Percent			
6					
7	SOLUTION		SOLUTION		
8					
9		Percentag	e	+A4*(A5*.01)	

CH11PR09

Chapter 11 Problem 9

Given
Base
Percentage

Required

Percent

SCREEN DISPLAY

```
Compute Percent
FACTS                   FACTS                   FACTS
      100  Base
       40  Percentage

SOLUTION                SOLUTION

         Percent                          40
```

CELL CONTENT

	A	B	C	D	E
1			Chapter 1	1 Problem	9
2	Compute P	ercent			
3	FACTS		FACTS		FACTS
4	100	Base			
5	40	Percent	age		
6					
7	SOLUTION		SOLUTION		
8					
9		Percent		(A5/A4)*100	

CH11PR10

Chapter 11 Problem 10

Given
Percent
Percentage

Required

Base

SCREEN DISPLAY

```
Compute  Base
FACTS                 FACTS                FACTS
       25  Percent
      100  Percentage

SOLUTION              SOLUTION

         Base                        400
```

CELL CONTENT

	A	B	C	D	E
1			Chapter 1	1 Problem	10
2	Compute	Base			
3	FACTS		FACTS		FACTS
4	25	Percent			
5	100	Percent	age		
6					
7	SOLUTION		SOLUTION		
8					
9		Base		(A5/A4)*100	

Allocated service department costs
FACTS FACTS FACTS
5000 Budgeted direct labor-hours

Variable overhead	Cost per labor hr.
Indirect labor	0.20
Indirect materials	0.10
Utilities	.05
Service department	0.15
Total	0.50
Fixed overhead	8500

SOLUTION

Direct Labor Hours	4000	5000	6000
Variable rate	0.50	0.50	0.50
Variable costs	2000	2500	3000
Fixed costs	8500	8500	8500
Total	10500	11000	11500
Predetermined rate		2.20	

Please work these problems
Check your answers with the solution

Item No.	Variable Costs	Fixed Costs	Budgeted Hours	Rate per Hour
1	2500	8500	5000	2.20
2	3500	8500	5000	2.40
3	4500	8500	5000	2.60
4	5500	8500	5000	2.80
5	6500	8500	5000	3.00
6	2500	9500	5000	2.40
7	2500	10500	5000	2.60
8	2500	11500	5000	2.80
9	2500	12500	5000	3.00
10	2500	13500	5000	3.20
11	2500	8500	6000	1.83
12	2500	8500	7000	1.57
13	2500	8500	8000	1.38
14	2500	8500	9000	1.22
15	2400	8500	10000	1.09
16	2300	8500	5000	2.16
17	2200	8500	5100	2.10
18	2100	8500	5200	2.04
19	2000	8500	5300	1.98
20	1900	8500	5400	1.93
21	5000	7500	5200	2.40
22	6000	6500	5000	2.50
23	7000	5500	4800	2.60
24	8000	4500	4600	2.72
25	9000	3500	4400	2.84

Allocation service department
Step method
FACTS FACTS FACTS

	DEPARTMENTS				
	Service		Producing		
	A	B	1	2	Total
Labor Hrs	---	5000	10000	25000	40000
Overhead	200000	45000	200000	300000	745000
SOLUTION					
Alloc. A	200000	25000	50000	125000	200000
Total	0	70000	250000	425000	745000

Please work these problems.
Compare your results with the prepared solution.

	DEPARTMENTS				
	A	B	1	2	Total
Item # 1					
Labor Hrs	---	5000	10000	25000	40000
Overhead	200000	45000	200000	300000	745000
Alloc. A	0	70000	250000	425000	745000
Item # 2					
Labor Hrs	---	10000	15000	30000	55000
Overhead	100000	45000	200000	300000	645000
Alloc. A	0	63182	227273	354545	645000
Item # 3					
Labor Hrs	---	10000	15000	30000	55000
Overhead	100000	45000	200000	300000	645000
Alloc. A	0	63182	227273	354545	645000
Item # 4					
Labor Hrs	---	10000	15000	20000	45000
Overhead	45000	45000	200000	300000	590000
Alloc. A	0	55000	215000	320000	590000
Item # 5					
Labor Hrs	---	15000	15000	20000	50000
Overhead	30000	45000	200000	300000	575000
Alloc. A	0	54000	209000	312000	575000
Item # 6					
Labor Hrs	---	30000	30000	40000	100000
Overhead	30000	45000	200000	300000	575000
Alloc. A	0	54000	209000	312000	575000

CH11PR03

Chapter 11 Problem 3

Allocation service department-Step method

FACTS FACTS FACTS

	DEPARTMENTS				
	Service		Producing		
	A	B	1	2	Total
Space-ft.			60000	40000	100000
Overhead		70000	200000	300000	570000
SOLUTION					
Alloc B		70000	42000	28000	70000
Total		0	242000	328000	570000

PRACTICE PRACTICE PRACTICE PRACTICE PRACTICE PRACTICE

Item No. 1	DEPARTMENTS				
	Service		Producing		
	A	B	1	2	Total
Space-ft.			50000	50000	100000
Overhead		70000	200000	300000	570000
Alloc. B		0	235000	335000	570000

Item No. 2	DEPARTMENTS				
	Service		Producing		
	A	B	1	2	Total
Space-ft.			30000	50000	80000
Overhead		80000	200000	300000	580000
Alloc. B		0	230000	350000	580000

Item No. 3	DEPARTMENTS				
	Service		Producing		
	A	B	1	2	Total
Space-ft.			20000	40000	60000
Overhead		60000	200000	300000	560000
Alloc. B		0	220000	340000	560000

Item No. 4	DEPARTMENTS				
	Service		Producing		
	A	B	1	2	Total
Space-ft.			20000	40000	60000
Overhead		60000	200000	300000	560000
Alloc. B		0	220000	340000	560000

Item No. 5	DEPARTMENTS				
	Service		Producing		
	A	B	1	2	Total
Space-ft.			40000	40000	80000
Overhead		40000	200000	300000	540000
Alloc. B		0	220000	320000	540000

Item No. 6	DEPARTMENTS				
	Service		Producing		
	A	B	1	2	Total
Space-ft.			40000	60000	100000
Overhead		50000	200000	300000	550000
Alloc. B		0	220000	330000	550000

Allocation service department

FACTS		Service depts.	Producing		
	A	B	1	2	Total
Labor Hrs		5000	10000	25000	40000
Space-ft.			50000	40000	90000
Overhead	200000	45000	200000	300000	745000
SOLUTION					
Alloc A	200000	25000	50000	125000	200000
Alloc B			38889	31111	70000
Total	0	0	238889	456111	745000

Please work these problems
Check your answers with the solution

Item No. 1

FACTS	FACTS	FACTS			
		Service depts.	Producing		
	A	B	1	2	Total
Labor Hrs		10000	10000	10000	30000
Space-ft.			40000	40000	80000
Overhead	100000	45000	200000	300000	645000
SOLUTION					
Alloc A	100000	33333	33333	33333	100000
Alloc B			39167	39167	78333
Total	0	0	239167	372500	645000

Item No. 2

FACTS	FACTS	FACTS			
		Service depts.	Producing		
	A	B	1	2	Total
Labor Hrs		5000	10000	10000	25000
Space-ft.			40000	40000	80000
Overhead	150000	45000	200000	300000	695000
SOLUTION					
Alloc A	150000	30000	60000	60000	150000
Alloc B			37500	37500	75000
Total	0	0	237500	397500	695000

Item No. 3

FACTS	FACTS	FACTS			
		Service depts.	Producing		
	A	B	1	2	Total
Labor Hrs		25000	25000	50000	100000
Space-ft.			60000	40000	100000
Overhead	30000	45000	200000	300000	575000
SOLUTION					
Alloc A	30000	7500	7500	15000	30000
Alloc B			31500	21000	52500
Total	0	0	231500	336000	575000

CH11PR05

Chapter 11 Problem 5

Allocation service department-Direct method

FACTS	FACTS	DEPARTMENTS			
	Service		Producing		
	A	B	1	2	Total
Labor Hrs		5000	10000	25000	40000
Space-ft.			50000	40000	90000
Overhead	200000	45000	200000	300000	745000
SOLUTION					
Alloc. A	200000		57143	142857	
Alloc. B		45000	25000	20000	
Total	0	0	282143	462857	745000

PRACTICE PROBLEMS

Item No. 1

FACTS	FACTS	DEPARTMENTS			
	Service		Producing		
	A	B	1	2	Total
Labor Hrs		5000	10000	25000	40000
Space-ft.			50000	40000	90000
Overhead	200000	45000	200000	300000	745000
SOLUTION					
Alloc. A	200000		57143	142857	
Alloc. B		45000	25000	20000	
Total	0	0	282143	462857	745000

Item No. 2

FACTS	FACTS	DEPARTMENTS			
	Service		Producing		
	A	B	1	2	Total
Labor Hrs		5000	10000	25000	40000
Space-ft.			50000	40000	90000
Overhead	200000	45000	200000	300000	745000
SOLUTION					
Alloc. A	200000		57143	142857	
Alloc. B		45000	25000	20000	
Total	0	0	282143	462857	745000

Item No. 3

FACTS	FACTS	DEPARTMENTS			
	Service		Producing		
	A	B	1	2	Total
Labor Hrs		5000	10000	25000	40000
Space-ft.			50000	40000	90000
Overhead	200000	45000	200000	300000	745000
SOLUTION					
Alloc. A	200000		57143	142857	
Alloc. B		45000	25000	20000	
Total	0	0	282143	462857	745000

CH11PR06

Chapter 11 Problem 6

Allocation service department-Fixed Cost

FACTS FACTS FACTS	Year 1	Year 2
Service dept. fixed	30000	30000
Machine hours		
Dept. A	15000	15000
Dept. B	15000	5000

SOLUTION SOLUTION		
Total Hours	30000	20000
Rate per machine hour	1.00	1.50

Please work these problems.
Compare your results with the prepared solution.

Item No. 1

FACTS FACTS FACTS	Year 1	Year 2
Service dept. fixed	30000	30000
Machine hours		
Dept. A	20000	15000
Dept. B	15000	6000

SOLUTION SOLUTION		
Total Hours	35000	21000
Rate per machine hour	0.86	1.43

Item No. 2

FACTS FACTS FACTS	Year 1	Year 2
Service dept. fixed	25000	25000
Machine hours		
Dept. A	24000	15000
Dept. B	15000	6000

SOLUTION SOLUTION		
Total Hours	39000	21000
Rate per machine hour	0.64	1.19

Item No. 3

FACTS FACTS FACTS	Year 1	Year 2
Service dept. fixed	42000	42000
Machine hours		
Dept. A	24000	22000
Dept. B	14000	12000

SOLUTION SOLUTION		
Total Hours	38000	34000
Rate per machine hour	1.11	1.24

Allocation service department

FACTS	FACTS	FACTS	Budgeted	Peak Period
Producing Dept. A hours			12000	18000
Producing Dept. B hours			10000	12000
Variable rate		0.10		
Fixed Cost		10000		
SOLUTION		SOLUTION		
			Dept. A	Dept. B
Variable			1200	1000
Fixed			6000	4000
Allocated cost			7200	5000

Please work these problems
Check your answers with the solution

			Budgeted	Peak Period
Producing Dept. A hours			12000	18000
Producing Dept. B hours			10000	12000
	Variable	Fixed	Department	
Item No.	Rate	Cost	A	B
1	0.10	10000	7200	5000
2	0.12	10000	7440	5200
3	0.14	10000	7680	5400
4	0.16	10000	7920	5600
5	0.18	10000	8160	5800
6	0.10	12000	8400	5800
7	0.10	14000	9600	6600
8	0.10	16000	10800	7400
9	0.10	18000	12000	8200
10	0.10	20000	13200	9000
11	0.09	10000	7080	4900
12	0.08	10000	6960	4800
13	0.07	10000	6840	4700
14	0.06	10000	6720	4600
15	0.05	10000	6600	4500
16	0.10	9000	6600	4600
17	0.10	8000	6000	4200
18	0.10	7000	5400	3800
19	0.10	6000	4800	3400
20	0.10	5000	4200	3000
21	0.15	12000	9000	6300
22	0.20	14000	10800	7600
23	0.25	16000	12600	8900
24	0.30	18000	14400	10200
25	0.35	20000	16200	11500

CH11PR08

Chapter 11 Problem 8

Compute Percentage

FACTS FACTS FACTS

100 Base
25 Percent

SOLUTION SOLUTION

Percentage 25

PRACTICE PRACTICE PRACTICE PRACTICE PRACTICE PRACTICE

Item No.	Base	Percent	Percentage
1	100	25	25
2	200	25	50
3	300	25	75
4	400	25	100
5	500	25	125
6	100	25	25
7	100	30	30
8	100	35	35
9	100	40	40
10	100	45	45
11	90	25	22.50
12	80	25	20.00
13	70	25	17.50
14	60	25	15.00
15	50	25	12.50
16	100	24	24.00
17	100	22	22.00
18	100	20	20.00
19	100	18	18.00
20	100	16	16.00
21	1000	30	300.00
22	2000	40	800.00
23	3000	50	1500.00
24	4000	60	2400.00
25	5000	70	3500.00

CH11PR09

Chapter 11 Problem 9

Compute Percent

FACTS FACTS FACTS

100 Base

40 Percentage

SOLUTION SOLUTION

Percent 40

Please work these problems.
Compare your results with the prepared solution.

Item No.	Base	Percentage	Percent
1	1000	400	40.00
2	1000	500	50.00
3	1000	600	60.00
4	1000	700	70.00
5	1000	800	80.00
6	500	250	50.00
7	500	260	52.00
8	500	270	54.00
9	500	280	56.00
10	500	290	58.00
11	490	25	5.10
12	480	25	5.21
13	470	25	5.32
14	460	25	5.43
15	450	25	5.56
16	100	60	60.00
17	200	65	32.50
18	300	70	23.33
19	400	75	18.75
20	500	80	16.00
21	1000	300	30.00
22	2000	400	20.00
23	3000	500	16.67
24	4000	600	15.00
25	5000	700	14.00

CH11PR10 Chapter 11 Problem 10

Compute Base

FACTS	FACTS	FACTS
25	Percent	
100	Percentage	

SOLUTION	SOLUTION	
	Base	400

PRACTICE PRACTICE PRACTICE PRACTICE PRACTICE PRACTICE

PRACTICE PROBLEMS PRACTICE PROBLEMS

Item No.	Percent	Percentage	Base
1	25	100	400.00
2	25	200	800.00
3	25	300	1200.00
4	25	400	1600.00
5	25	500	2000.00
6	500	250	50.00
7	500	260	52.00
8	500	270	54.00
9	500	280	56.00
10	500	290	58.00
11	490	25	5.10
12	480	25	5.21
13	470	25	5.32
14	460	25	5.43
15	450	25	5.56
16	60	60	100.00
17	60	65	108.33
18	60	70	116.67
19	60	75	125.00
20	60	80	133.33
21	1000	300	30.00
22	2000	400	20.00
23	3000	500	16.67
24	4000	600	15.00
25	5000	700	14.00

12 Statement Analysis

Condensed List of Items

Item No.		*Problems*
CH12PR01	Earnings per share	5
CH12PR02	Price-earnings ratio	5
CH12PR03	Dividend payout ratio	5
CH12PR04	Dividend yield ratio	5
CH12PR05	Return on assets	5
CH12PR06	Return on common equity %	5
CH12PR07	Return on common equity %	5
CH12PR08	Book value per share	5
CH12PR09	Current ratio	5
CH12PR10	Acid-test ratio	5
CH12PR11	Current, acid-test and working capital	5
CH12PR12	Turnover—Accounts receivable	5
CH12PR13	Return on investment	25
CH12PR14	Collection period—Accounts receivable	10
CH12PR15	Turnover—Inventory	10
CH12PR16	Times interest earned	25
CH12PR17	Debt to equity ratio	25
	Total	155

CH12PR01

```
Chapter 12 Problem 1
Compute Earnings Per Share

  Net Income                      213000
- Preferred Dividends              12000
  To common stock                 201000
/ Common Stock Outstanding         60000
  Earnings Per Share                3.35
```

SCREEN DISPLAY

```
FACTS               Earnings Per Share
 213000 Net Income
  12000 Preferred Dividends
  60000 Common stock outstanding
Solution            Solution

Earnings Per Share              3.35
```

CELL CONTENT

	A	B	C	D
1	FACTS		Earnings	Per Share
2	213000	Net Inco	me	
3	12000	Preferre	d Dividen	ds
4	60000	Common s	tock outs	tanding
5	Solution		Solution	
6				
7	Earnings	Per Share		(+A2-A3)/A4

CH12PR02

Chapter 12 Problem 2
Compute Price-earnings ratio

	Market Price	25
/	Preferred Dividends	2.50
	Price-earnings ratio	10

SCREEN DISPLAY

```
FACTS              Price-earnings ratio
       25 Market Price
      2.5 Earnings Per Share

Solution           Solution

Price-earnings ratio               10
```

CELL CONTENT

	A	B	C	D	
1	FACTS		Price-ear	nings rat	io
2	25	Market P	rice		
3	2.5	Earnings	Per Shar	e	
4					
5	Solution		Solution		
6					
7	Price-ear	nings rat	io	+A2/A3	

CH12PR03

```
Chapter 12 Problem 3
Compute Dividend Payout Ratio

  Dividends Per Share               3.00
/ Earnings per share                6.00

  Dividend Payout Ratio               50 %
```

SCREEN DISPLAY

```
FACTS             Dividend Payout Ratio
     3.00Dividends per share
     6.00 Earnings Per Share

Solution          Solution

Dividend Payout Ratio          50.00 %
```

CELL CONTENT

	A	B	C	D	E
1	FACTS		Dividend	Payout Ra	tio
2	3	Dividends	per shar	e	
3	6	Earnings	Per Shar	e	
4					
5	Solution		Solution		
6					
7	Dividend	Payout Ra	tio	(+A2/A3)*100	%

CH12PR04

Chapter 12 Problem 4

Compute Dividend Yield Ratio

Dividends per share	3.00
Ave market price per share -common stock	60.00
Dividend Yield Ratio %	5

SCREEN DISPLAY

```
FACTS                Dividend Yield Ratio
   3 Divdends per share
  60 Ave. Market Price per share - Common Stock

Solution             Solution

Dividend Yield Ratio                5 %
```

CELL CONTENT

	A	B	C	D	E	F
1	FACTS		Dividend	Yield Rat	io	
2	3	Divdends	per shar	e		
3	60	Ave. mar	ket price	per shar	e - commo	n stock
4						
5	Solution		Solution			
6						
7	Dividend	Yield Rat	io	(+A2/A3)*1 00	%	
8						
9						
10						
11						

CH12PR05

Chapter 12 Problem 5
Return on Assets

	Net Income	3000
+	Interest expense	450
		3450
/	Average Assets	50000
	Return on Assets	6.90

SCREEN DISPLAY

```
FACTS              Return on assets
  3000.00 Net income
   450.00 Interest expense
    40.00 Tax rate %
 40000.00 Assets-beginning of year
 60000.00 Assets-end of year
Solution           Solution
Income + interest              3450.00
Average assets                50000.00

Return on assets   %              6.90
```

CELL CONTENT

	A	B	C	D
1	FACTS		Return on	assets
2	3000	Net inco	me	
3	450	Interest	expense	
4	40	Tax rate	%	
5	40000	Assets-b	eginning	of year
6	60000	Assets-e	nd of yea	r
7	Solution		Solution	
8	Income +	interest		+A2+A3
9	Average a	ssets		+A5+A6/2
10				
11	Return on	assets	%	(+D8/D9)*100

CH12PR06

Chapter 12 Problem 6
Return on Stockholder's Equity

	Net Income		3000
-	Preferred dividends		300
	Net Income - common		2700
/	Average common equity		12000
	Return on common equity	%	22.50

SCREEN DISPLAY

```
FACTS  Return on common stockholder's equity
  3000.00 Net income
   300.00 Preferred dividends
 15000.00 Average stockholders's equity
  3000.00 Preferred stock
Solution            Solution
Net Income                    3000.00
Preferred dividends            300.00
Net Income - common           2700.00
Average common equity        12000.00
Return on common equity %       22.50
```

CELL CONTENT

	A	B	C	D	E
1	FACTS Re	turn on c	ommon sto	ckholder'	s equity
2	3000	Net inco	me		
3	300	Preferre	d dividen	ds	
4	15000	Average	stockhold	ers's equ	ity
5	3000	Preferre	d stock		
6	Solution		Solution		
7	Net Incom	e		+A2	
8	Preferred	dividend	s	+A3	
9	Net Incom	e - commo	n	+D7-D8	
10	Average c	ommon equ	ity	+A4-A5	
11	Return on	common e	quity %	(+D9/D10)*100	

CH12PR07

```
Chapter 12 Problem 7
Leverage Preferred Long term debt
                              Dollars    Rate %
EBIT                                                20000
Long term debt             50000          10         5000
Net Income                                          15000
Tax                                       40         6000
                                                     9000
Common stockholder's equity     50000
Return-common equity  %                                18
```

SCREEN DISPLAY

```
FACTS    Leverage Preferred Long term debt
    20000 Earnings before interest and taxes
    50000 Long term debt
       10 Interest Rate %
       40 Tax Rate %
    75000 Preferred Stock
        8 Preferred dividend rate %
    50000 Common stockholder's equity
SOLUTION Net income -common     15000
         Taxes                   6000
         Income after tax        9000
Return-equity - common          18.00
```

CELL CONTENT

	A	B	C	D	E
1	FACTS	Leverage	Preferred	Long ter	m debt
2	20000	Earnings	before i	nterest a	nd taxes
3	50000	Long ter	m debt		
4	10	Interest	Rate %		
5	40	Tax Rate	%		
6	75000	Preferre	d Stock		
7	8	Preferre	d dividen	d rate %	
8	50000	Common s	tockholde	r's equit	y
9	SOLUTION	Net incom	e -common	+A2-(50000*(A4*.01)	
10		Taxes		+D9*(A5*.01)	
11		Income af	ter tax	+D9-D10	
12	Return-eq	uity - co	mmon	(+D11/A8)*100	

CH12PR08

Chapter 12 Problem 8
Book Value per share

	Stockholders Equity	20000
-	Preferred Stock	2000
	Common Stock	18000
/	Common Shares outstanding	7500
	Book Value per share	2.40

SCREEN DISPLAY

```
FACTS    Book value per share
    20000 Stockholders equity
     2000 Preferred stock
     7500 Common outstanding

SOLUTION

Book value per share              2.4
```

CELL CONTENT

	A	B	C	D
1	FACTS	Book valu	e per sha	re
2	20000	Stockhol	ders equi	ty
3	2000	Preferre	d stock	
4	7500	Common o	utstandin	g
5				
6	SOLUTION			
7				
8	Book valu	e per sha	re	+A2-A3/A4

CH12PR09

Chapter 12 Problem 9

Working Capital	
Current Assets	20000
- Current Liabilities	12500
Working Capital	7500
Current Ratio	
Current Assets	20000
/ Current Liabilities	12500
Current Ratio	1.60

SCREEN DISPLAY

```
FACTS    Working Capital
    20000 Current Assets
    12500 Current Liabilities


SOLUTION

Working capital                 7500

Current ratio                    1.6
```

CELL CONTENT

	A	B	C	D
1	FACTS	Working C	apital	
2	20000	Current	Assets	
3	12500	Current	Liabiliti	es
4				
5				
6	SOLUTION			
7				
8	Working c	apital		+A2-A3
9				
10	Current r	atio		+A2/A3

CH12PR10

Chapter 12 Problem 10

Acid-test ratio	
Cash	4000
+ Accounts Receivable	2520
Total Quick Assets	6520
/ Current Liabilities	5000
Acid-test ratio	1.304

SCREEN DISPLAY

```
FACTS    Acid-test ratio
     4000 Cash
     2520 Accounts Receivable
     5000 Current Liabilities
SOLUTION

Acid-test ratio                 1.304
```

CELL CONTENT

	A	B	C	D
1	FACTS	Acid-test	ratio	
2	4000	Cash		
3	2520	Accounts	Receivab	le
4	5000	Current	Liabiliti	es
5	SOLUTION			
6				
7	Acid-test	ratio		(+A2+A3)/A4

```
CH12PR11
                Chapter 12 Problem 11
          Compute acid-test ratio,working capital and W.C. ratio
                Cash
              + Accounts Receivable
                Total Quick Assets
              + Inventory
              + Prepaid Expenses
                Total Current Assets
              / Current Liabilities
                Acid-test ratio
                Working Capital
                Working Capital ratio
```

SCREEN DISPLAY

```
FACTS    Acid-test ratio
    25000 Cash
    60000 Accounts Receivable
    85000 Inventory
     5000 Prepaid Expenses
    87500 Current Liabilities
SOLUTION

Acid-test ratio              .9714286
Working capital                 87500
Working capital ratio               2
```

CELL CONTENT

	A	B	C	D
1	FACTS	Acid-test	ratio	
2	25000	Cash		
3	60000	Accounts	Receivab	le
4	85000	Inventor	y	
5	5000	Prepaid	Expenses	
6	87500	Current	Liabiliti	es
7	SOLUTION			
8				
9	Acid-test	ratio		(+A2+A3)/A6
10	Working c	apital		+A2+A3+A4+A5 -A6
11	Working c	apital ra	tio	(+A2+A3+A4+A 5)/A6

CH12PR12

```
          Chapter 12 Problem 12
Compute accounts receivable turnover
          Sales
          Accounts Receivable - Beg
          Accounts Receivable - End
          Average Accounts Receivable

          Accounts Receivable turnover
```

SCREEN DISPLAY

```
FACTS    Accounts receivable turnover
     8000 Accounts Receivable - Beg.
    10000 Accounts Receivable - End
    45000 Sales


SOLUTION
Sales                          45000
Average accounts receivable     9000
Accts. Rec - turnover              5
```

CELL CONTENT

	A	B	C	D	
1	FACTS	Accounts	receivabl	e turnove	r
2	8000	Accounts	Receivab	le - Beg.	
3	10000	Accounts	Receivab	le - End	
4	45000	Sales			
5					
6					
7	SOLUTION				
8	Sales			+A4	
9	Average a	ccounts r	eceivable	(+A2+A3)/2	
10	Accts. Re	c - turno	ver	+D8/D9	

CH12PR13

Chapter 12 Problem 13

Return on Investment

```
   Given
100000  Sales
 10000  Net Operating income
 50000  Average operating assets
   Solution
        Margin
        Turnover
        Return on Investment
```

SCREEN DISPLAY

```
                 Return on Investment
   Given
100000  Sales
 10000  Net Operating income
 50000  Average operating assets
   Solution
        Margin                              10 %
        Turnover                             2
        Return on Investment                20
```

CELL CONTENT

	A	B	C	D	E	F
1						
2						
3			Return o	n Investm	ent	
4	Giv	en				
5	100000	Sales				
6	10000	Net Ope	rating in	come		
7	50000	Average	operatin	g assets		
8	Sol	ution				
9		Margin			(+A6/A5)*1 00 %	
10		Turnove	r		+A5/A7	
11		Return	on Invest	ment	+E9*E10	

CH12PR14

```
          Chapter 12 Problem 14
Compute accounts receivable collection period
          Sales
          Accounts Receivable - Beg
          Accounts Receivable - End
          Average Accounts Receivable
          Days per year
          Accounts Receivable turnover
          Average collection period
```

SCREEN DISPLAY

```
FACTS     A R collection period
     7000 Accounts Receivable - Beg.
     6000 Accounts Receivable - End
   104000 Sales
      365 Days per year

SOLUTION
Sales                            104000
Average accounts receivable        6500
Accts. Rec - turnover                16
Average collection period     22.8125 days
```

CELL CONTENT

	A	B	C	D	E
1	FACTS	A R colle	ction per	iod	
2	7000	Accounts	Receivab	le - Beg.	
3	6000	Accounts	Receivab	le - End	
4	104000	Sales			
5	365	Days per	year		
6					
7	SOLUTION				
8	Sales			+A4	
9	Average a	ccounts r	eceivable	(+A2+A3)/2	
10	Accts. Re	c - turno	ver	+D8/D9	
11	Average c	ollectio	n period	+A5/D10	days

CH12PR15

Chapter 12 Problem 15			
Compute inventory turnover			
Days per year			365
Cost of goods sold		36000	
Inventory - Beg	8000		
Inventory - End	10000		
Average inventory		9000	
Inventory turnover times			4
Inventory days			91.25

SCREEN DISPLAY

```
FACTS    Inventory turnover
   36000 Cost of Goods Sold
    8000 Inventory - Beg.
   10000 Inventory - End
     365 Days per year

SOLUTION
Cost of goods sold              36000
Average inventory                9000
Inventory turnover times            4
Inventory turnover              91.25 days
```

CELL CONTENT

	A	B	C	D	E
1	FACTS	Inventory	turnover		
2	36000	Cost of	Goods Sol	d	
3	8000	Inventor	y - Beg.		
4	10000	Inventor	y - End		
5	365	Days per	year		
6					
7	SOLUTION				
8	Cost of g	oods sold		+A2	
9	Average i	nventory		(+A3+A4)/2	
10	Inventory	turnover	times	+D8/D9	
11	Inventory	turnover		+A5/D10	days

CH12PR16

Chapter 12 Problem 16	
Times interest earned	
EBIT	45000
Interest expense	4000
Times interest earned	11.25

SCREEN DISPLAY

```
FACTS    Times interest earned
    45000 Earnings before interest & taxes
     4000 Interest expense


SOLUTION
Times interest earned          11.25
```

CELL CONTENT

	A	B	C	D	E
1	FACTS	Times int	erest ear	ned	
2	45000	Earnings	before i	nterest &	taxes
3	4000	Interest	expense		
4					
5					
6					
7	SOLUTION				
8	Times int	erest ear	ned	+A2/A3	

CH12PR17

Chapter 12 Problem 17	
Debt to equity ratio	
Total liabilities	8500
Stockholder's Equity	10000
Debt to equity ratio	.85

SCREEN DISPLAY

```
FACTS     Debt to equity ratio

     8500 Total liabilities
    10000 Stockholder's equity


SOLUTION
Debt to equity ratio              .85
```

CELL CONTENT

	A	B	C	D
1	FACTS	Debt to e	quity rat	io
2				
3	8500	Total li	abilities	
4	10000	Stockhol	der's equ	ity
5				
6				
7				
8	SOLUTION			
9	Debt to e	quity rat	io	+A3/A4

Problem 1

Compute Earnings Per Share

	Net Income	213000
-	Preferred Dividends	12000
	To common stock	201000
/	Common Stock Outstanding	60000
	Earnings Per Share	3.35

Item No.	Net Income	Pfd Div.	Com Stk. Out	EPS
1	213000	12000	60000	3.35
2	218000	12000	60000	3.43
3	223000	12000	60000	3.52
4	228000	12000	60000	3.60
5	233000	12000	60000	3.68

Problem 2 PRACTICE PRACTICE PRACTICE PRACTICE PRACTICE PRACTICE

Compute Price-earnings ratio

	Market Price	25
/	Preferred Dividends	2.50
	Price-earnings ratio	10

Item No.	Market Price	EPS	PE Ratio
1	25	2.5	10.00
2	26	2.5	10.40
3	27	2.5	10.80
4	28	2.5	11.20
5	29	2.5	11.60

Problem 3

Compute Dividend Payout Ratio

	Dividends Per Share	3.00
/	Earnings per share	6.00
	Dividend Payout Ratio	50 %

Item No.	Dividend		Dividend
1	Per Sh	EPS	Payout Ratio
2	3.00	6.00	50.00 %
3	3.25	6.00	54.17 %
4	3.50	6.00	58.33 %
5	3.75	6.00	62.50 %

Please work these problems.

Problem 4

Compute Dividend Yield Ratio

Dividends per share	3.00
Ave market price per share -common stock	60.00
Dividend Yield Ratio %	5

Item No.	Div. Per Share	Ave. M.P. Common	Dividend Yield Ratio %
1	3.00	60.00	5.00
2	4.00	60.00	6.67
3	5.00	60.00	8.33
4	6.00	60.00	10.00
5	7.00	60.00	11.67

Problem 5 PRACTICE PRACTICE PRACTICE PRACTICE PRACTICE PRACTICE

Return on Assets

Net Income	3000
+ Interest expense	450
	3450
/ Average Assets	50000
Return on Assets	6.90

Item No.	Income	+Int.After Tax	Average Assets	ROA
1	1500	375	27860	5.38
2	1510	375	27860	5.42
3	1520	375	27860	5.46
4	1530	375	27860	5.49
5	1540	375	27860	5.53

Problem 6

Return on Stockholder's Equity

Net Income	3000
- Preferred dividends	300
Net Income - common	2700
/ Average common equity	12000
Return on common equity %	22.50

Item No.	Net Income	Pfd Dividends	Average Common Equity	Return on Common Equity
1	3000.00	300.00	12000	22.50
2	2900.00	300.00	12000	21.67
3	2800.00	300.00	12000	20.83
4	2700.00	300.00	12000	20.00
5	2600.00	300.00	12000	19.17

Problem 7

Leverage Preferred Long term debt

	Dollars	Rate %	
EBIT			20000
Long term debt	50000	10	5000
Net Income			15000
Tax		40	6000
			9000
Common stockholder's equity		50000	
Return-common equity %			18

Tax Rate	40 %
Preferred Stock	75000
Preferred Rate	8 %
Common Stock	50000
Interest Rate	10 %

Item No.	Earnings Before Int & Tax	Long Term Debt	Earnings After Int & Tax	Net Inc. Common	Return Equity-Common
1	20000	50000	15000	9000.00	18.00
2	20000	55000	14500	8500.00	17.00
3	20000	60000	14000	8000.00	16.00
4	20000	65000	13500	7500.00	15.00
5	20000	70000	13000	7000.00	14.00

Problem 8 PRACTICE PRACTICE PRACTICE PRACTICE PRACTICE PRACTICE

Book Value per share

Stockholders Equity	20000
- Preferred Stock	2000
Common Stock	18000
/ Common Shares outstanding	7500
Book Value per share	2.40

Item No.	Stkhldrs Equity	Pfd. Stock	Common Stock	Bk. Val. Per Shr.
1	20000	2000	7500	2.40
2	21000	2000	7500	2.53
3	22000	2000	7500	2.67
4	23000	2000	7500	2.80
5	24000	2000	7500	2.93

Problem 9

PRACTICE PROBLEMS

Please work these problems.
Compare your results with the prepared solution.

Working Capital	
Current Assets	20000
- Current Liabilities	12500
Working Capital	7500
Current Ratio	
Current Assets	20000
/ Current Liabilities	12500
Current Ratio	1.60

Item No.	Current Assets	Current Liab.	Working Capital	Current Ratio
1	20000	12500	7500	1.60
2	22000	12500	9500	1.76
3	24000	12500	11500	1.92
4	26000	12500	13500	2.08
5	28000	12500	15500	2.24

PRACTICE PRACTICE PRACTICE PRACTICE PRACTICE PRACTICE

Problem 10

Acid-test ratio
Cash
+ Accounts Receivable
Total Quick Assets
/ Current Liabilities

Acid-test ratio

Item No.	Cash	A. R.	Current Liab.	Acid-test Ratio
1	25000	60000	87500	0.97
2	25500	60000	87500	0.98
3	26000	60000	87500	0.98
4	26500	60000	87500	0.99
5	27000	60000	87500	0.99

PRACTICE PROBLEMS

PRACTICE PROBLEMS

Please work these problems.
Compare your results with the solution.

Problem 11

Compute acid-test ratio, working capital and W.C. ratio

Cash	25000	
+ Accounts Receivable	60000	
Total Quick Assets		85000
+ Inventory	85000	
+ Prepaid Expenses	5000	
Total Current Assets		175000
/ Current Liabilities		87500
Acid-test ratio		.9714286
Working Capital		87500
Working Capital ratio		2.00

Item No.	Cash	A. R.	Inventory	Current Liab.	Acid-test Ratio	Working Capital	W. C. Ratio
1	25000	60000	90000	87500	0.97	87500	2.00
2	25500	60000	90000	87500	0.98	88000	2.01
3	26000	60000	90000	87500	0.98	88500	2.01
4	26500	60000	90000	87500	0.99	89000	2.02
5	27000	60000	90000	87500	0.99	89500	2.02

PRACTICE PRACTICE PRACTICE PRACTICE PRACTICE PRACTICE

Problem 12

Compute accounts receivable turnover.

Sales		45000
Accounts Receivable - Beg	8000	
Accounts Receivable - End	10000	
Average Accounts Receivable		9000
Accounts Receivable turnover		5

Item No.	Accts. Rec. Beg.	End	Sales	Average A.R.	AR Turnover
1	8000	10000	45000	9000	5.00
2	9000	9000	45000	9000	5.00
3	10000	8000	45000	9000	5.00
4	11000	7000	45000	9000	5.00
5	12000	6000	45000	9000	5.00

CH12PR13

Chapter 12 Problem 13
Return on Investment

Given

100000 Sales
10000 Net Operating income
50000 Average operating assets

Solution

Margin	10	%
Turnover	2	
Return on Investment	20	

Item No.	Sales	Net Oper Income	Ave Oper Assets	Margin	Turnover	Return on Invest.
1	100000	10000	50000	10.00	2.00	20.00
2	120000	10000	50000	8.33	2.40	20.00
3	140000	10000	50000	7.14	2.80	20.00
4	160000	10000	50000	6.25	3.20	20.00
5	180000	10000	50000	5.56	3.60	20.00
6	100000	12000	50000	12.00	2.00	24.00
7	100000	14000	50000	14.00	2.00	28.00
8	100000	16000	50000	16.00	2.00	32.00
9	100000	18000	50000	18.00	2.00	36.00
10	100000	20000	50000	20.00	2.00	40.00
11	100000	10000	55000	10.00	1.82	18.18
12	100000	10000	60000	10.00	1.67	16.67
13	100000	10000	65000	10.00	1.54	15.38
14	100000	10000	70000	10.00	1.43	14.29
15	100000	10000	75000	10.00	1.33	13.33
16	100000	10000	50000	10.00	2.00	20.00
17	90000	10000	50000	11.11	1.80	20.00
18	80000	10000	50000	12.50	1.60	20.00
19	70000	10000	50000	14.29	1.40	20.00
20	60000	10000	50000	16.67	1.20	20.00
21	110000	12000	48000	10.91	2.29	25.00
22	120000	14000	46000	11.67	2.61	30.43
23	130000	16000	44000	12.31	2.95	36.36
24	140000	18000	42000	12.86	3.33	42.86
25	150000	20000	40000	13.33	3.75	50.00

Please work these problems.

Problem 14

Compute accounts receivable collection period		
Sales		104000
Accounts Receivable - Beg	7000	
Accounts Receivable - End	6000	
Average Accounts Receivable		6500
Days per year		365
Accounts Receivable turnover		16
Average collection period		22.8125

Item No.	Sales	Average A. R.	A. R. Turnover	Ave. Coll. Period
1	104000	6500	16.00	22.81 Days
2	105000	6500	16.15	22.60 Days
3	106000	6500	16.31	22.38 Days
4	107000	6500	16.46	22.17 Days
5	108000	6500	16.62	21.97 Days
6	109000	6500	16.77	21.77 Days
7	110000	6500	16.92	21.57 Days
8	111000	6500	17.08	21.37 Days
9	112000	6500	17.23	21.18 Days
10	113000	6500	17.38	21.00 Days

PRACTICE PRACTICE PRACTICE PRACTICE PRACTICE PRACTICE

Problem 15

Compute inventory turnover			
Days per year			365
Cost of goods sold		36000	
Inventory - Beg	8000		
Inventory - End	10000		
Average inventory		9000	
Inventory turnover times			4
Inventory days			91.25

Item No.	COGS	Average Inventory	Inventory times	Turnover days
1	36000	9000	4.00	91.25
2	37000	9000	4.11	88.78
3	38000	9000	4.22	86.45
4	39000	9000	4.33	84.23
5	40000	9000	4.44	82.13
6	35000	9000	3.89	93.86
7	34000	9000	3.78	96.62
8	33000	9000	3.67	99.55
9	32000	9000	3.56	102.66
10	31000	9000	3.44	105.97

CH12PR16

PRACTICE PROBLEMS

PRACTICE PROBLEMS

Please work these problems.
Compare your results with the solution.

Problem 16

Times interest earned	
EBIT	45000
Interest expense	4000
Times interest earned	11.25

Item No.	EBITT	Interest Expense	Times Earned
1	45000	4000	11.25
2	46000	4000	11.50
3	47000	4000	11.75
4	48000	4000	12.00
5	49000	4000	12.25
6	44000	4000	11.00
7	43000	4000	10.75
8	42000	4000	10.50
9	41000	4000	10.25
10	40000	4000	10.00
11	45000	3500	12.86
12	45000	3000	15.00
13	45000	2500	18.00
14	45000	2000	22.50
15	45000	1500	30.00
16	45000	3900	11.54
17	45000	3400	13.24
18	45000	2900	15.52
19	45000	2400	18.75
20	45000	1900	23.68
21	45000	5000	9.00
22	44000	4500	9.78
23	43000	4000	10.75
24	42000	3500	12.00
25	41000	3000	13.67

PRACTICE PRACTICE PRACTICE PRACTICE PRACTICE PRACTICE

Please work these problems.
Compare your results with the solution.

Problem 17

Debt to equity ratio

Total liabilities	8500
Stockholder's Equity	10000
Debt to equity ratio	.85

Item No.	Total Liab.	Stkhldrs Equity	Debt to Equity
1	8500	10000	0.85
2	9000	10000	0.90
3	9500	10000	0.95
4	10000	10000	1.00
5	10500	10000	1.05
6	8500	11000	0.77
7	8500	12000	0.71
8	8500	13000	0.65
9	8500	14000	0.61
10	8500	15000	0.57
11	9500	10000	0.95
12	10500	9000	1.17
13	11500	8000	1.44
14	12500	7000	1.79
15	13500	6000	2.25
16	14500	10000	1.45
17	15500	11000	1.41
18	16500	12000	1.38
19	17500	13000	1.35
20	18500	14000	1.32
21	17500	15000	1.17
22	16500	16000	1.03
23	15500	17000	0.91
24	14500	18000	0.81
25	13500	19000	0.71

Index